Crucible
of
Liberty

---

200 YEARS OF
THE BILL OF RIGHTS

Edited by

Raymond Arsenault

THE FREE PRESS
A Division of Macmillan, Inc.
NEW YORK

Maxwell Macmillan Canada
TORONTO

Maxwell Macmillan International
NEW YORK   OXFORD   SINGAPORE   SYDNEY

For Amelia and Anne,
who never let me forget
that children have rights, too

The Free Press
A Division of Macmillan, Inc.
866 Third Avenue, New York, N.Y. 10022

Maxwell Macmillan Canada, Inc.
1200 Eglinton Avenue East
Suite 200
Don Mills, Ontario M3C 3N1

Macmillan, Inc. is part of the Maxwell Communication
Group of Companies.

Printed in the United States of America

printing number
1   2   3   4   5   6   7   8   9   10

Library of Congress Cataloging-in-Publication Data

Crucible of liberty: 200 years of the Bill of Rights / edited by
    Raymond Arsenault.
        p.   cm.
    Includes bibliographical references and index.
    ISBN 0-02-901054-3   ISBN 0-02-901055-1 (pbk.)
    1. United States—Constitutional law—Amendments—1st–10th—
History.   2. Civil rights—United States—History.   I. Arsenault,
Raymond.
KF4749.A2C78   1991
342.73′085—dc20   91-24005
[347.30285]   CIP

Contents

Acknowledgments

This book had its origins in an experiment in public education. For twelve weeks during the winter and early spring of 1991, the University of South Florida, St. Petersburg, hosted an interdisciplinary course and public lecture series commemorating the bicentennial of the ratification of the Bill of Rights. Each week several hundred individuals—students and non-students, academic specialists and ordinary citizens—gathered together to consider the history and contemporary meaning of the first ten amendments to the United States Constitution. The lecturers in the series included several distinguished legal practitioners and some of the nation's finest constitutional scholars, but the most noteworthy aspect of the series was the character of the audience, a diverse mix which cut across the traditional divisions of class, race, ethnicity, regional background, age, and gender. Interactive and inclusive, the series reflected the spirit of openness espoused by James Madison and the framers of the Bill of Rights two centuries ago.

Each essay in this volume, with the exception of David J. Bodenhamer's contribution, represents a revised version of a lecture delivered during the series. I would like to thank all of the contributors—Kermit Hall, John Hope Franklin, Samuel Walker, Stephen Whitfield, David Bodenhamer, Paul Murphy, and James Carey—for their cooperation and consummate professionalism. Despite severe time constraints, they were able to maintain a uniformly high standard of intellectual rigor and literary craftsmanship. I would also like to express my gratitude to the other lecturers in the series—John Egerton, Ramsey Clark, Lili Levi, Robyn Blumner, Stanford M. Lyman, Richard John Neuhaus, Jon Butler, Peter Bensinger, and Lewis Maltby—whose lectures could not be included in a volume limited to the historical development of the Bill of Rights. Their efforts were essential to the overall success of the series. I am also deeply indebted to Mike Killenberg and Tim Reilly, two talented and dedicated colleagues who devoted countless hours to the planning, administration, and teaching stages of this project. In addition, I want to thank the members of the Program Advisory Committee: Louie N. Adcock, Jr., Gardner Beckett, Jr., John Berglund, Stephen M. Bragin, Robert Brister, Mark Brown, Sevell Brown, Dean Winston T. Bridges, Jr., David Carr, David Cozad, Roy Peter Clark, Ed Cole, Jr., Andrew Corty, Judith Flynn, Sister Margaret Freeman, James R. Gillespie, Julie F. Gillespie, Sidney M. Goetz, Cecil E. Greek, Robert J. Haiman, Denise Hart, Hazel Hough, Dean Bruce Jacob, Douglas L. Jamerson, Herb Karl, Cecil Keene, Deborah Kurelik, Jan Majewski, Thomas M. Mieczkowski, Pat Miller, Jacob Neusner, Sharon Nolte, Darryl Paulson, Paul H. Pohlman, George K. Rahdert, Frank Reinhart, Perkins Shelton, James Simmons, Helen H. Stambaugh, Margaret Tappan, Sally Wallace, Cynthia R. White, and Gene Windham.

I would like to express my appreciation to the staff of the Nelson Poynter Memorial Library at the University of South Florida, St. Petersburg—especially to Melissa Conlin, Jackie Jackson, Jerry Notaro, and Bob Thrush; to Pamela Burdett and the staff of the Stetson College of Law Library; and to several other individuals who contributed to the success of this project—Ellen Babb, Marion Ballard, Herman Brames, Alison Brereton, Khaleah Bryant, Thom Foley, Paul Getting, Joan Hesler, Rae Howe, Pat Kemp, David McCally, William McKee, Bob McKenzie, Al Mells, Linda Meuntener, Gary Mormino, Heather Nichol, Valerie Prosser, James Schnur, Richard Scott, Kenneth Shaw, David Shedden, Sarah Shoup, Anthony Smith, Karen Spear, Tracy Storm, Nancy Teets, Sudsy Tschiderer, Jacob Vonk, Christian Warren, Nigel Watson, Constance Woulard, Mike Wright, Margo Yazell, Ray Yazell, and the intrepid civil libertarians of the Pinellas County ACLU.

A generous grant from the Florida Endowment for the Humanities provided most of the funding for this project. I would like to thank the FEH's Board of Directors and its staff—especially Joan Bragginton, Ron Cooper, Ann Henderson, and Susan Lockwood—for unflagging support and expert advice. Several other organizations—most notably, the University of South Florida, St. Petersburg; the University of South Florida Foundation; the Stetson University College of Law; the Poynter Institute for Media Studies; the St. Petersburg Chamber of Commerce; the *St. Petersburg Times*; WUSF and Florida Public Radio; the St. Petersburg Bar Association; Friends of the First Amendment; Fisher and Sauls, P.A.; Harris, Barrett, Mann, and Dew; Rahdert and Anderson; and Canteen Corporation—also deserve thanks for their support and encouragement.

I also want to express my appreciation to Joyce Seltzer and the staff of The Free Press, especially Loretta Denner, Lise Esdaile, and Cherie Weitzner. From start to breathless finish, it has been a great pleasure working with them.

Finally, I want to thank my family. As always, my wife Kathy provided expert editorial guidance, common sense, and affectionate but telling criticism. This book is lovingly dedicated to my daughters, Amelia and Anne, two budding civil libertarians. May they grow up to live in a world that cherishes civil liberties and human rights.

1

The Crucible of Liberty

RAYMOND ARSENAULT

*T*he year 1991 marks the two-hundredth anniversary of the Bill of Rights, the third in a series of national bicentennials that began in 1976. The first bicentennial, which commemorated the signing of the Declaration of Independence, was a lighthearted affair that produced a dazzling array of red, white, and blue souvenirs, several memorable fireworks displays, and a spectacular flotilla of tall sailing ships. Not surprisingly, an American public in need of a post-Watergate, post-Vietnam catharsis responded with enthusiasm. Eleven years later, in 1987, former Chief Justice Warren Burger presided over the bicentennial of the framing of the United States Constitution, an elaborate and expensive enterprise that combined serious academic inquiry and show-business hype. The result was an impressive number of scholarly conferences and monographs devoted to constitutional themes, and a dizzying series of public extravaganzas—including a Ben Franklin look-alike contest in Bluefield, West Virginia; a hot-air balloon race in Philadelphia involving thirteen balloons (one for each of the original states); the unfurling of the world's largest flag in St. Louis; and a glitzy television production titled "The Splendiferous Wham-Bam Constitution Special." Predictably, the 1987 bicentennial celebration received mixed reviews, even though the scholarly achievements of "Project 87" were undeniable. Despite the best efforts of Justice Burger and his colleagues, the bicentennial of the Constitution failed to capture the imagination of the American people. Most Americans, it seems, revere the Constitution and all that it stands for, but they do not find it very interesting. With the exception of a few clauses dealing with the electoral college, the original document of 1787 is not a subject for public or private debate; instead, like the Declaration of Independence, it is an icon in black and white.

This is not the case with the Bill of Rights. Two centuries after the ratification of the first ten amendments, the Bill of Rights remains a subject of controversy and compelling interest for millions of Americans. Historical experience tells us that the reinterpretation of rights and liberties is an inescapable part of American life. It also tells us that in a complex nation such as the United States, judicial review seldom results in consensus. Indeed, the most divisive domestic controversies of our time—from George Bush's challenge to the card-carrying members of the American Civil Liberties Union, to the bitter struggle over Robert Bork's nomination to the United States Supreme Court, to the movement to overturn *Roe v. Wade*—have revolved around conflicting interpretations of one or more of the first ten amendments. Abortion, women's rights, gun control, capital punishment, the rights of criminal defendants and prison inmates, the protection of privacy, mandatory drug testing, the burning of flags and draft cards, radical political dissent and academic freedom, affirmative action and racial equality, prayer in schools and crèches in public parks, pornography and obscenity, government censorship and freedom of the press—all of these important issues require an ongoing consideration of the contemporary meaning and implications of the Bill of Rights.

For this reason, the metaphor of a crucible—a refractory cauldron in which ores and metals are melted down—seems appropriate. In a sense, the Bill of Rights is a *constitutional* cauldron, a vessel in which the contradictions and ambiguities of liberty are transformed into national law. The melting process which extracts individual and minority rights from the ore of majoritarian democracy gives off heat and sparks and requires careful supervision. But maintaining the crucible is well worth the effort; without it the materials of American democracy would remain raw and untempered, and the tyranny of the majority that James Madison and the framers warned us about would almost certainly become a reality.

The Bill of Rights has always served the difficult function of mediating between community interests and individual liberties, but in recent years the "crucible of liberty" has taken on a superheated quality. In the absence of a national consensus, an increasingly active judiciary has mobilized its powers of judicial and appellate review to address problems that no other governmental institution has been able to resolve. The courts have assumed this pivotal role largely by default, since from the late 1960s onward a persistent stalemate between a Democratic-controlled Congress and a Republican-controlled White House has limited the power and influence of the legislative and executive branches of the federal government. Some observers applaud the judiciary's willingness to fill this void, while others, such as the historian Fred Siegel, are sharply critical of a "judicialized politics" that "bypasses public consent . . . by placing public policy in the private hands of lawyers and litigants." But nearly everyone agrees that, for better or for worse, the courts have taken center stage in the determination of domestic public policy.

To the dismay of political and legal conservatives, this new wave of judicial activism has helped to foster a powerful movement known as the "rights revolution." The intertwining of law and politics is as old as recorded history, but the translation of political debate into a discourse on fundamental rights is a relatively recent phenomenon. Though clearly foreshadowed in earlier times, the "rights revolution" that emerged from the cultural and political upheavals of the 1950s and 1960s has radically altered the relationship between constitutional law and civic culture. As Joel B. Grossman, a professor of political science and law at the University of Wisconsin, recently observed, " 'rights consciousness' . . . is now probably the dominant form of interaction and perception between citizens and government." This reality transcends divisions of class, race, gender, and geography, as every group from the homeless to the handicapped seeks inclusion in the widening circle of rights protection.

In this context, access to the levers of constitutional history represents a major source of empowerment. Indeed, since revisions and reinterpretations of rights are invariably grounded in legal precedent and historical understanding, a rudimentary knowledge of constitutional history is now almost a prerequisite for responsible citizenship. A citizen does not really know his or her rights until he or she has some sense of how and why these rights developed over time. Fortunately, the rich historical scholarship of the past three decades offers a wealth of insights and informed judgments on the origins and evolution of the Bill of Rights.

In *Crucible of Liberty,* eight scholars—seven historians and one journalist—have combined forces to create a thought-provoking volume on the history of the Bill of Rights. Organized chronologically, the seven essays in this book present a rough narrative of the past two centuries of American constitutional history. But it is not our intention to provide an encyclopedic treatment of that history. Instead, we have chosen to focus on the major themes and turning points that have punctuated the historical evolution of the Bill of Rights. Readers seeking a comprehensive knowledge of American constitutional history should consult some of the general works cited in the Selected Bibliography, especially Leonard Levy's magisterial *Encyclopedia of the American Constitution.* The present volume also includes two appendices; the first provides the text of the United States Constitution, and the second offers an annotated chronology of important judicial and legislative decisions that relate to the Bill of Rights.

In the first essay, Kermit L. Hall argues that the Bill of Rights is a living document, a flexible set of principles that each generation must rework and clarify for its own purposes. The words of the framers remain the same, but the meaning and implications of the first ten amendments vary with changing social circumstances. Exposing the folly of basing constitutional interpretation on the doctrine of "original intention," Hall reminds us that the Bill of Rights, as promulgated in 1791, was a creature of both philosophy and politics. In his words, "the history of the creation of the Bill of Rights leads us to one clear conclusion—the framers adopted broadly stated limitations on government, leaving to courts and judges the task of giving precise meaning to these majestic generalities." The system by which judges and lawyers and ordinary citizens reshape constitutional law may be cumbersome and difficult to embrace without ambivalence. But there can be little doubt that this system of constitutional reinterpretation has become an essential element of American democracy. Without it, we might achieve security, but not liberty.

John Hope Franklin's contribution focuses on the long constitutional nightmare visited upon African-Americans during the eighteenth and nineteenth centuries. The fledgling nation's experiment in democratic constitutionalism benefited many white Americans, but this new calculus of freedom rarely applied to black Americans. Indeed, liberty for whites often depended upon the absence of liberty for blacks. In the South, the institution of chattel slavery and its attendant racial ideologies placed blacks, free or enslaved, beyond the reach of constitutional protection. And in the North, where blacks were nominally "free," a culture of white supremacy created obstacles, both legal and extralegal, which few individuals could overcome. Prior to the Reconstruction Era, the Constitution was a slaveholders' document that legitimized racial oppression. And even after the ratification of the Thirteenth, Fourteenth, and Fifteenth Amendments, constitutional protection of black rights was little more than a rhetorical hoax. By refusing to endorse the principle of incorporation, the Supreme Court of the late nineteenth century allowed and even encouraged state and local governments to treat blacks as second-class citizens. Thus, for more than a century the Bill of Rights was an empty vessel for African-Americans. Only in the twentieth century, through a long process of struggle and persuasion, has the Bill of Rights become a document in which all Americans can invest their hopes.

Samuel Walker's essay traces the evolution of American civil liberties from the Progressive Era to the end of World War II. Focusing on the critical period between the world wars, he examines the emergence of "rights consciousness" as a national phenomenon. After the domestic and international crises of World War I and the first "Red Scare" forced Americans to reevaluate the limits of dissent and liberty, judicial and legislative interpretations of the Bill of Rights, and especially of the First Amendment, became a matter of national concern. A series of dramatic public confrontations, from the 1925 Scopes trial to the World War II debate over Japanese-American internment, revealed the salience and power of "rights," nudging the American democratic ethos into a new stage of philosophical and legal sophistication. Though seldom acknowledged by historians, this foreshadowing of the "rights revolution" of the 1960s, in Walker's view, ranks in importance with industrialization, urbanization, and immigration as a primary determinant of modern American life.

Stephen J. Whitfield extends Samuel Walker's cultural analysis of constitutional history into the Cold War era of 1945–1965. His essay reveals the bitter irony of Cold War America: in attempting to counter the threat of Stalinist totalitarianism, a self-professed democracy jettisoned its own libertarian ideals. When a majority of Americans concluded that the Soviet Union had established a fifth column of spies and subversives in the United States, public commitment to the constitutional protections guaranteed by the Bill of Rights weakened. Goaded by the political demagoguery of McCarthyism, America's major institutions, from government to religion, from education to the arts, joined forces to inoculate the nation against the Communist "virus." This broad effort not only crippled the American Communist Party, placing radical political dissenters beyond the bounds of constitutional protection; it also disrupted the lives and ruined the careers of thousands of other Americans caught in the web of distrust and suspicion. As Whitfield demonstrates, from the novels of Mickey Spillane to the activities of J. Edgar Hoover and the FBI, the culture of the Cold War was a pervasive force, one that seriously threatened the openness and vitality of political discourse and cultural creativity in postwar America. Thanks to the Warren Court and the easing of Cold War tensions in the 1960s, the Bill of Rights survived. But the memory of what transpired during the 1950s provides fair warning to anyone who doubts the difficulty of sustaining civil libertarian values in a dangerous world.

David J. Bodenhamer's essay examines one of the most controversial aspects of the modern "rights revolution": protecting the rights of the

accused, before, during, and after trial. In theory, due process of law—
the right to a speedy public trial, the right to be judged by a fair and
impartial jury, the right to adequate counsel, and the protection against
double jeopardy, self-incrimination, and cruel and unusual punishment—
has a long history in Anglo-American jurisprudence. But, in reality, due
process has been an elusive commodity, especially for racial minorities
and the poor. As Bodenhamer points out, the nationalization of the rights
guaranteed by the Fourth, Fifth, Sixth, and Eighth Amendments has been
a slow and uneven process. The Supreme Court did not apply the Bill of
Rights to criminal trials in state courts until the 1930s, and even then it
did so hesitantly and incompletely. Finally, in the 1960s, the Warren
Court issued a series of landmark decisions that unequivocally incorporated specific due process protections into state law. Since 1969, the
Burger and Rehnquist Courts have taken a more conservative approach to
due process questions, but they have not overturned the basic principles
established by the Warren Court. Due process guarantees are still in
force, even though certain elements of the due process revolution—the
exclusionary rule, *Miranda* rights, the extended rights of appeal for death
row inmates, and other restraints placed upon police power and penal
retribution—remain controversial.

The pivotal role of the Supreme Court in recasting the social reality of
modern American law is also the subject of Paul L. Murphy's essay. For
Murphy, the Court's attempt to balance the libertarian implications of the
Warren Court's rulings with the cultural and political conservatism of the
1970s and 1980s is the central theme of recent constitutional history. For
better or for worse, the Court has assumed a mediating role in a complex
national culture that is deeply divided over a number of important issues.
To prove his point, Murphy examines several controversial issues that
have come before the Court with increasing frequency in recent decades:
racial equality and affirmative action; gender discrimination and women's
rights; political dissent and the right of free expression; campaign financing and commercial speech; freedom of the press; obscenity, community
standards, and artistic freedom; and the separation of church and state. In
most of these areas, the recent Court has proceeded cautiously and judi-
ciously, resisting the temptation to disregard the daring precedents of the
1960s. Indeed, in the area of gender discrimination and women's rights,
Murphy finds that the Burger and Rehnquist Courts have exhibited considerable sensitivity and sophistication, ''pushing far ahead of the Warren
Court.''

The final essay, written by the noted journalist James W. Carey, places
the Bill of Rights in the post–Cold War context of the 1990s. The renewal

of democratic discourse in the age of glasnost almost compels us to evaluate the present condition and future prospects of American democracy. Undertaking such an evaluation is no simple matter, however. As Carey points out, the quality of liberty rests on more than legal and constitutional forms; it is also a function of public spirit and moral philosophy. Repeating Louis Hartz's shrewd observation that "law has flourished on the corpse of philosophy in America," he reminds us that institutionalized expression is no substitute for a true "marketplace of ideas." Laws can control human behavior, and judges can provide instruction in civic virtue, but only free intellectual exchange and serious moral deliberation can sustain a culture of liberty. Regrettably, when measured by philosophical rather than legal standards, American democracy falls far short of Carey's ideal of an open "conversational" society. We can take comfort in the knowledge that the libertarian values of the Western democracies have helped to inspire the regeneration of hope and freedom in Eastern Europe. But we also have much to learn from the spirit of democratic resistance that has swept across the Eastern bloc. The energy, exhilaration, and sense of purpose that surround acts of democratic creation are chastening to citizens of an established democracy that has accumulated two centuries' worth of compromise and declension. The simple truths uttered by the survivors of the gulag and the police state are humbling reminders of the difficulty of achieving true freedom of expression in a nation dominated by technological and institutional sophistication. The two-hundredth anniversary of the Bill of Rights is a milestone worth celebrating, but it is also a time for sober reflection and renewed dedication.

2

The Bill of Rights, Liberty, and Original Intent

KERMIT L. HALL

*A*ny consideration of rights in American history begins with the simple observation that we are deeply conflicted about them. Survey after survey has disclosed as much. Asked, for example, if an individual has a right to see or show a pornographic movie, or to send or receive lewd materials through the mails, a majority of Americans respond negatively. Time and again, when offered a choice between liberty and community control, many Americans select the latter. Yet these same respondents routinely insist—and insist in overwhelming numbers—that, of the Constitution's provisions, the Bill of Rights is sacred. For example, recent efforts to amend the federal Constitution through a national convention have foundered because so many Americans worry that its delegates just might tamper with the Constitution's first ten amendments. We love to hate, it would seem, those provisions of our fundamental law that we most cherish.

This tension is readily explained. Liberty is not an absolute; indeed, granting total freedom to any individual could theoretically result in the restriction of freedom for everyone else. Social control is essential if rights are to have meaning. The far more difficult issue is how liberty is distributed within the social order, and in what institutions we lodge responsibility for this task. This concern about the distribution of rights forms the very fabric of American legal culture.

Many Americans seem to feel somewhat as Daniel Webster did when a friend visited him on his deathbed. The friend said to the faltering Webster: "Well, cheer up, Senator, I believe your *constitution* will pull you through." "Not at all," Webster responded, "my *constitution* was gone long ago, and I am living on my *by-laws* now." Like Webster more than a century ago, many Americans feel today that we live not so much by virtue of our Bill of Rights, as by its more pastel judicial interpretations. The by-laws promulgated by an unelected Supreme Court, we often hear, have replaced our original Bill of Rights.

Today, two centuries after the ratification of the Bill of Rights, we are being treated to the odd spectacle of public officials arguing about how best the Supreme Court can balance rights with community control amidst massive social change. Former Attorney General Edwin Meese and Chief Justice William Rehnquist, on the one hand, and Justice Thurgood Marshall and recently retired Justice William J. Brennan, on the other, have exchanged bitter comments about the devotion of the Court to the framers' wishes when interpreting the Bill of Rights. Meese complains that, with the chief justiceship of Earl Warren in the 1950s and 60s, the Court became little more than a continuing constitutional convention, in which the justices rewrote our fundamental law to suit their own prejudices and redistributed rights in a way that favored minorities. The Court, they charge, has become an *imperial judiciary* awash in its own personal excesses and locked in a kind of rapturous fit of liberalism and welfare statism in which the rights of minorities have taken precedence over the rights of the majority, and in which reverse discrimination has replaced just plain old discrimination. If, the argument runs, the justices only heeded the wishes—the intentions—of the framers, the present mess—in which we find the courts supposedly subverting community control and unfairly redistributing rights—would cease.

Of course, liberals have praised the Court's sensitivity to contemporary demands for social justice through law. Former Justice Brennan and Justice Marshall have ridiculed Meese and other conservative commentators for their commitment to the doctrine of original intent. Brennan has observed that "an awareness of history and appreciation of the aims of the Founding Fathers seldom resolve concrete problems of rights." Justice Marshall has been more direct, factiously urging African-Americans and women to take the original-intent doctrine seriously and boycott the bicentennial altogether. After all, Marshall argues, the all-white male framers in 1790 respected neither blacks nor women before the law. More generally, liberals insist that, given the heavy emphasis in American politics on majority will, the judiciary is the only institution capable of making more equal in law those who are less equal in life.

Recently, this debate took a dramatic turn with the failed nomination of Judge Robert Bork to the Supreme Court. Bork's Senate confirmation proceedings revealed the profoundly different visions that public leaders hold about how best to interpret what Justice Robert H. Jackson once aptly described as the "majestic generalities" of the Bill of Rights. These same proceedings also raised the perennial question of whether there are liberties protected by the Bill of Rights that are not explicitly provided for in the first ten amendments. For example, even though the Constitution nowhere mentions it, is there a right of privacy? Can the universe of liberties expand beyond those enumerated in the Bill of Rights? If so, what branch of government is to determine what they are and how they are to be distributed? Courts and judges? Legislatures and legislators? Or, should such changes come only through the amending process?

These questions have special urgency today because of the startling social and cultural changes that have generated them. It is self-evident that the Constitution and American society have changed enormously since 1791. Just in this century, for example, great changes can be discerned in patterns of parental authority; in attitudes toward treason, patriotism, and national defense; and in the rights of women, ethnic and racial minorities, students, and various other categories of persons previously at the bottom of the social pecking order. There have been profound and rapid changes in public and official attitudes toward so-called victimless crimes, such as prostitution, and striking shifts in the standards of permissible conduct governing dress, sexual habits, and styles of cohabitation. All of these have made issues of pornography, obscenity, and—most recently—nude cocktail-lounge dancers, subjects for constitutional scrutiny under the Bill of Rights. Changes in the field of law enforcement have been important as well. The right to be apprised of one's legal rights and to be represented by attorneys has become part of the Fifth and Sixth Amendments. Courts are far more likely to question the use of evidence under the Fourth Amendment than was true even forty years ago. Groups that were once silenced or unorganized—the aged, homosexuals, prisoners, and the physically and mentally handicapped—have entered the constitutional arena demanding a share of the national wealth and fuller protection for their rights.

At no time in our own history have law and the courts figured so prominently in at once responding to social demands and nationalizing rights. We have come to rely on the law and judges in ways that would truly astound our forebears. We hear today of a litigation explosion, of "hyperlexis," of excessive law, of everyone suing everyone else. We live in the era of the giant lawsuit—of the federal government, for example, pursuing from 1969 to 1980 an antitrust suit against the IBM corporation that resulted in more than 100,000 pages of testimony and over 7,000 separate documents being brought into the discovery process. The Pennzoil corporation has won a judgment of $11 billion against Texaco—a judgment larger than the gross national product of 75 percent of the nations of this earth. Awards are given in personal injury cases amounting sometimes to tens of millions of dollars. There is today one lawyer for every 350 people in the United States, a ratio unmatched in the rest of the world and unprecedented in our own history. By 1995, America will have one million lawyers.

The growing demands for the expression of rights that this law explosion represents, however, has not been universally welcomed. Commentators such as Bork, Meese, and Rehnquist characterize them as problems, attributable in part to excessive governmental interference in the operation of the marketplace for rights, with the resulting consequence that we are over-lawyered and over-judged, and that the federal government has simply gained too much power over our day-to-day lives. Others, such as Brennan and Marshall, explain these developments not as problems but as responses to unprecedented racial, gender, economic, and technological demands. The so-called law explosion, in this view, is not a sign of any impending breakdown in the system, but rather a healthy manifestation of its functional response to an underlying culture which has come to enshrine an ideology of *rights consciousness* and given priority to the quest for *total justice*.

These are powerful cultural assumptions, far different from those posed by our ancestors. Medical, technical, and social developments have so profoundly raised our expectations about the quality of life that we have generated demands for rights far in excess of anything we have previously known. In this century, we have moved toward the idea of recompensing all injuries and losses that are not the victim's fault, and even of making the government itself into an engine to protect rights, through programs such as affirmative action. Such notions were alien to the generation that framed the Bill of Rights. And as courts expand rights and give government a greater role in their maintenance, their judges, in turn, create fresh expectations for even greater rights. Yet it is our inability to deliver total justice that spurs demands for greater community control of the pornographer, the political dissenter, and the social outcast who seem to threaten the system.

Digesting all these social changes, while attempting to balance freedom and control, renders us a bit schizophrenic. We are at once proud of the gifts of freedom in a bountiful land, yet deeply introspective. Some of us brood about our rights in an indeterminate future in which community control is threatened and in which the only constant is change. Are we moving fast enough to fulfill the promise of the Bill of Rights, of equality before the law? Or have we broken from what Thomas Jefferson called the great promise of the Bill of Rights—that it would provide "equal rights for all, special privileges for none?" Does freedom of religion still have meaning in a country in which one million churches dot the landscape, but only one-third of the population regularly attends church? Aren't we only inviting anarchy by coddling smut peddlers and drug dealers when we clothe them with rights? Some see in this resort to constitutional protections the evidence not only of a collapse of community authority but of moral authority generally. Others argue that, over the long haul, fidelity to the Bill of Rights will save us from ourselves.

The simple truth of the matter is that we live in a constitutional system that forces us repeatedly to reexamine the Bill of Rights in the light of social change. One of the simple lessons of the anniversary just beginning is that the Bill of Rights as it is, is always becoming—and so too is American society. We can grasp the indeterminate nature of the relationship between social change and rights in this country by placing both in a comparative if admittedly stereotypical perspective. Thus, as one sage has recently observed:

> In Germany, under the law, everything is prohibited except that which is permitted.
> In France, under the law, everything is permitted, except that which is prohibited.
> In the Soviet Union, under the law, everything is prohibited, *including* that which is permitted.
> In Italy, under the law, everything is permitted, *especially* that which is prohibited.
> And in the United States, under the law, everything is *both* permitted *and* prohibited, because Americans are forever deciding the law but nothing ever seems to get decided.

There are many reasons for this peculiar turn to the relationship between rights and social change in our culture, but the most important, and most controversial, is judicial review. This is the practice by which judges—unelected judges in the case of the Supreme Court—review the merits of state and federal legislative enactments in the light of the Bill of Rights. This process has emerged as the chief means by which the federal Bill of Rights has been adapted to social change, making it an instrument of social reform and reconstruction.

There are two points to make about this development. First, judicial review has been important historically to the Bill of Rights because the

United States does not have a *social constitution,* as many Third World countries do. What distinguished the social constitutions of such nations as the Philippines, Nigeria, and Brazil, are the extensive commitments of governments to guarantee economic rights, equality for different ethnic groups, and the rights of the urban poor. These lengthy documents make the allocation of rights *explicit.* The problem with such social constitutions is that if the explicit promises go unfilled, the people lose faith in the constitution itself. The American scheme is different, because it has come to leave to courts the task of giving substance to, and adapting to, those "majestic generalities" of the Bill of Rights.

Second, while judicial review has many virtues, it has also stirred great concern about the power of unelected judges to readjust the balance between liberty and community control. A recent poll published in the *New York Times* indicated the depth of public concern about the Court and its powers. That poll revealed that Americans revere the Bill of Rights, but that they are deeply troubled by what seems to be the unaccountable nature of the Supreme Court. More than 60 percent of the respondents concluded that the present system of tenure during good behavior should be changed to make the justices less independent. The polling data revealed, as well, that the decisions in matters of school prayer, busing to achieve racial balance, and abortion have promoted social division and even outright hostility to the Supreme Court.

Much of this hostility stems not just from political differences about the appropriateness of judges mandating a redistribution of rights, but also from concerns about who is benefiting as a result. The doctrine of original intent has appeal because it promises to limit judicial discretion while promoting stability amid unrelenting social change. Its proponents insist that by invoking it we can link the present to a seemingly stable and secure past, while simultaneously restoring genuine liberty by reemphasizing community control.

Yet even the most casual reading of the history used by judges ought to give us pause. Too often, what judges do with the past brings to mind a cartoon that recently appeared in the *New Yorker* magazine. This cartoon depicts two Puritans who are all decked out in black—they have black hats, black cloaks, and black buckles on their shoes. They are standing on the deck of a sailing ship in Boston Harbor. In the background behind them, one sees the modern-day skyline of Boston. One Puritan looks at the other and asks, "What brought you to the New World?" The other Puritan answers, "I came in quest of religious freedom." There are a few dashes, followed by "I hope someday, however, to get into the real estate business in Boston." Or, to put the matter another way, Mark Twain's comment about the stock market is something like the way liberals as well as conservatives on the Court have abused the past. Twain observed: "Buy low and sell high. And if your stocks do not go up, don't buy." The invocation of history by judges from either end of the political spectrum is merely a way of indicating how, with 20/20 hindsight, one side or the other would have liked the world to be.

Bluntly put, the idea of original intention as a way of understanding our rights carries with it problematical methodological assumptions, and the potential to abuse the past; as a result, it raises profound ethical problems. As Justice Oliver Wendell Holmes, Jr., observed at the beginning of this century: historical continuity in the law is "not a duty, it is only a necessity." We root answers to contemporary disputes about rights in historical terms because our legal culture, with its common law roots and its emphasis on precedent, requires as much. But we should, at the same time, be alert to the limits of doing so.

What ought to make us worry about the doctrine of original intention is the realization that the Supreme Court is the only institution in our national experience that has the power to *declare* history: that is, to articulate some understanding of the past and then compel the rest of society to conform its behavior based on that understanding. No Ministry of State Security, no Thought Police, has ever succeeded in establishing such authority. This power exists irrespective of the degree to which judicial perceptions of the past conform to reality or even to a consensus of trained historians. Even where the Court's history is at odds with the past, that judicial history, as absorbed into a decision, and then into a doctrine, becomes the progenitor of a rule of law. So without belaboring Justice Robert H. Jackson's concession that "judges are often not thorough or objective historians," it is worth reiterating that judicial history has had an impact on the evolution of our rights in the form of constitutional doctrines that govern us all.

The selective use of historical facts and interpretations, while doubtless suitable to writing a legal brief, is often disastrous in judicial opinions. Moreover, this use of history has often been undertaken to break precedent and enable a justice to get around established law. The famous *Dred Scott* case of 1857, which involved the Fifth Amendment to the Constitution, found Chief Justice Roger B. Taney declaring that, as a matter of history, persons of African-American descent had no rights that white persons were bound to respect. Since, Taney concluded, the framers had not intended for African-Americans to be covered by the Bill of Rights, then there was no way they could share in those rights—ever.

More recently, Justice William Rehnquist, in *Carey v. Population Services International,* provided us with a nice example of this form of history when considering whether a New York state law limiting access by persons under sixteen years of age to contraceptives would have violated the wishes of the framers of the Fourteenth Amendment. Justice Rehnquist concluded that if the soldiers who fought at ''Shiloh, Gettysburg, and Cold Harbor could have lived to know that their efforts had enshrined in the Constitution the right of commercial vendors of contraceptives to peddle them to unmarried minors through . . . vending machines located in the men's rooms of truck stops, it is too difficult to imagine their reaction.'' One has to agree with Justice Rehnquist: it is difficult to imagine their reaction, since it was probably the furthest thing from their minds with bullets whizzing about.

Conservatives, I hasten to add, have not been alone in such moral pontificating.

The past, unfortunately, reveals itself only ambiguously, and, once we recognize as much, there are real questions to be asked about whether sound public policy can actually rest on judicial interpretation rooted in original intentions. A few examples drawn from our early history will underscore how difficult it can be to apply the past to the present.

Proponents of original intent argue that judicial power is legitimate only as long as it remains faithful to the wishes of the framers of the Bill of Rights. Unfortunately, the framers' intentions are insufficiently clear on a number of important matters.

Take, for example, the seemingly simple question of what were the origins of the Bill of Rights. There is no doubt that its framers believed that the power of government was and would continue to be a constant threat to individual liberty. They drew this lesson from several sources rather than from just one, including the Magna Carta of 1215, subsequent English constitutional history leading up to and then flowing from the Glorious Revolution of 1689, and the common law tradition. But the American framers of the Bill of Rights had more immediate experience to draw on, including lessons from establishing their own colonial governments, of protecting their rights within the empire, and of fighting, winning, and then securing a revolution. But which of these sources most influenced the framers of the Bill of Rights?

One way of answering this question is to ask another question: was a bill of rights necessary in the first place? The framers of the Constitution in 1787 did not think so. They worried incessantly about protecting liberty from encroaching governmental power, but most of them concluded that a separate bill of rights was unnecessary. James Madison, the

single most influential person at the Philadelphia convention, argued that
since the Constitution was one of strictly enumerated powers, the federal
government was prevented from passing legislation that would trample
individual rights. Madison was hardly alone; for most delegates to the
Philadelphia convention agreed that a bill of rights was unnecessary. It
became essential only when its absence complicated significantly the
process of ratifying the Constitution. Within hours of the delegates' signing the Constitution, George Mason, of Madison's Virginia, published a
pamphlet, the central theme of which was that the absence of a "declaration of rights" made the Constitution unacceptable. Without limitations, Mason believed, the federal government would infringe the basic
rights of the citizenry. Because the laws of the general government,
according to Mason, would be paramount to the laws and constitutions of
the states, state bills of rights would provide no protection at all against
that central government.

The Anti-Federalist opponents of the Constitution repeated these arguments in the state ratification debates over the next ten months. While the
federal convention had withheld from the ratifying conventions the power
to propose amendments, the delegates in the states nonetheless adopted
the tactic of offering "recommendatory amendments."

Madison was impressed by the strength of demands in his home state
for the addition of a bill of rights, which was the one issue that seemed
to coalesce the Constitution's various opponents. Virginia and New York
both voted to ratify the Constitution, but they did so with the proviso that
the first Congress would consider the addition of a bill of rights. The
Federalists in general, and Madison in particular, gained ratification by
promising to address the issue of a bill of rights in the first Congress.
Thus, Madison, who originally discounted the necessity of such a bill,
quickly grasped how essential it was in order to preserve his handiwork
in Philadelphia. At the same time, Anti-Federalist critics reversed field.
They now worried that its adoption would secure the strong central government that they did not want.

The point is not to accuse Madison—or the Anti-Federalists, for that
matter—of being unprincipled. Instead, it is to affirm that compromise
and political sagacity, as much as constitutional principles, shaped the
framers' original reasons for adopting the Bill of Rights. Was the Bill of
Rights necessary? Yes, but for reasons entirely different from those that
the proponents of original intent would have us believe.

In discerning the original intentions of the framers, we need some idea
of where they turned for authority. One of the most important problems
presented by the doctrine of original intention is the matter of whose

intentions we are speaking of: Madison's, as the chief architect? Or the intentions of the members of the conference committee that redrafted Madison's work? Or the intentions of the state legislatures that ratified only ten of the twelve amendments sent to them?

Madison borrowed conspicuously from several sources, and often what is most revealing is what he ignored. Of the twenty-six rights ultimately declared in the Bill of Rights, only four—due process, illegal seizures, fines, and jury trials—can be traced to the Magna Carta. While many present-day commentators point to our English inheritance of liberty, that connection was in fact quite weak.

Nor did Madison give much heed to the ninety-seven "recommendatory" amendments proposed by the ratifying conventions. His draft included only 17 percent of the rights they urged upon him. He purposefully ignored most of the proposed amendments because they seriously constrained the power of the new central government, something that even Madison, for all of his states' rights sympathies, could not tolerate.

Where, then, did Madison turn? Existing state bills of rights were certainly an important source. More than 60 percent of the rights proclaimed in Madison's draft were taken from these documents, and if one adds those rights that were ultimately put in the Bill of Rights—that is, the additions made to Madison's initial nine-amendment proposal—then more than 75 percent were from the state bills of rights.

The most comprehensive body of authority for Madison, however, actually predated the Revolution itself. This important source consisted of the various charters, compacts, and governing documents drawn up by the colonists themselves in the century and a half before the Revolution. Everything that was included in Madison's draft, in the revised draft of the conference committee, and in the federal Bill of Rights had previously been treated in these precursor documents such as the Mayflower Compact, the Massachusetts Charter of Liberties, and the Fundamental Orders of Connecticut. In short, the federal Bill of Rights summed up and encapsulated what colonial Americans had already taken to be their rights. There is, in fact, no single source to which we can turn today to discern these rights authoritatively. Instead, there are many sources.

Yet even if we know in a general way where these rights came from, we do not know what, in most instances, their framers and ratifiers actually thought they meant. The framers' own words are of little help. Proponents of an originalist reading of the Bill of Rights suggest that we can know, but such is certainly not the case. The problem with the originalists' position is that there is so little evidence left behind about what actually was said, let alone intended. The 1789 debates in Congress are sketchy, the discussions in the conference committee that revised Madison's proposed amendments are even sketchier, and the debates over ratification in the states are essentially nonexistent. We search, in vain, to find out exactly what the framers and ratifiers meant with regard to "free speech," the right to "bear arms," or "cruel and unusual punishment." Most often the evidence suggests that these Bill of Rights provisions were cast broadly not because a consensus existed over their precise meaning, but for just the opposite reason. There was sufficient disagreement about them that a consensus could be achieved only by stating them as majestic generalities. To have done otherwise would have threatened the fragile consensus upon which the new Constitution and government rested.

Furthermore, these very same pressures meant that all sides recognized that the rights listed in the Bill of Rights were not meant to be exhaustive. That is why Madison, Congress, and the states agreed to the Ninth and Tenth Amendments, which, while guaranteeing no specific rights, as did the first eight amendments, did outline divisions of powers within the Constitution. Both of these amendments were critical to fashioning written guarantees that would protect individual rights against encroachment by the national government. Their inclusion is particularly instructive because both of them affirm that the entire thrust of the Bill of Rights was not to list rights but instead to set broad substantive and procedural guarantees designed to bridle government. Indeed, the proponents of original intent misapprehend what the framers of the Bill of Rights did. The Bill of Rights was really not a catalog of rights; instead, it was a "bill of restraints," one that told the government where it could not encroach.

There remain, of course, the final issues of who was to interpret the Bill of Rights and against whom was it to apply—the nation or the states? These issues are at the heart of the contemporary criticism of the High Court and judicial review, since critics charge that the justices have usurped power that the framers never intended them to exercise, and that they have meddled in local and state affairs to a degree that would have horrified the framers. Once again, we have to be impressed by the ambiguity of the record.

The creation of an independent federal judiciary with status coequal to that of the other branches was one of the important innovations of the federal Constitution. It was also a source of great concern among proponents of states' rights, who feared that the federal government would become, through the courts, an engine to oppress them. We know, however, that Madison shared none of this uncertainty when it came to the role of the federal judiciary in implementing the Bill of Rights. He advanced the key argument that the reason to adopt the Bill of Rights was that it offered additional *legal* protection against excessive legislative power. Since these guarantees would go into the Constitution, Madison insisted that "independent tribunals of justice will consider themselves in a peculiar manner the guardians of those rights." Madison intended that the newly created federal courts would be a countermajoritarian legal force to protect individual rights against the excesses of the political and popularly elected branches. He also expected that, as agents of the law, judges would give an impartial, lawful interpretation to rights that would bind the public in a way the political branches could never do.

We also know that, at least in its most important provisions, Madison expected that the Bill of Rights would be applied against the states and not just against the national government. Madison's original draft included exactly such a provision.

But once again what Madison wanted was not what others agreed to. The Congressional conference committee that reviewed Madison's draft struck the state action provision from the Bill of Rights, making it apply only against the national government. Even after this action, considerable difference of opinion persisted over whether federal judges could invoke the Bill of Rights against state legislation, and whether state judges could invoke its terms against legislatures in their own states. As early as 1810, Chancellor James Kent of New York relied on the Fifth Amendment provision against the taking of property without just compensation to strike down an act of the New York state assembly. Moreover, throughout the pre–Civil War period all but the most extreme abolitionists argued not only that the framers had intended the Bill of Rights to apply against the states but that it could be used as a basis upon which to eradicate the peculiar institution of slavery. Chief Justice John Marshall in 1833 became so worried about the consequences to the Union of this antislavery vision of the Bill of Rights that in *Barron v. Baltimore* he rendered his famous opinion that the Bill of Rights applied only to the nation and not to the states. Yet, thirty-five years later, when the Reconstruction Congress debated the Fourteenth Amendment's due process, equal protection, and privileges and immunities clauses, several moderate and radical Republicans argued that the Bill of Rights had *always* applied to the states. Conservative Democrats were equally emphatic that it had not, and that by passing the Fourteenth Amendment it would not. There is, in sum, no clear answer to either the question of whether the framers of the Bill of Rights originally intended that it apply to the states or whether the framers of the Fourteenth Amendment meant to do so.

Today, of course, most of the Bill of Rights has been incorporated through the Fourteenth Amendment and applies against the states. The most controversial High Court decisions of this century—involving free speech and the press, separation of church and state, and the rights of the accused—have resulted from justices broadly construing the meaning of the Bill of Rights, often doing so, somewhat ironically for proponents of original intent, with a strong reliance on historical arguments.

What the framers of the Bill of Rights did was to put forth certain broad *concepts*—there could be no cruel and unusual punishment, there had to be due process—but they did not attempt to put forth *conceptions* (what exactly cruel and unusual punishment was, what a denial of due process precisely amounted to). Instead, they left to the judiciary the task of defining those notions, and of conceptualizing them. In essence, the history of the creation of the Bill of Rights leads us to one clear conclusion—the framers adopted broadly stated limitations on government, leaving to courts and judges the task of giving precise meaning to these majestic generalities.

This excursion into the historical meaning, scope, and interpretation of the Bill of Rights ought to give us pause in resorting to a doctrine of original intention. The current prophets of this doctrine argue that judicial power is only legitimate so long as it remains faithful to principles embraced by the framers. Unfortunately, the framers held often contradictory views and, as a result, the thin surviving historical record is marked by ambiguity, not clarity.

But does this conclusion mean that the framers themselves had no sense of original intent on matters of rights? Simply put, did the framers believe that what they did was going to bind future generations? The answer to that question is certainly, *yes*. These men had fought a revolution, seen the blood of friends and brothers shed, and passionately believed in what they were doing. As the words of the Constitution indicate, they meant to create a more perfect Union that was intended to endure for the ages. They did invoke the concept of original intent, but it differed significantly from that espoused by modern critics, such as Judge Bork and Attorney General Meese, of judicially protected constitutional rights. As James Madison observed in 1796: "Whatever veneration might be entertained for the body of men who formed our Constitution, the sense of that body could never be regarded as the oracular guide in expounding the Constitution."

Of course, as citizens of a nation blessed with a written constitution, Americans must be bound by its words, must presume that those words have meaning, and must understand that meaning in light of how those words were used by their authors and by subsequent generations. But the Bill of Rights does not, like a cookbook, specify which ingredients, combined in what orders and amounts, will yield "liberty." Even more important, this character of the Bill of Rights was no accident, as we have seen. On many crucial questions, its framers, in order to establish a nation, selected language flexible enough to anticipate social, economic, and political crises. That is what Chief Justice John Marshall meant when he wrote that the Constitution was intended to "endure for ages to come and adapt to the various crises of human affairs."

That, in sum, was the framers' original "original intent." They expected Americans pragmatically, through the legal process, to fit the Bill of Rights to changing exigencies, but to do so in ways that would preserve the Union, sustain broad principles of human worth, maintain skepticism about government's power, and leave sufficient room for the community control that all of the framers knew was essential to true liberty.

Imagining what the framers would have said is often a sterile and all but meaningless historical exercise. Too much has changed. Moreover, there is the real danger, as our constitutional history shows, that we will come to believe that choices of law can be passively made by the discovery of a single "original intent" that will free our own generation from the difficult social choices that it must make. As the great Englishman Sir Thomas More observed at his own trial: "The world must construe according to its wits. The courts must construe according to the law." History offers no relief from such obligations.

The danger that judges might wield power not in the name of the Constitution but in the service of their own personal moral predilections is *heightened, not reduced,* by the habit of couching judicial determinations of rights in the form of historical explanations. As Justice Felix Frankfurter once observed: "[T]he problem is not whether the judges make law, but when and how and how much." To accept any other view is to cloak the Bill of Rights—and the entire Constitution—in mystery, miracle, and unquestioned authority, and to retard rather than expand our liberties.

Moreover, far from liberating judges to impose purely personal values on each of us, an appreciation on their part for the essentially indeterminate nature of history forces them to *explain* their distributive choices, and the reasons supporting those choices, in ways that are accessible to meaningful public discussion.

The point is certainly *not* that the Supreme Court is a weak institution or that history should be ignored when we consider the meaning of the Bill of Rights. Far from it. But we should take care not to be trapped by rhetorical flourish, whether it is from the right or the left. Perhaps Paul

Freund was right, when he observed: "Of history it may be said briefly that its usefulness varies inversely with the weight of the demands made upon it."

The federal judiciary is not an imperial force and the law explosion is not a catastrophe. The federal courts remain the branch with the least discretionary power and the one best suited to balancing freedom and community control while doing what the political branches—because they are political branches—cannot do: protect the rights of minorities from majority tyranny. In the circumstances of contemporary society, in which racial and gender equality are professed to a degree unknown to the framers, any other approach seems unsound. The great problem with the concept of original intent is not that it lacks validity, but that it lacks the importance with which it has been so solemnly invested. The notion that we can return to a simpler past and purer time, of less law and government, is illusory. So, too, is the belief that we can find through history a specific set of particular intentions that will give a sense of certainty to the present and the future. To accept any other view would, in the words of Harold Bloom, condemn us to read the past backwards from the present in such a way that we would end up imitating our ancestors.

Moreover, we should recognize that even amid the rights explosion of this century, liberty and community control remain unbalanced and justice remains unevenly distributed throughout the social order. The social categories of class, race, ethnicity, and gender continue to have powerful influence in shaping the distribution of rights. We know that white middle-class Americans are far more likely to benefit from the recent expansion of the right to counsel and Miranda warnings than are persons of color at the lower end of the social spectrum. In the case of the death penalty, the evidence is overwhelming that, despite the cruel and unusual punishment clause of the Eighth Amendment, African-Americans—especially lower class African-Americans that kill white persons—are far more likely to die at the hands of the state than are white offenders.

Yet even as we recognize these limitations, we can take comfort in the fact that the history of the Bill of Rights does teach us an important lesson—a lesson quite different from that of original intent. In the hands of the federal judiciary, the Bill of Rights has developed as a living organism. Justice Thurgood Marshall rightly says that "the true miracle was not the birth of the Bill of Rights, but its life, a life nurtured through two turbulent centuries of our own making, and a life embodying much good fortune that was not." It is fitting, therefore, to use this bicentennial celebration to "commemorate the suffering, struggle, and sacrifice that has triumphed over much of what was wrong with the original Bill of Rights, and observe the anniversary with hopes not realized and promises not fulfilled.'' Yet it is precisely those hopes, and the possibility that at every turn of social development we have the opportunity to readdress the balance between liberty and community control, that sustain the importance of the Bill of Rights.

The debate we are living through about original intent, social change, and the Bill of Rights is precisely what the framers intended. As Daniel Webster's friend observed over a century ago, we should cheer up and understand at this bicentennial that the clamor over our judicially constructed by-laws of liberty is really a sign of constitutional health that will pull us through the third century of government with liberty for all. That was, after all, exactly what the framers intended.

3

African-Americans and the Bill of Rights in the Slave Era

JOHN HOPE FRANKLIN

The Bill of Rights was no afterthought. Virtually every provision in the group of resolutions that became the Bill of Rights received considerable attention, at one point or another, at the Constitutional Convention in 1787. Indeed, matters that later were incorporated into the first ten amendments to the Constitution had been debated before and during the Convention, but did not become a part of the original Constitution for a variety of reasons. Some members of the Convention agreed with Alexander Hamilton that a bill of rights was more than unnecessary: "Why declare that things shall not be done which there is no power [in Congress] to do?" Others supported James Wilson in his view that any attempt to include a bill of rights would be impracticable. "Enumerate all the rights of men?" Wilson asked. "I am sure that no gentlemen in the late convention would have attempted such a thing." In further attempting to provide reasons for omitting a bill of rights, Wilson argued that the Constitution was not a body of fundamental law, but a code of reference, providing for a framework of government. Still others had no objection to a bill of rights, but thought it would be catastrophic if an attempt were made to enumerate them and some rights were omitted.

One suspects, moreover, that some Founding Fathers steadfastly opposed the Bill of Rights because they did not believe in freedom of religion, or speech, or speedy jury trials for the accused, or other practices which, from their point of view, were too radical to countenance. To include such matters in the original Constitution would unleash a debate that would seriously jeopardize the ratification of the Constitution itself. They had hoped that the Constitution would be ratified without reference to such matters. And should it be impossible to do that, then such thorny questions should be postponed at least until after the Constitution was ratified. Then, perhaps some consideration would be given to those questions by the Congress that met after the new government was inaugurated. There were those who agreed with James Wilson that the Constitution was a code of reference, but they thought the Bill of Rights went too far in dealing with matters of detail. Excessive bail, cruel and unusual punishment, trial by jury in cases exceeding twenty dollars—these were matters, they argued, best handled by the legislative branch as it sought to carry out the mandates set forth in the Constitution itself. In any case, the general argument that prevailed in 1787 was that the Bill of Rights had no place in the Constitution itself and should be kept out at all possible costs.

But the Constitution itself *did* contain matters of detail, such as provisions regarding the slave trade and fugitive slaves or those prohibiting bills of attainder and ex post facto laws. It would appear that consistency was not so much the goal as was the belief that if a detail was best handled in the Constitution, then that is where it would be handled.

But arguments against incorporating the Bill of Rights in the Constitution did not prevail, no matter how closely reasoned and eloquent they were. And many who voted for the ratification of the Constitution in 1787 and 1788 did so with the clear understanding that the Bill of Rights would be added to the Constitution, and would be at the top of the agenda with the convening of the First Congress in 1789.

Looking back into the late eighteenth century, it hardly seems possible that the framers of the Constitution could have seriously entertained the possibility of omitting the Bill of Rights from the Constitution altogether. One can only be grateful to Sam Adams, Elbridge Gerry, Patrick Henry, and the others who were intransigent enough and sufficiently strong in their opposition to the Constitution as it had been written that its proponents agreed to mollify them by promising to include the Bill of Rights after the Constitution was ratified.

If the Bill of Rights celebrated and protected certain very fundamental privileges that were a part of the legacy of free men since the signing of the Magna Carta in 1215, it was somewhat fastidious in its protection of the rights of certain individuals and not of others. I do not know what Richard Allen, a black Philadelphian, thought of the First Amendment that ostensibly guaranteed freedom of religion. At best he must have been skeptical of it or even wondered whether it was worth the paper on which it was written when he was dragged from his knees at St. George's Methodist Church in Philadelphia in November 1787, simply because he was using the front-row pew instead of a rear-row pew in the balcony of the church.

Since this incident occurred two months after the United States Constitution was signed by its framers and just when the arguments for a Bill of Rights were being formulated, it was reasonable for Richard Allen to conclude that the grand fight to include a Bill of Rights in the Constitution had nothing whatever to do with the free exercise of *his* religion. The only thing he was free to do was to leave St. George's Church, which he promptly did, and worship in a church of his own making, which he also promptly did.

The experience of Richard Allen and other blacks similarly situated as worshippers in predominantly white churches raises other questions regarding the extent to which the framers of the Constitution—and, indeed, white worshippers—were truly committed to the free exercise of religion. If religious brotherhood was to be maintained in a setting characterized by segregation and discrimination, the question inevitably arises concerning the consistency, integrity, and commitment of those who claimed that they stood for the free exercise of religion. Had they so chosen, the proponents of the new Constitution could not have had a better example of the need to protect freedom of religion than its denial to Allen and his confreres by the trustees of St. George's Church. They chose not to. And if they could countenance discrimination against worshippers on the basis of race, it would be easy and convenient to deny religious freedom to those whose beliefs were regarded as unorthodox or even heretical. It was easy to protect religious freedom among the white orthodox believers. It was obviously not so easy to protect the religious freedom of blacks and those holding strange, unpopular religious views. All too often, the Bill of Rights did not help such individuals or groups.

That same First Congress that passed the resolution forbidding Congress to interfere with the free exercise of religion and that guaranteed freedom of speech, the press, and of assembly, also passed a Second Amendment that, in some quarters, remains controversial to this day. It says, "A well regulated militia, being necessary to the security of a free State, the right of the people to keep and bear arms, shall not be infringed." A careful, casual, even reckless reading of the Second Amendment reveals that it deals exclusively with the establishment and maintenance of the militia. It has *absolutely nothing* to do with a private individual's owning a Saturday night special or an AK-47, notwithstanding claims to the contrary by the National Rifle Association and its life members, including George Herbert Walker Bush.

Perhaps the most fascinating aspect of the passage of this Second Amendment is that once it was ratified Congress then proceeded to exclude blacks from whatever it was that it was protecting in that Amendment. In an act establishing a ''Uniform Militia Throughout the United States,'' the Congress said: ''Each and Every free able-bodied white male citizen of the respective states . . . who is or shall be of the age of eighteen years and under the age of forty-five . . . shall be . . . enrolled in the Militia. . . .'' In a word, the Act told the 5,000 blacks who saw service in the War for Independence, and all or most of whom were freed after the war, that their services were no longer needed and that once independence was achieved, with their help, they were not worthy to serve in the militia of the United States. This declaration was not only lacking in grace, it was also lacking in gratitude. One would be compelled to conclude, upon reading the provision, that a certain kind of illness would be required for a people—in this case white Americans—to think up and then impose such forms of humiliation on others.

The ''white only'' militia law repudiated the policy reluctantly accepted by George Washington that blacks could serve in the armed forces of the United States, and embraced the view that the protective arm of the United States must be white in order to be effective. No exception was made of free blacks who numbered some 59,000 in 1790 and who were as entitled under the Constitution as any other citizens to participate in the military activities and in the political process of the United States. Such a policy and such a view launched this country on a systematic program of racial bigotry, carefully conceived and executed, that would in the future mar race relations in war as well as in peace.

The Constitution and the Fugitive Slave Laws of 1793 and 1850 gave ample protection to slaveowners in their efforts to recover runaway slaves. Congress had exclusive jurisdiction, moreover, in all procedural and other matters regarding their recovery, as Justice Joseph Story pointed out in *Prigg v. Pennsylvania* in 1842. One would have thought that the Bill of Rights—either the Fifth, Sixth, or Seventh Amendment—would have extended *some* protection, *some* due process, in the litigation growing out of contests over slaves having allegedly run away. It is well to remember that there were always free blacks in the United States, and the number grew steadily with every passing decade before the Civil War. By 1860 there were about a half-million free blacks divided almost evenly between the slave states and the free states. Every free black person was constantly at risk of losing his or her freedom, for every white person assumed that if a person was black, that person was a slave.

Laws current at the time authorized all whites to challenge any black whom the white person suspected of being a runaway. (One need not dwell on the psychological headiness it gave to a white who had no slaves, and had no reasonable chance of ever having any, to challenge a black as a runaway, seize him, and deliver him to the authorities.) It made the hapless white feel that he was part of the system. As James De Bow aptly put it in 1860:

> Upon the sure testimony of God's Holy Book, and upon the princi-
> ples of universal policy, they [the non-slaveholders] have defended
> and justified the institution. . . . The non-slaveholder of the South
> preserves the status of the white man, and is not regarded as an in-
> ferior or a dependent. . . . No white man at the South serves an-
> other as a body servant, to clean his boots, wait on his table, and
> perform the menial services of his household. His blood revolts
> against this, and his necessities never drive him to it. He is a com-
> panion and an equal.

As such, he enthusiastically joins in the defense and protection of the institution of slavery. Thus, in the slave states, slaves and free blacks alike had to defend themselves from the power and force of the entire white population in their effort to escape from slavery or, if they were already free, to maintain their freedom.

Even in the free states, blacks who were accused of being fugitive slaves had no protection from false arrest or frivolous or erroneous ac-cusations. If some white person in the North accused a black person of being a runaway, all the alleged owner or his agent had to do was to bring the so-called fugitive before any federal or state court and, upon proof of identity, the magistrate would turn him over to the owner or his agent. The Fifth Amendment, a very central feature of the Bill of Rights, de-clared that no person could be deprived of life, liberty, or property with-out due process of law. Mere personal identification, in the absence of one word of defense or refutation on the part of the alleged fugitive, was hardly due process of law. The Sixth Amendment provided that the accused shall enjoy the right to a speedy and public trial by an impartial jury of the state, to be confronted by witnesses against him, to have compulsory process for obtaining witnesses in his favor, and to have the assistance of counsel for his defense. The summary manner in which a magistrate accepted the declaration of an alleged owner that the person appearing before the magistrate was his property is a clear indication that the rights protected in the Sixth Amendment were not extended to blacks, whether they were actual runaways or merely unfortunate free blacks who happened to cross the path of a slaveowner or his agent looking for his runaway slave.

The Seventh Amendment provided that in suits at common law, where the value in controversy shall exceed twenty dollars, the right to trial by jury shall be preserved. Any slave was worth at least twenty dollars and surely any alleged runaway would contest his recapture. The controversy thus ensuing was one that should have guaranteed the accused a trial by jury. Yet, this ancient and honorable practice, venerated and adhered to since medieval times, meant nothing in American courts of law where the accused was black and where his status as a fugitive slave or a free black person was yet to be established. There are no records, so far as I know, of an alleged fugitive slave enjoying the rights ostensibly protected by the Seventh Amendment.

These, then, were the rights guaranteed by the Fifth, Sixth, and Seventh Amendments—the centerpiece of the Bill of Rights guaranteed to all persons living within the jurisdiction of the United States. If one were to read these provisions in, say, 1830, they must have been reassuring. Yes, they were reassuring to white Americans, but meant nothing to black Americans, even if they were free. It is remarkable how the future well-being and, indeed, the very life of a free black could hang in the balance awaiting the verdict of a judge who was called upon to determine his status. In 1836 one John Pedro, declaring himself to be a free man of color, was confined to jail in Vicksburg, Mississippi, charged with no crime but accused of being a runaway slave:

> He states that he is not a slave, but is a free man and that he was born of free parents and that he is a native of Curracou [sic.] in South America and that he is a sailor by profession and that he came to New Orleans, where he has resided nine years, making occasional voyages to different parts of the United States; that he shipped on the Steamboat Chickasaw as a sailor at New Orleans in October 1836 and came on here to Vicksburg, where he was taken from said Boat and confined as before stated as a runaway slave.

Pedro asked the court to grant a writ of habeas corpus and that he be brought before the court where he would prove his freedom. The judge granted the writ, but there is no account in the records of the disposition of the case. One can only hope that Pedro was given an opportunity to establish his freedom to the satisfaction of the court.

Samuel Bryan, a well-traveled Jamaican, had unusually good fortune

in establishing his freedom, even without some of the protections provided by the Bill of Rights. In 1837, after being taken up as a slave, he
presented his case to Judge John J. Guion of the Criminal Court of
Warren County, Mississippi.

> The petition of Samuel Bryan a free man of color now confined in
> custody of the Jailor of Warren Co . . . Miss., since the 5th day of
> June, 1836, without being charged with any crime that he has been
> informed of but is informed that he is confined as a runaway slave.

Bryan's petition then declared that he was born in Kingston, Jamaica, of
free parents, the subjects of the King of Britain, that he was apprenticed
to James Johnson, a carpenter, to learn the trade for five years. Johnson
died, which ended the apprenticeship. Bryan then went by ship to New
York, settled there, and became a citizen. He worked as an assistant cook
on board ships sailing to ports such as Savannah and Charleston.

In April 1836, Bryan left New York aboard the *Mary* as assistant
steward and arrived in New Orleans. He had his certificate of freedom on
board, but it was in the belongings of his half-brother, with whom he had
a disagreement. He decided to return to New York by some other means,
leaving behind his free papers. He began working on a ship up the
Mississippi River, but when the captain discovered that Bryan had no
certificate of claim to freedom, he had him committed to jail as a runaway
slave. Bryan requested and was granted a writ of habeas corpus so that he
could appear before the court and establish his freedom. In court one
white witness swore that he knew Bryan in New York and in 1834 had
sailed with him to Liverpool on a ship in which Bryan was second cook.
He was regarded as a free man and no one ever claimed him as a slave.
Another white man sent an affidavit saying that he knew Bryan in New
York where he passed as a free man. After receiving the affidavit, Judge
Guion discharged Bryan as a free man, but required him to pay the court
costs. It is somewhat ironic that the ship's captain who falsely turned
Bryan in as a fugitive received a reward of six dollars, while Bryan, who
was not a fugitive, had to pay the court costs.

Many other free blacks, whose claims to freedom were doubtless as
valid as those of John Pedro and Samuel Bryan, had no such good luck.
One by one, in Northern and Southern courts, they were paraded before
a magistrate and, after a perfunctory hearing, with none of the protections
of the Bill of Rights, were hustled off to a lifetime of service on a
Southern plantation. It is obviously not possible to determine the numbers
of the victims who were unable to defend themselves and consequently
were sent into slavery. One can only say that, unless the evidence and

testimony were irrefutable, as in the case of Samuel Bryan, there was simply no chance to remain free if that was just a claim, or to become free if that is what a runaway hoped to do. With slaveholders and their agents combing the countryside from New Orleans to Boston in search of runaways, virtually every free person of color was in immediate danger of being taken up and delivered into slavery with no opportunity whatever to establish a valid claim to freedom. And the Constitution and the Bill of Rights provided no protection whatever to free blacks who could easily be falsely accused of being runaway slaves.

Even in death a free black person was not protected by the provisions of the Bill of Rights. The case of William Johnson is an example of this tragic fact. Johnson, a free black of Natchez, Mississippi, in the antebellum years, was a barber, real estate dealer, and money lender who amassed a fortune. He owned several valuable properties in Natchez as well as several plots of rural land. His social life was restricted, of course, since few blacks had the resources or interests that he had. Whites would patronize his barber shop, even borrow money from him, but would have nothing to do with him socially. For recreation, he frequently traveled to New Orleans on the same ship with some of his customers, but they avoided him en route and in the city. Indeed, some of them were fiercely jealous of his success; and that was his ultimate undoing.

In the late 1840s Johnson became embroiled in a dispute with one Baylor Winn over the accuracy of the boundary line that separated adjacent lands which they owned. Although the dispute was settled, with Johnson making concessions favorable to Winn, bad feelings remained between the two men. Some claimed that Winn was a free Negro, but he had always argued that, while he had some Indian ancestry, he had no African forebears. He had voted, had married a white woman, and was generally accepted as a white person. One evening in 1851, while Johnson was returning on horseback to his home with two other blacks, he was shot from ambush. Before he died several hours later, Johnson said that he had been shot by Winn, and his two black companions also attested to Winn's guilt. Winn was tried three times, but each time his attorneys successfully argued that he was innocent. There were no competent witnesses, since those who claimed that Winn shot Johnson were of African descent and under the laws of Mississippi could not testify against a white person. The irony is that under the Bill of Rights the accused was guaranteed a fair and speedy trial before a jury and, at the same time, was protected by state law from testimony against him by blacks. Meanwhile, Johnson was denied his life without due process of law, despite the Fifth Amendment, because in 1851 the protection did not extend to the state.

Even if it had, neither the Constitution of the United States nor the laws of Mississippi gave credence to testimony given by a black person against a white man.

Black Americans were delivered from slavery in a variety of ways. In addition to being born free, they ran away, purchased their freedom, were manumitted by their owners, or were set free by the state for supplying information on plots of rebellion. Desperately anxious to enjoy a measure of that freedom, they joined with antislavery groups in seeking the civil and legal rights that others enjoyed. It is interesting to observe, however, that in their national conventions that met annually after 1831, and in numerous addresses to public officials and to their own people, black leaders almost never invoked the Constitution and the Bill of Rights as the source of their anticipated support and protection. From time to time they asked Congress to repeal all laws that made distinctions on the basis of race or color, of course to no avail.

When the Pennsylvania Constitution of 1837 disfranchised black voters, some forty thousand Pennsylvania free blacks bitterly protested this insult to their status as persons and as citizens. They took their stand, they said, on the basis of the electrifying words of the Declaration of Independence which proclaimed that to protect the inalienable rights of all peoples "governments are instituted among men, deriving their just powers from the consent of the governed." Not once did they refer to the Constitution or its Bill of Rights, for their examination of those documents revealed nothing to relieve them in their solemn hour of grievance.

When Congress enacted a more stringent fugitive slave law in 1850 that had no provision for a jury trial or for an alleged fugitive to testify in his or her own behalf, an important guarantee in the Bill of Rights, the 435,000 blacks who were free should have been convinced that they had no reasonable protection under the Constitution and laws of the United States. Speaking before the State Convention of Ohio Negroes in January 1851, one delegate said:

> No man can consistently vote under the United States Constitution. That instrument also provides for the return of fugitive slaves. And, sir, one of the greatest lights now adorning the galaxies of American literature declares that the 'Fugitive Law' is in accordance with that stipulation; it is a law unequaled in the worst days of Roman despotism, and unparalleled in the annals of heathen jurisprudence.

No wonder the reaction of many free blacks to the Fugitive Slave Law of 1850 was to flee *en masse* to Canada, convinced, as Henry McNeal

Turner would say a generation later, that there was ''no manhood future for Negroes in the United States.''

African-Americans were not only sensitive to the rights to which they were entitled under the Constitution and did not enjoy; they were also especially anxious to argue that under the Second Amendment they were as fully entitled as anyone else to organize militia that would become a part of the American military establishment. And yet, just as the federal government had barred blacks from the militia in 1791, many states, acting as their agents in organizing the militia, excluded blacks from the state military units. In 1851 blacks requested the Massachusetts legislature to authorize the establishment of a black militia company, but were not successful. Ten months later, in 1853, sixty-five blacks submitted a petition to the legislature pleading for a charter to establish an independent military company, but their appeal brought no result. This unsuccessful bid prompted William J. Watkins, one of the black petitioners, to address the Massachusetts Legislative Committee on the Militia in which he argued the case for black militiamen. He said that the petitioners were

> among the most respectable men in the community. They are law-abiding, tax-paying, liberty-loving, native-born American citizens; men who love their country despite its heinous inequities. . . . the very fact that some of those who have signed this petition are descendants of those who faced the cannon's mouth, and quaked not when it bellowed forth its dreadful thunders, who quailed not beneath its lurid lightnings, and yet are denied rights and privileges accorded to the descendants of those who shot down the brave patriots of the Revolution, should be enough to cause the blood to boil within you and cause 'horror upon horror's head accumulate.'

In his peroration, Watkins appealed to the legislature not on the basis of the rights guaranteed in the Constitution, but on the basis of the principles set forth in the Declaration of Independence:

> We ask no favors, Mr. Chairman . . . all we demand is the unrestricted right to breathe unmolested, the pure, unadulterated atmosphere of heaven. We are told we cannot rise! Take the millstone from off our necks. We are inferior to the white man! *Give us our rights.* We can't be elevated in the land of our birth! Give us our rights, we ask no more. Treat us like men; carry out the principles of your immortal declaration: 'All men are born free and created equal, and are endowed by their Creator with certain unalienable rights, among these are life, liberty and the pursuit of happiness.'

And *then*, if we do not equal you in every respect, let us be the recipients of your intensified hate, your vituperative anathemas, then let your ponderous Juggernaut roll on, or like Nebuchadnezzar, let us be driven beyond the pale of humanity, to herd with the beasts of the field.

In 1859 a bill authorizing blacks to join the state militia was passed by the legislature, but was vetoed by Governor N. P. Banks. His veto was sustained. Thus, as far as serving in the militia was concerned, Massachusetts blacks were no better off at the middle of the century than they had been at the beginning.

If there was needed any final declaration that blacks in the United States were not protected either by the Constitution itself or by its first ten amendments—the Bill of Rights—the Chief Justice of the United States, Roger Brook Taney, provided that declaration in the decision he handed down in 1857 in the Dred Scott case. Dred Scott, a slave in Missouri who had traveled with his owner to a free state and a free territory, sued for his freedom on the ground that his residence on free soil had emancipated him. When the case came to the Supreme Court, Chief Justice Taney rejected Scott's claim. He said that an owner's slave was property protected by the Constitution whether the slave resided in a so-called slave state or a so-called free state or free territory. In any case, a black man was not a citizen and therefore had no standing in a court of law.

Speaking specifically about the status of blacks, slave and free, at the time of the Constitution and in the early days of the Republic, the Chief Justice said:

It is difficult at this day [1857] to realize the state of public opinion in relation to that unfortunate race, which prevailed in the civilized and enlightened portions of the world at the time of the Declaration of Independence and when the Constitution of the United States was framed and adopted. . . . They had for more than a century before been regarded as beings of an inferior order, and altogether unfit to associate with the white race, either in social or political relations; and so far inferior, that they had no rights which the white man was bound to respect. . . .

Regarding the status of African-Americans at the time of the formation of the Constitution and the Bill of Rights, Taney unfortunately rendered an accurate reading. There can be no doubt that he was more than pleased to provide such a reading, but it was the framers of the Constitution and the authors of the Bill of Rights and the members of the First and Second

Congresses who made it easy for Taney and his contemporaries to exclude blacks from the protections of the Constitution. Unfortunately and unwittingly he provided much grist for those who, almost a century and a half later, continued to seek ways to exclude African-Americans from the full enjoyment of the Constitution and the Bill of Rights.

4

The Growth of Civil Liberties, 1900–1945

SAMUEL WALKER

*B*y early 1925 the Director of the American Civil Liberties Union (ACLU) was in despair. After five years Roger Baldwin had virtually nothing to show for his tireless efforts on behalf of civil liberties. Overt repression of dissent had lessened somewhat since the Red Scare, Baldwin conceded, but that was because there was almost nothing to repress. Despondent about the future, he asked for a leave of absence from the ACLU and seriously considered abandoning the civil liberties fight altogether.

Baldwin's pessimism was justified. Educating the American public about the civil libertarian implications of the Bill of Rights had always been an uphill struggle. But the disappointments of the postwar era seemed especially harsh to reformers who had been cautiously optimistic before the war, reformers who had come to believe that the "progressive" spirit would eventually spread to the realm of civil liberties. The mood of the country was as hostile to civil liberties in early 1925 as it had been at the height of the feverish repression during World War I. There were no Supreme Court decisions affirming constitutional protection of freedom of speech, press, or assembly. State and federal courts routinely granted sweeping injunctions barring strikes, picketing, union meetings, and even discussions of unions. Race relations were at the lowest point since before the Civil War. In a naked display of political strength, the Ku Klux Klan staged a massive march in the nation's capital.

Communism was only one of many "dangerous ideas" that could not be freely discussed in public. Birth control advocate Margaret Sanger was

36

prevented from speaking in New York City, Boston, and other cities. The Post Office Department and the United States Customs Bureau barred a long list of literary classics and new works on sexuality. Local officials, meanwhile, suppressed books, magazines, and plays.

Then, subtly but perceptibly, the mood of the country began to change. The long-term trend was not evident until many years later, and the initial events appeared to be random and unrelated events. Two events in the year 1925 heralded the portentous changes that lay ahead in American attitudes toward civil liberties. The first was the celebrated Scopes "monkey trial" over a Tennessee law banning the teaching of evolution. The second was a Supreme Court decision (*Gitlow v. New York*) holding that the free speech guarantees of the First Amendment applied to the states—a doctrine that laid the foundation for much of the subsequent revolution in civil liberties and civil rights law.

Two decades later, at the end of World War II, the status of civil liberties in American society had completely changed. The Supreme Court had created an impressive body of First Amendment law: protecting freedom of speech for Communists and other political dissidents; prohibiting prior restraint of publications; granting constitutional protection to the free exercise of religion; assuring a broad freedom of assembly for labor union organizers and others. On two other important issues, the Court had taken the first tentative steps toward dismantling de jure segregation and establishing constitutional standards in the criminal process.

Perhaps even more important than the cases themselves was the new role of the Supreme Court as the defender of civil liberties. In a major shift, the Court embraced the role of protecting powerless minorities against majority will. This shift created an opportunity that civil liberties and civil rights groups quickly took advantage of. Both the ACLU and the NAACP gave new emphasis to Supreme Court litigation in the late 1930s. In 1946 they were joined by the Commission on Law and Social Action of the American Jewish Congress. This marked the emergence of the "rights industry," the network of public interest law groups seeking social change through constitutional law litigation. In the post-1945 years, despite serious setbacks as a result of the Cold War, there were even greater advances in the areas of civil rights, opposition to censorship, separation of church and state, and due process of law.

The tremendous gains in civil liberties in the twenty years between 1925 and 1945 are beyond dispute. Unfortunately, historians have not done a very good job of explaining this major change in American society. Virtually every account either explicitly or implicitly presents the Supreme Court as the principal if not the only agent of change. The growth of civil liberties is defined entirely in terms of Supreme Court cases, with accounts tracing the development of legal doctrine and the changing composition of the Court.

A few historians have offered a different perspective, shifting the focus from the Court to the place of constitutionalism in society. Constitutionalism may be defined as the sense of the constitution among the American people. One important manifestation of that sense is the phenomenon of "rights consciousness," the belief on the part of individuals and/or groups that they are entitled to certain rights.

While the contributions of the Supreme Court to the growth of civil liberties in the first half of the twentieth century cannot be ignored, the broader social phenomenon of constitutionalism clearly deserves more attention. Ideas and lifestyles changed with the emergence of modern urban industrial life. In many instances, these changes produced the conflicts that eventually led to a landmark Supreme Court case. And in some instances the expectation of certain rights among large segments of the public outpaced the Court.

Kermit L. Hall, quoting Oliver Wendell Holmes, describes the law as a "magic mirror" which reveals our history and our culture. Assuming this to be so, what does the magic mirror reveal? The growth of civil liberties between the mid-1920s and mid-1940s can be explained in large part by long-term changes in the fabric of American society, in the way people live, their ideas, their values, their conception of the good life and the good society. The magic mirror reveals that the growth of civil liberties has not been something imposed upon society by an imperial and undemocratic Court, as some contemporary critics of the Court argue. While the Court is indeed an undemocratic institution—and was designed as such—its role in the growth of civil liberties reflects deeper changes in society.

Of course, as already noted, social change in early twentieth century America also had the capacity to diminish civil liberties, at least in the short run. The sweeping suppression of freedom of speech, press, and assembly during World War I has often been described as the greatest single violation of civil liberties in American history. Regrettably, there is a great deal of competition for that dubious honor and no definitive judgment is possible. Wartime dissent was ruthlessly crushed by the combined forces of the federal and state governments and private vigilantes. Eugene V. Debs and other prominent war critics were convicted and imprisoned. In Debs's case he was prosecuted for a speech that did not even criticize World War I, but merely opposed war in general. The Post Office Department barred the entire socialist press from the mails.

The Socialist Party, which had great political strength prior to the war, was crushed and never recovered. The radical IWW was also smashed by federal prosecution. Meanwhile, private vigilantes, some acting with government authorization, rounded up thousands of suspected draft dodgers and tarred and feathered people deemed unpatriotic.

The most significant aspect of the wartime crisis was its *national* character. First, it put the issue of civil liberties on the national political agenda for the first time, and put it there permanently. Second, for the first time in American history the machinery of the federal government was mobilized to suppress unpopular opinion. Third, repression was justified in the name of the national interest and of majoritarian democratic theory.

Intolerance was nothing new in American life by 1917. There was a long history of censorship, racism, religious persecution, and suppression both of political radicals and of conventional trade unionists. The vigilante committee was the true expression of majoritarian democratic theory: the community could take the law into its own hands to suppress ideas and practices it did not like.

Perhaps the most revealing aspect of American legal culture before the war was the absence of any serious attention to civil liberties. The notable civil liberties crises of the past—the Alien and Sedition Act controversy (1798–1799); the abolitionist free speech fights; Lincoln's suspension of habeas corpus during the Civil War; political and civil rights during Reconstruction—these remained isolated episodes, without producing a sustained attention to the general question of civil liberties.

The repression of unpopular ideas and groups had been primarily private and local in nature. The mob that sacked and burned the Catholic convent in Charlestown, Massachusetts (1834), the bigots who terrorized the Mormons across the country, the Ku Klux Klan in the South, the San Francisco Vigilance Committee that staged a political coup (1856) were all manifestations of this essentially private and local pattern. By contrast, the World War I suppression of free speech was led by the federal government and done in the name of the national interest. This was symptomatic of a general phenomenon in industrial societies: the centralization of power by the national government and the subordination of the individual to national interests. If the United States avoided the totalitarianism that engulfed so many other countries it was in part because of its unique countertrend of civil libertarianism.

The wartime events also posed a crisis for majoritarian theory. President Woodrow Wilson justified the government's actions in terms of majority rule: when Congress declared war, the matter was settled; once the people's representatives had debated and voted, there was no longer any room for dissent. On the national level, the country had never squarely faced the question of the extent to which the First Amendment created exceptions to majority rule, particularly in a time of national crisis. This question reached the Supreme Court in a series of cases in 1919, and in each the Court upheld the criminal convictions of the dissenters. Justice Oliver Wendell Holmes fashioned a majoritarian rationale with his "clear and present danger" test in *Schenck v. United States.* A few months later, however, he had an evident change of heart and his dissent in *Abrams v. United States*, in which he affirmed First Amendment protection for dissent, ultimately shaped the growth of First Amendment law.

The wartime crisis also nationalized civil liberties by provoking the creation of the American Civil Liberties Union in 1920 (although the creation in 1917 of the ACLU's predecessor, the National Civil Liberties Bureau, is the pivotal event). This marked the advent of a special interest group dedicated to the advancement of civil liberties. Historian Robert Wiebe has argued that the lesson of the Progressive Era was "organize or perish." To succeed in the complex society that the United States had become, an idea needed an organized advocate. With the ACLU, the Bill of Rights found its advocate. The success of the civil libertarian countertrend was due in large part to the ACLU's advocacy.

Events in England provide an interesting perspective on the ACLU and the subsequent growth of civil liberties in the United States. During World War I, England had its own civil liberties defense organization, the National Council for Civil Liberties (NCCL); however, it lapsed after the war and was not reorganized until 1934. The different histories of the ACLU and NCCL highlight important differences in national legal cultures. The role of a written Bill of Rights in the United States was crucial. It provided a frame of reference for Americans that allowed the defense of civil liberties to be cast in terms of "old-fashioned American liberties," of freedoms that had somehow been lost and needed to be restored. This gave the defense of civil liberties a certain conservative cast that helped to offset the role of civil liberties in protecting new and often radical ideas.

The wartime hysteria continued into the postwar years, reaching its climax in the famous "Red Scare" of 1919–20. In a series of massive raids, government agents rounded up thousands of suspected radicals. The raids and the resulting detentions and deportations involved wholesale violations of free speech and due process.

In the early 1920s, "free speech" remained tainted by its association with "Huns," "Bolsheviks," and disloyalty. The courts, legislatures, and public opinion were all equally hostile to any notion of civil liberties. This was the bleak picture that Roger Baldwin confronted in 1925 and which nearly caused him to give up the fight. Yet, just at that point, new forces in American life began to assert themselves—forces that began to build support for civil liberties.

The famous Scopes "monkey trial" was the first great ACLU case. It became a national and international sensation—a "media event" in today's terms. A flood of reporters descended on Dayton, Tennessee. The *Baltimore Sun* sent five, including H. L. Mencken who largely fashioned the stereotypes that continue to define the image of the case. It was the first trial ever covered live by the fledgling radio networks.

Scopes was tried for violating the Tennessee law prohibiting the teaching of evolution. The trial quickly turned into a circus. The basic legal issue concerning control of public school curricula was eclipsed in favor of a debate over the respective merits of the theory of evolution and the Bible. Darrow badgered Bryan about the literal interpretation of the Bible and succeeded in making him look like a fool. Scopes was eventually convicted, but the Tennessee Supreme Court overturned the conviction on a technicality, thereby preventing a Supreme Court test case on the constitutional issues. Tennessee officials, clearly embarrassed by the entire episode, declined to enforce the law, and no new test case arose.

From our standpoint, the important aspect of the case was the public reaction to it. Darrow and his co-counsel Arthur Garfield Hayes from the ACLU played the trial as political theater, seeking to dramatize the issue of freedom of thought. It was an approach that many activists in the 1960s would have applauded. Mencken played a principal role in presenting the trial as a confrontation between religious intolerance and freedom of thought. Although most ACLU leaders were appalled by Darrow's tactics, his approach played very well with the national audience. Scopes was the first case that attracted favorable notice to the ACLU. Darrow's success in lining up eminent scientists and theologians as expert witnesses (although they were never allowed to testify) was another first. The ACLU had never been able to recruit a similar group of respectable and esteemed figures to testify on behalf of Communists or labor unions, the organization's major clients to that point. Finally, the Scopes case was the first occasion where the ACLU raised more money than it needed. A single mailing to the American Academy for the Advancement of Science covered all the expenses and left a small surplus.

The various responses to the case—the media coverage, the expert witnesses, the fundraising success—indicated that it touched a sensitive nerve. In the brief history of the ACLU, no previous controversy had framed the defense of civil liberties in terms that appealed to established and even to conservative elements of society. Support did not come from the mass of society, by any means, but it did include important segments of opinion-makers in education and journalism. They saw the case in terms of issues that were vital to them and to the future of the country. Education and science were the keys to progress. This, in turn, required freeing education from the restrictions of religious dogma. In Mencken's stereotyped version of events, southern fundamentalists served as very convenient foils. Civil liberties was no longer a concept that smacked of bearded, bomb-throwing anarchists. At the same time, simple majoritarianism no longer automatically represented the best interests of the community or the nation.

The Scopes case was quickly followed by others that also reflected the impact of social change on attitudes toward civil liberties.

The most important long-term change was the sexual revolution. As ideas and habits about sexuality changed, there were new expectations about free discussion of sexual matters, access to contraceptives, and the uninhibited treatment of sexual themes in literature. One indicator of the rapidity of social change was the transformation of the birth control issue. At the time of World War I it was identified with anarchists and radicals, with Emma Goldman and Margaret Sanger. Sanger was prosecuted in 1914, and her 1917 film, *Birth Control,* was suppressed. But by the 1920s, birth control had become an upper middle-class issue. Sanger now drew her support from the medical establishment and from wealthy Republican club women.

One of the first cases to signal a major shift in public thinking about sexuality was the prosecution of Mary Ware Dennett. Civil libertarian and prominent birth control advocate, Dennett was convicted in 1928 for mailing *The Sex Side of Life*, a sex education pamphlet she had written for teenagers. The federal Comstock Law defined literature on contraception as obscene. Her conviction was overturned on appeal a year later, but the controversy evoked a response similar to that of the Scopes case. The ACLU again found itself supporting a highly popular case, with support from prominent, wealthy, and conservative people. These included Mrs. Marshall Field of Chicago and publisher Roy Howard. They saw the Dennett case as dramatizing issues of great personal and social importance. Frank discussion of sexuality, including sex education for children, was one of the hallmarks of an enlightened family. Birth control was a necessary part of planning a rational and successful life course. On a broader scale, many people saw population control as an important matter of social policy. This was fueled to a great extent by racist concern about high birth rates among black Americans and East European immigrants. Even more than the Scopes case, the Dennett prosecution struck home. Here was an issue, framed in civil liberties terms, that touched peoples' lives directly.

The Dennett defense committee also found itself with unexpected financial surplus. It turned the $1,265 over to the ACLU for a "permanent agency" to wage a broad fight against all forms of censorship, and the ACLU created the National Committee to Combat Censorship (NCCC). This was the ACLU's first concerted attack on censorship in the arts. One of the remarkable aspects of ACLU history is that the organization gave almost no attention to censorship of literature during the 1920s. In the aftermath of World War I it had concentrated on political speech and the defense of the rights of labor. Its own view of the scope of the First Amendment was, by later standards, rather limited.

The ACLU's new interest in censorship was quickly reinforced by the "Battle of Boston." Beginning in 1926, local officials began an aggressive campaign of censorship in which they banned a series of novels and plays by some of the greatest names in American literary history: Ernest Hemingway, Theodore Dreiser, Sinclair Lewis. The campaign popularized the phrase "Banned in Boston." In nearly every case, officials banned the work because of its treatment of sexuality. A bit hesitant at first, the ACLU eventually threw itself into the fray. Once again it quickly found considerable support from influential segments of society, especially in higher education, journalism, and the publishing industry.

The response to the Scopes and censorship campaigns convinced Roger Baldwin that the time had come for the ACLU to expand its program and its organizational structure. In 1929 he proposed a bold new program of activity which included a vigorous campaign against censorship, challenges to segregation and police misconduct, and support for the rights of Native Americans and aliens. He also planned to expand the ACLU organizationally, conceding that it had been too small and too concentrated in New York City. In short, there was far more support for civil liberties than he or any other ACLU leader had imagined.

What a difference four years had made. The despair of early 1925 had given way to a bold vision of a comprehensive campaign for civil liberties issues. Nor had he misread the temper of the country. A series of victories quickly followed. The Supreme Court issued its breakthrough decisions on freedom of speech and press in 1931. The following year Congress passed the Norris-LaGuardia Act restricting the use of injunctions against labor unions—a major victory in what had been the ACLU's principal issue through the Twenties. President Herbert Hoover's crime commission issued a searing report on police brutality in 1931. The report was written by attorneys active in the ACLU (including Walter Pollak who argued *Gitlow* and several other breakthrough cases in the Supreme Court) and was based heavily on material in the ACLU files. In 1934 Congress passed the Indian Reorganization Act which embodied the ACLU's recommendations. The campaign against censorship achieved its first great victory when a federal court overturned the ban on James Joyce's famous novel *Ulysses* in 1933.

By the mid-1930s the ACLU was out of the wilderness. It could legitimately claim to have had a remarkable impact on public policy. Most of these gains, moreover, preceded and were independent of developments in the Supreme Court. The Court's historic turnabout on civil liberties did not occur until 1937.

The Court delivered its first decisions affirming civil liberties in 1931. *Stromberg v. California* overturned the conviction of an avowed Communist persecuted under the California "Red Flag" statute. The decision marked the Court's acceptance of ideas first articulated in the *Abrams* dissent and developed through the *Gitlow* dicta and Brandeis's opinion in *Whitney v. California*. Then, in *Near v. Minnesota*, the Court affirmed a constitutional protection of freedom of the press from prior restraints, even for a scurrilous and willfully offensive publication.

The two 1931 decisions, momentous as they were, evoked no outpouring of public hostility. This was all the more surprising, given the fact that the country was sinking deeper into the depression, and that the repression of radical union organizers was increasing. A year later, in a case arising from the famous Scottsboro case (*Powell v. Alabama*), the Court overturned a conviction and death penalty on the grounds that the defendant had not had adequate legal counsel. This marked the Court's first step in imposing constitutional standards on state and local criminal proceedings. The *Powell* decision laid the foundation for the "due process revolution" that flowered in the 1960s under the Warren Court.

By the end of 1936 there were at most a handful of Court decisions affirming civil liberties principles. Important as they are in retrospect, they were not perceived as a new direction for the Court at the time. Nor did the Court articulate a new doctrinal orientation. This shift occurred in 1937–38. The constitutional revolution consisted of two parts. First, in a major reversal, the Court upheld the constitutionality of New Deal economic measures. This ended the era of substantive due process during which the Court had struck down economic regulations on the grounds that they violated liberty of contract under the Fourteenth Amendment.

At the same time, the Court embraced a new role of protecting political and civil rights under the Constitution. In January 1937 the Court overturned the conviction of Communist Party organizer Dirk DeJonge on the grounds that he had not advocated violence but had been convicted solely for his Communist Party membership. Later that year the Court reversed the conviction of Communist Party organizer Angelo Herndon, who had been prosecuted under an old Georgia insurrection law. Herndon, the Court held, had also not advocated the violent overthrow of the state but had merely distributed literature on political issues.

The Court made it clear that these would not remain isolated decisions. In two other cases it offered a philosophical rationale for its new role in protecting political and civil rights. In *Palko v. Connecticut* (1937) it held that freedom of speech and of the press represented the "indispensable condition, of nearly every form of freedom" and were "the very essence of a scheme of ordered liberty." A year later, in a footnote in an otherwise obscure case (*United States v. Carolene Products Company*), Justice Harlan Fiske Stone indicated the Court's intention to impose "exacting judicial scrutiny" on laws that restricted the political process or were "directed at particular religious, or national, or racial minorities."

The Jehovah's Witnesses provided the greatest opportunity for the Court to protect an unpopular group. A small religious sect, the Witnesses underwent an internal transformation in the Thirties, adopting both a wildly paranoid vision of the world and an aggressive proselytizing campaign. Adherents descended on entire communities in what they called their "locust" technique and confronted people in "streetcorner witnessing." Their message was, among other things, viciously anti-Catholic, and they deliberately entered predominately Catholic neighborhoods and provoked confrontations with individual Catholics.

Their message and tactics aroused tremendous hostility. Vigilante groups across the country assaulted Witnesses, in some cases driving them en masse out of town. Local communities responded with criminal prosecution for breach of the peace and ordinances restricting leafletting, door-to-door canvassing, and other tactics. These measures led to court cases that eventually produced an impressive body of First Amendment law. In the annals of Supreme Court advocacy, the Witnesses lawyer, Hayden Covington, has a civil liberties "batting average" rivalled only by the NAACP's Thurgood Marshall.

In a series of landmark decisions, the Supreme Court ruled that a leafletting ordinance unduly restricted First Amendment rights, and that door-to-door canvassing was constitutionally protected. In a breach of the peace case (*Cantwell v. Connecticut*), it established a broad protection of the free exercise of religion. The Witnesses won nearly all of their cases. One of the most important exceptions was *Chaplinsky v. New Hampshire* which created a "fighting words" exception to free speech.

The most celebrated confrontation between the Witnesses and authorities involved saluting the American flag. The aggressive campaigns of the Witnesses happened to coincide with an upsurge of American nationalism in the late 1930s. One manifestation of this was a series of laws and regulations requiring school children to salute the flag. Witnesses refused to allow their children to salute on the grounds that to do so would violate their religious principles. This refusal only heightened public antagonism toward the Witnesses. Eventually a case (*Minersville School District v. Gobitis, 1940*) reached the Supreme Court, and the Court upheld the salute requirement.

Later, however, several justices publicly admitted that they had changed their minds. Thus, when a second flag salute case reached the Court in 1943, the majority upheld the Witnesses' right to refuse to salute the flag on religious grounds. Justice Robert Jackson's majority opinion in *West Virginia State Board of Education v. Barnette* remains one of the great affirmations of respect for individual conscience in the entire history of the Court. "If there is one fixed star in our constitutional constellation," he wrote, "it is that no official, high or petty, can prescribe what shall be orthodox in politics, nationalism, or other matter of opinion. . . ." The Court rendered its decision on June 14, Flag Day, with obvious awareness of its symbolic impact. Moreover, the country was then in the midst of a two-front World War and patriotic feelings were running high. The Court was clearly saying that the hallmark of American democracy was the constitutionally guaranteed tolerance for minorities, even obnoxious minorities, and even during wartime.

The *Barnette* decision marked the high point of the defense of civil liberties under the Roosevelt Court (1937–49). In standard histories of constitutional law the posture of the Roosevelt Court is explained primarily in terms of its personnel. Between 1937 and 1941 President Roosevelt completely refashioned the Court, appointing seven new justices. They included two of the greatest civil libertarians ever to sit on the bench: Hugo Black and William O. Douglas.

The changing composition of the Court, however, offers only a partial explanation of the Court's new role. If the Roosevelt appointees embraced new ideas about the Bill of Rights, we need to ask where those ideas came from. This forces our attention back to society at large. The Supreme Court, after all, does not initiate cases or write briefs; it responds to the cases and arguments that come before it. The Court's new role then cannot be separated from the social and political context that raised new issues and offered new interpretations of the Bill of Rights.

The changing face of American constitutionalism in the late 1930s cannot be understood apart from the international context. In subtle but powerful ways the rise of totalitarianism, especially in Germany and the Soviet Union, heightened the consciousness of Americans about the uniqueness of their own form of constitutional democracy.

Nothing dramatized the shift in public attitudes toward civil liberties in the late 1930s better than the contrast between the respective celebrations of the 150th anniversaries of the Constitution and the Bill of Rights. The anniversary of the Constitution in 1937 was a dispirited affair, and for good reason. The country was locked in a profound constitutional crisis. The Supreme Court had struck down all of the major New Deal measures, despite an overwhelming political sentiment for positive government action to end the depression. Many people asked whether the Constitution itself was a barrier to government by the people. President Roosevelt tried to resolve the impasse by changing the size of the Court. His court-packing proposal aroused a storm of opposition, however, and was quietly killed. The crisis was resolved when the Supreme Court, in a dramatic reversal, approved the constitutionality of two major New Deal measures.

By the time of the anniversary of the Bill of Rights two years later (the introduction of the Bill of Rights in Congress was celebrated in 1939; ratification in 1941) the public mood was celebratory. A number of developments indicated this shift in public attitudes. Particularly important were steps taken by several prominent professional associations.

The American Bar Association (ABA) created a Committee on the Bill of Rights in 1938. Modelled after the ACLU (and cooperating with it on some cases), it filed *amicus* briefs in several important Supreme Court cases. The committee represented a complete turnabout for the ABA, which had previously made no official report on behalf of political and civil rights. The ABA Committee on the Bill of Rights organized local committees across the country. These gave many young lawyers their first taste of civil rights and civil liberties litigation; in a broader sense, they were an affirmation of civil libertarian values by the profession.

The American Library Association (ALA) adopted a Library Bill of Rights in 1939, affirming the right to read and defining the role of the library as a public forum. In 1940, university presidents, through the

Association of American Universities (AAU), reached an agreement on academic freedom and tenure with the professoriate, acting through the American Association of University Professors (AAUP). The 1940 statement remains the basic document on academic freedom and tenure.

Finally, in 1939, Attorney General Frank Murphy established the Civil Liberties Division of the Justice Department. The forerunner of the present Civil Rights Division, it represented the first time the federal government had assumed responsibility for an affirmative role in the defense of individual rights.

These developments signaled a dramatic shift in public attitudes about civil liberties, certainly among the leaders of key organizations. A number of factors helped to produce these changes. The New Deal fostered an atmosphere of tolerance. It brought to office people sensitive to the protection of individual rights, even if Roosevelt himself expressed no concern for civil liberties. The New Deal coalition also marked the arrival of groups which had long been the targets of discrimination, notably Catholic and Jewish Americans, and black Americans, who would begin to assert their rightful place in American society in the 1940s.

American consciousness of international totalitarianism reinforced this trend. Indeed, the word *totalitarianism* itself first entered public discourse in this period, as political observers concluded that there were important similarities between the nominally right wing Nazi Germany and the nominally left wing Soviet Union. This consciousness put American constitutionalism in a new perspective: the uniqueness of American society was seen to lie in its constitutional framework and, in particular, in its capacity to respect minority viewpoints.

This consciousness of American uniqueness found explicit expression in the *Hague v. Congress of Industrial Organizations* case. The efforts of Mayor Frank Hague of Jersey City to suppress labor unions in his city became one of the most celebrated cases of the late 1930s and eventually produced a landmark Supreme Court decision. Hague's tactics included denying permits for union meetings, arresting union organizers, and physically assaulting organizers. Alan Reitman, later a long-time ACLU staff person, recalled the police padlocking the synagogue his parents attended because a union meeting was scheduled there. Norman Thomas was only one of many people rudely ''deported'' back to New York City by being thrown down the steps to the subway.

The significance of the Jersey City battle lay in its larger context. Hague's repression of union organizers was typical of the anti-union suppression of free speech and assembly that prevailed through the mid-

1930s. By the late 1930s, however, things had changed in industrial cities. The Wagner Act guaranteed workers the right to organize, and the CIO had organized most of the mass production industries. Suddenly, Hague's anti-union tactics stood out as the exception (in the industrial cities, at any rate; anti-unionism still ran strong in the South and in rural areas). The anti-Hague literature and editorials across the country portrayed Hague as a domestic Mussolini. Even conservative papers editorialized against him, arguing that his tactics were un-American and that they did not represent the true spirit of American democracy.

References to international developments were explicit in the District Court opinion written by Judge William Clark. Imposing a sweeping injunction on Hague, Clark concluded with an observation on international affairs: "Ultimately, Russia will not be judged by how much bread it has given its people . . . but by how much freedom, self-respect, equality, truth, and human kindness it has brought into the world." By the same token, the many decisions upholding the rights of the Jehovah's Witnesses were informed by the awareness of Nazi persecution of Jews, along with suppression of the Witnesses in Germany.

The rising consciousness of the unique aspects of American constitutionalism had another side to it, however. Celebration of Americanism implied its counterpart, un-Americanism. It is no accident that the same period that saw the flowering of civil liberties law also saw the birth of the House Un-American Activities Committee, loyalty oaths for teachers, the Smith Act, renewed FBI spying on alleged subversives, and the first federal loyalty program. The entire apparatus of the post–World War II Cold War was created in the prewar years. The magic mirror of the law reveals the complex and often contradictory currents in American life during the late 1930s. The same shift in public consciousness that enhanced civil liberties in so many respects also set the stage for one of the most serious assaults on those same liberties.

The fate of civil liberties during World War II dramatized how much the country had changed since the first Great War. The contrast between the two periods could not have been greater. With one notable exception—the Japanese-American internment—there was remarkably little suppression of civil liberties.

Even before the United States entered the war, Roosevelt administration leaders took great pains to remind the country that freedom at home had to be preserved during wartime. Messages of tolerance were delivered by Attorneys General Frank Murphy, Francis Biddle, and the President himself.

Once the war began, there were relatively few restrictions on expression. The administration made a few half-hearted efforts to censor the Socialist Workers Party, while the FBI investigated but did not act against the black press. Attorney General Biddle held the line against prosecution as best he could, but finally had to yield to strong pressure from the President. The few prosecutions for political dissent were largely token gestures, designed to appease those elements of Congress that wanted to suppress domestic fascists. Significantly, the official Left—the Communist Party and many non-Communist leftists—were among the more aggressive advocates of suppression. The prowar posture of the left dramatized the fact that this was an extremely popular war, with no large-scale dissent. And in that sense, the national commitment to freedom of speech during wartime was not really tested.

The 1940 Selective Service Act provided far broader protection for conscientious objection than did the World War I law, extending it to anyone who objected on the basis of religious training and belief and not just to members of the three historic peace churches, as had been the case during World War I. The fact that many more objectors went to prison was not due to the content of the law; instead, it was a measure of the growth of pacifist thought, and of the activism of Jehovah's Witnesses who claimed ministerial status for all their members.

The war years also dramatized the changed status of the ACLU. During World War I the offices of the Civil Liberties Bureau were raided by the Justice Department and the organization's top leadership barely escaped indictment under the Espionage Act. In World War II ACLU leaders regularly met with government officials, in some instances to challenge government policy, and in others to advise officials in a friendly manner. ACLU leaders met with the heads of the Justice and War Departments, the Director of the FBI, and even President Roosevelt himself. If they were usually unsuccessful in pressing the claim they brought that day, the fact that they received a cordial and respectful hearing indicated the elevated status of both the organization and the idea of civil liberties.

The great exception to this generally favorable picture, of course, was the evacuation and internment of the Japanese-Americans. About 120,000 people, including 90,000 citizens, lost their liberty and millions of dollars of property. Even more appalling was the limited opposition to the government's action. The political left, giving top priority to the defeat of Hitler, declined to criticize the government. Attorney General Earl Warren of California actively lobbied the federal government to act. And in the Supreme Court, two of the greatest civil libertarians ever to sit on the Court—Hugo Black and William O. Douglas—voted with the majority to uphold the government. Only a few church groups voiced any opposition to the government's program, while the ACLU received little support as it pressed the two most important test cases: *Hirabayashi v. United States* and *Korematsu v. United States*.

The treatment of the Japanese-Americans was a sobering reminder of the fragility of civil liberties. Despite the recent progress, the episode illustrated the extent to which the government, the Supreme Court, and most of the public could countenance a gross violation of civil rights.

Still, we should not allow this wartime affront to civil libertarian values to obscure the real progress that had been achieved during the previous two decades. "Rights consciousness" had become a powerful force in American life, and a broad range of social issues had been "constitutionalized," in the sense of being transformed into issues of constitutional law. As World War II gave way to the Cold War, public attitudes toward the first ten amendments remained complex and contradictory, but the relevance of the Bill of Rights to the quality of life and liberty in the United States was no longer in doubt.

5

Civil Liberties and the Culture of the Cold War, 1945–1965

STEPHEN J. WHITFIELD

*T*he framers did not intend the Bill of Rights to be a suicide pact, in which license for insurrectionaries might undermine American society itself. But the latitude and opportunity promised in that document were not supposed to be suspended in times of crisis, either. Basic freedoms of expression and association were nowhere more imperiled—and perhaps imperiling—than during a war; and when a majority of citizens believed, as they did in, say, August 1950, that World War III had already begun, the Bill of Rights became more vulnerable to hedging and fudging, a process of civic declension that eventually became one of the most troubling legacies of the Cold War.

The postwar animus against Communism, far from being built on fantasy, was rooted in reality. If judged in the light of liberal democratic ideals, of the promise inherent in personal autonomy and of the conventions of ordinary decency, Stalinism *was* evil. Because this form of totalitarianism had activated champions in the United States, a relatively open society confronted a unique threat to its operations; and those who wished to reform as well as defend democratic institutions had to puzzle through the appropriate means of resisting such a movement. In 1925, in his lapidary dissent in *Gitlow v. New York,* Justice Oliver Wendell Holmes had proclaimed that, "if . . . the beliefs expressed in proletarian dictatorship are destined to be accepted by the dominant forces in the community, the only meaning of free speech is that they should be given their chance and have their way.'' But less than three decades later, such libertarianism seemed even more marginal, and even rather naive, especially after the exposure of one of his own former clerks, Alger Hiss, as a Soviet espionage agent.

The secrecy and authoritarianism of Communist cadres flung down a peculiar challenge, for they sought to enjoy the rights and benefits of a largely free society in order to demolish it. These clandestine and cohesive parties took their signals from a foreign power hostile to Western political values, and had no principled objections to violent revolution under the right circumstances. American Communists were enemies of civil liberties, which they disdained as "bourgeois," but which they invoked in their own behalf when opportune. They themselves remained mini-totalitarians, even when incurring penalties in the United States for beliefs that they had voluntarily chosen. Because their commitment to civil liberties was so fraudulent, party members earned little sympathy when their rights were unfairly withdrawn—and thus bore some responsibility for the suppression they endured.

So unappealing an organization helps explain the phobic overreaction of the American political system in the late 1940s and the 1950s. Communism was a threat *to* the United States, as the literary critic Philip Rahv phrased it in 1952; but it was not a threat *in* the United States, where the danger was often wildly overestimated. The battalion of Stalinists may have been secret, but it was too negligible to divert the course of American history. Though evidence of infiltration could be detected from Hollywood to Harvard, party membership, which had touched 80,000 immediately after World War II, hovered around 43,000 by 1950, around 32,000 a year later in a nation of about 150 million people. True, the party and its outriders could inflict mischief in a few trade unions or in some advanced social movements; but the cost that American society paid to crush domestic Communism was disproportionate—for the repression weakened the legacy of civil liberties, impugned standards of tolerance and fair play, and tarnished the very image of a democracy. The United States thus repudiated two of the Four Freedoms for which the Second World War had so recently been fought; freedom of speech and freedom from fear were among the entitlements that the late President Franklin D. Roosevelt had enunciated. Within a decade after the ghastly slaughter that the Four Freedoms were supposed to redeem, the United States had transparently violated those ideals. This Red Scare was not a collective tragedy, but it was a disgrace.

The political tests that were applied to thought and expression were not systematic, but they were not entirely haphazard either. Sometimes the tests were imposed by agencies of the federal government, and were designed to intimidate other branches or the private sector. The demands of hyperpatriotism sometimes reflected the efforts of private employers, sometimes those of self-appointed monitors of political morality who acted with official complicity. Sometimes the private sphere was ahead of the government in such efforts at regulation and purification. But the effect was the same: the suffocation of liberty and the debasement of culture itself. Even by the narrowest chauvinistic criteria of the Cold War, the United States thus diminished itself in the global struggle to be seen as a just society.

And though the state was intimately involved in restricting liberty, it acted with popular approval and acquiescence; the will of the majority was not thwarted. The citizenry imposed a starchy repression upon itself, without denying rights to minorities—at least, to certain political factions, anyway. Indeed American Legionnaires and the Catholic War Veterans were among the "veto groups" exercising their First Amendment rights, such as seeking to prevent other Americans from attending particular films and plays. The opportunity to dissuade other citizens from patronizing an institution or an individual has long been included in the definition of a democracy, and the marketplace—including the marketplace of ideas—has accepted the notion that unpopularity is decisive. No company, including a movie studio or a television network, is obligated to keep on its payroll those from whom the public has explicitly withdrawn its favor. Nor did foes of the right to boycott condemn such tactics in principle; differences arose only over the choice of targets.

Government agencies acted improperly because they barged into areas where they did not belong and thus corrupted the sphere of expression that the First Amendment was designed to protect. In denying a level playing field to the assorted talents who contributed to the nation's culture, the House Committee on Un-American Activities, the Subcommittee on Investigations of the Senate Committee on Government Operations, the Senate Internal Security Subcommittee, and the Federal Bureau of Investigation were the most conspicuous offenders. To acknowledge that their efforts were often clumsy, spasmodic, and feckless, or that some folks were plucky and independent enough to defend themselves, is proof that a genuinely totalitarian impulse could gain little traction on American soil, where the banners emblazoned with "Don't Tread on Me" had been unfurled less than two centuries earlier.

But historians should not ignore the dangers of majoritarian tyranny either, even as the happy conclusion can be drawn that the culture of the Cold War was by no means synonymous with the culture of the 1950s. In that asymmetry one can distinguish a relatively free society from a political system with totalitarian tendencies. Central to the latter, for example, was the denial of what the political philosopher Hannah Arendt had called "the right to have rights." Both the Third Reich and the Soviet Union had turned certain groups into pariahs, whose exclusion from the political community was so complete that they could make no claims upon it. Nothing so absolute happened in the 1950s to American Communists, or to those believed to be Communists, or to those who might be sympathetic to Communists. But their "right to have rights" was imperiled. Their opportunities for political association and utterance, their freedom of movement, their chances of employment (even when the risk to national security was irrelevant) were all withdrawn or seriously curtailed. "There will be no witch-hunts at Yale," its president declared in 1949, "because there will be no witches. We do not intend to hire Communists." The penalties for political dissidence were generally economic and social rather than legal. The victims of this Red Scare were deprived of their livelihood, but not—with a handful of exceptions—of their lives.

But Dwight D. Eisenhower's 1954 State of the Union address had nevertheless proposed depriving Communists of their citizenship. According to a national poll that Harvard's Samuel A. Stouffer administered, 80 percent of the populace agreed with the President's suggestion; 52 percent wanted all Communists jailed; 77 percent wanted them banned from the radio. For good measure, 42 percent of those polled thought that *no* member of the press should be permitted to criticize the "American form of government." The demonic peril that the party incarnated suggested to many citizens that its destruction was warranted within the law. Because the Communists could exploit the Constitution, all three branches of the federal government united to destroy their political freedom, paying the Stalinist apparatus at least the tribute of sneaky imitation. Thus Andrei Vishinsky's notorious 1938 treatise on Soviet law, which denied the legitimacy of political opposition, came to be adopted by American anti-Communists, who abandoned the Jeffersonian faith in the ultimate wisdom of the electorate.

Confidence in the suffrage was widely jettisoned. Alabama not only kept blacks from voting but also kept Reds from running, and in 1947 became the first state to honor the call of the American Legion to outlaw the Communist Party. Other states and localities found increasingly imaginative ways to immunize themselves against the bacillus. In a state like Texas, a Communist was more likely to be exotic than dangerous. Its legislature nevertheless made party membership a felony, for which the punishment could be twenty years' imprisonment. Governor Allan Shivers was reluctant to sign the bill because he disagreed with the penalty, which he thought should be death. With even more "subversives" living in New York, a loyalty oath was imposed there on applicants who wanted to fish in municipal reservoirs. Indiana also forced professional wrestlers to take a loyalty oath. Ordinances in Jacksonville, Florida and McKeesport, Pennsylvania required Communists and even fellow-travellers to be out of town within forty-eight hours. Perhaps it is surprising that other communities did not follow, though the city council of New Rochelle, New York limited itself to an ordinance in 1950 that obligated Communists living there or "regularly passing through" to register. One law-abiding citizen on the morning train for Manhattan got off to present himself at the New Rochelle city hall, where he was reassured that the registration was for Communists—not commuters. In March 1947 a member of Harry Truman's cabinet, Secretary of Labor Lewis B. Schwellenbach, became the first national politician to demand that the Communist Party be outlawed. In the Republican primaries the following spring, the "liberal" ex-governor of Minnesota, Harold Stassen, echoed that call; and Senator Arthur H. Vandenburg (R-Mich.) warned: "We are suicidal fools if we do not root out any treason at home which may dream of bringing world revolution to the United States."

The most powerful national instrument for the political elimination of Communism was a law that bore the name of Congressman Howard W. Smith (D-Va.). Mr. Smith had gone to Washington in 1940 and convinced Congress to pass its first peacetime sedition act in almost a century and a half. The genesis of its use against the Communist Party was the Truman administration's need to demonstrate its sensitivity to national security, when GOP attacks encouraged the Department of Justice to reconcile the outside Soviet peril that the foreign policy of the Democrats recognized ("containment") with the nearby danger that Stalin's disciples posed at home. Indeed a possible case against the party had been built within the administration as early as the summer of 1945. Enforcement of the Smith Act was the anticipated responsibility of the FBI, which, in the event of war with the Soviet Union, would round up Americans whose loyalty was highly questionable. This "Custodial Detention Program" would require the compilation of names, based not on previous criminal conduct but on beliefs and associations. Because such an emergency was unprecedented and only potential, the FBI recommended early in 1948 that the Communist leadership be prosecuted under the Smith Act to establish a Constitutional basis for future use. Then, if the Cold War were to escalate into a superpower military conflict, party members could be legally arrested as "substantive violators" of the Smith Act. The public also had to be persuaded to sanction the unprecedented notion of an emergency "Custodial Detention Program." The FBI's educational crusade was therefore designed to explain how imminent and serious a danger domestic Communism represented.

When J. Edgar Hoover presented Attorney General Tom Clark with the brief that became the case against the party, the director of the FBI did not bother to present evidence that any individual member had actually committed illegal acts. George Kneip, the attorney for the Department of Justice who was instructed to draw up the prosecution case based on the FBI brief, acknowledged that "the Government will be faced with a difficult task in seeking to prove beyond a reasonable doubt, in a criminal prosecution, that the Communist Party advocates revolution by violence." Section 11, the conspiracy provision of the Smith Act, enabled the Department of Justice to go after the party itself rather than any particular individuals, about whom the department knew so little that, when it was about to indict them, the FBI was asked for the names of the party's current leaders.

Their threat to the Republic was wildly overestimated, especially against the backdrop of the extremely close 1948 election campaign. But the FBI was certainly right to question their loyalty. In Europe the Communist leaders Palmiro Togliatti of Italy and Maurice Thorez of France issued a joint declaration that, in the event of war, their parties would come to the aid of Soviet troops (in resisting "aggression"), even if within the national borders of Italy and France. Four American apparatchiks wanted to issue a similar statement; but in early March 1949 the National Committee hammered out a compromise that proclaimed: "If, despite the efforts of the peace forces of America and the world, Wall Street should succeed in plunging the world into war, we would oppose it as an unjust, aggressive, imperialist war, as an undemocratic and anti-Socialist war." By then the party leaders were already on trial, though the jury had not yet heard the evidence—much less reached a conclusion—when President Truman found the defendants guilty of something worse than the conspiracy for which they had been indicted: "I have no comment on a statement made by traitors." The repression that ballooned into the Red Scare was manifestly bipartisan.

Irving Howe and Lewis Coser's standard scholarly history of American Communism notes that "conviction was almost a foregone conclusion." The eleven leaders who went on trial in February 1949 in Foley Square in New York were charged with intending to conspire to advocate violence sometime in the future. Because the Smith Act made words treasonable, much depended on their exegesis—especially since the director of the New York Public Library testified that all the Marxist texts that the government introduced as evidence were available in the general circulation division of his library. Interpretation of those classics was the role of the thirteen "expert" witnesses for the prosecution, who explained the "Aesopian language" of the Communist Party. Budenz, for example, read into the record passages from Lenin's *Imperialism: The Highest Stage of Capitalism,* and *State and Revolution;* from Stalin's *Foundations of Leninism,* and the *History of the Communist Party of the U.S.S.R.;* and from other works that sanctioned or promoted revolutionary violence. One section of the constitution of the American Communist Party nevertheless required the immediate expulsion of any advocate of such violence, a contradiction which the former managing editor of the *Daily Worker* resolved by applying the appropriate critical method: If Marxist-Leninist texts preached the violent extinction of the ruling class, the words were to be taken literally. But if a peaceful transition to socialism was expected, they were to be distrusted as deliberately misleading.

Yet even the government's first witness—Herbert Philbrick, who as an undercover agent in the party since 1940 had risen to its middle ranks—had never reported to his FBI superiors any violent or criminal acts among his Marxist-Leninist comrades. (He also conceded that he had never met the eleven leaders on trial.) The absence of any overt acts among these alleged conspirators enabled defense attorney Abraham Isserman to claim that the Department of Justice had failed to prove a "clear and present danger," which was Justice Holmes's test of the limits of free speech in *Schenck v. U.S.* (1919). That particular standard was too strict for the prosecution even to try to meet during the nine-month trial, and Judge Harold R. Medina ruled that the Smith Act need not be so interpreted for the jury to find the defendants guilty. Medina thus scrapped Holmes's celebrated test, instructing the jury that "there is a sufficient danger of a substantive evil that the Congress has a right to prevent to justify the application of the statute under the First Amendment." The eleven defendants were duly convicted. For good measure Medina imprisoned all five defense attorneys (plus Eugene Dennis, who defended himself) for contempt of court. A six-month jail sentence also alerted other members of the bar to the risks of vigorous representation of Communist clients.

The *New York Times* editorially applauded the verdict, and reported on its front page that the defendants had been "convicted of secretly teaching and advocating, on secret orders from Moscow, overthrow of the U.S. Government and destruction of American democracy by force and violence." The newspaper of record got it wrong: the charge had been the looser legal test of *conspiracy* to advocate revolution by violence. The following year the Court of Appeals unanimously upheld the Smith Act convictions as consistent with the U.S. Constitution, though Chief Judge Learned Hand altered Medina's "substantive evil" to "grave evil" and wondered "how one could ask for a more probable danger, unless we must wait till the actual eve of hostilities." The Supreme Court agreed, even though Chief Justice Fred M. Vinson conceded that the party was too small and weak to overthrow the government, and that its leadership had not attempted to put revolutionary theory into practice during the period (1945–48) in question. Only Justices Hugo L. Black and William O. Douglas dissented in *Dennis v. U.S.* (1951). Justice Black clearly wrote for posterity:

> Public opinion being what it now is, few will protest the conviction of these Communist petitioners. There is hope, however, that in calmer times, when present pressures, passions and fears subside, this or some later Court will restore the First Amendment liberties to the high preferred place where they belong in a free society.

Not all liberals agreed with the dissenters, however. Former Attorney General Francis Biddle believed that the party leadership had been properly convicted of "the secret teaching of a preparation for sabotage and espionage" and of plans "to act violently when the time comes." Adlai Stevenson's valiant opposition to McCarthyism in this era was compromised when the Illinois governor supported the Smith Act itself and then extolled Truman for having "put the leaders of the Communist Party . . . where they belong—behind bars." Professor Arthur M. Schlesinger, Jr., urged the repeal of the provision of the Smith Act that penalized advocacy, but proposed new legislation outlawing the Communist Party as "a criminal conspiracy systematically utilizing perjury and espionage in the interests of a foreign totalitarian power" (even though perjury and espionage were already illegal). Traditional civil liberties would thus be safeguarded by denying them to the conspiratorial movement that would have destroyed them, were it ever to seize power. Perhaps somewhat inconsistently, the Harvard historian opposed any further prosecutions under the act. By the end of 1952, another thirty-three Communists had nevertheless been convicted, three others had been acquitted, and further trials were scheduled. One hundred and twenty-six party leaders were eventually indicted, of whom ninety-three were convicted. Four of the original Foley Square defendants also jumped bail, fearing the imposition of an "American fascism." These paranoids had real enemies, however. Hoover, the chief official responsible for rounding them up, concurred that a war emergency was imminent; and the FBI was indeed making plans to arrest and "detain" them.

Other legislation was designed to enfeeble American Communism even further. Over a Truman veto in 1950, Congress passed the Internal Security Act, which established concentration camps in Pennsylvania, Florida, Oklahoma, Arizona (2), and California. A Subversive Activities Control Board was also charged with registering Communists and Communist fronts. Such organizations could be fined up to $10,000, and its officers imprisoned for five years as well as fined. The Communist Control Act of 1954, which Senator Hubert H. Humphrey (D-Minn.) championed, defined Communism itself as "a clear, present and continuing danger to the security of the United States," and deprived the party itself of "all rights, privileges, and immunities attendant upon legal bodies." The Americans for Democratic Action had long opposed treating the party like other political groups because it did not compete openly in the marketplace of ideas and its methods were secretive rather than persuasive. Humphrey's law blocked the possibility of open competition by banning Communists from seeking political office. Forcing the party underground reinforced the accusation that it was—well, an underground organization. The Loss of Citizenship Act, also passed in 1954, compounded the penalties already imposed under the Smith Act by adding one that had been historically reserved for those convicted of treason. Through tax liens of $400,000, the Department of Justice also sought to extinguish the *Daily Worker*, the party newspaper which ran an annual deficit of $200,000.

Such pressures guaranteed that, by 1956 at the very latest, this minuscule movement was twisting slowly, slowly in the wind. Party membership had skidded from its post–World War II high of 80,000 to about 5,000—of whom so many were FBI operatives that Hoover considered taking control of the Communist Party, simply by massing his informants behind one faction at the national convention scheduled for early 1957. The proper dialectical approach, the FBI ideologists concluded, was "middle of the road" because, if the Bureau's own cadres swung too openly to a losing faction, they risked expulsion from the party. But they did wreak further internal havoc by raising vexing questions about Soviet Premier Nikita S. Khrushchev's de-Stalinization campaign as well as his invasion of Hungary. Beginning in 1956 the FBI's Counter Intelligence Program (COINTELPRO) conducted an aggressive demolition campaign that spread disruptive rumors about individual comrades and engaged in various "dirty tricks" to deepen the apprehensions and distrust that already rippled through the party. Such clandestine influence did not, however, make the director of the FBI more realistic about the "masters of deceit" who menaced the Republic. After 1956, when the Federal Bureau of Prisons closed the detention camps that had been set up six years earlier, Hoover complained about the "growing public complacency toward the threat of subversion." The party was not a subject of realistic assessment, for anti-Communism had become an addiction. Other right-wingers expressed alarm as well, showing reluctance to awaken from their nightmares—or to abandon the repressive instruments that vigilance required. "I am not willing to accept the idea that there are no Communists left in this country," Senator Barry Goldwater (R-Ariz.) remarked in 1959. "I think that if we lift up enough rocks, we will find some."

Hoover in particular could hardly have been pleased when the Supreme Court began gutting the Smith Act and "privileging" the Bill of Rights. In *Yates v. U.S.* (1957), the Court ruled that a criminal prosecution for advocacy had to be of some future *action*, not for belief that something in the future was *desirable*. By holding that the testimony of the FBI's paid informers had to be made available to the defense, the Court in *Jencks v. U.S.* (1957) forced the government to retry the cases of several Communists—or drop the prosecutions. *Pennsylvania v. Nelson* (1956) brought to a halt state prosecutions for sedition. Other decisions also signaled that the Court was giving civil liberties greater weight on the scales of justice, as Black had hoped his brethren would.

Recognition of the rights of Communists convinced Eisenhower that Chief Justice Earl Warren was not the political moderate whom the President thought he had appointed to the Court in 1953. Warren's memoirs disclose that, while traveling with the ex-President to Winston Churchill's funeral in 1965, he was asked about "those Communist cases" of the previous decade. Warren wondered which particular decisions. "All of them," Eisenhower answered. The former President candidly acknowledged that he had not read the opinions (despite the oath he had twice taken to "preserve, protect and defend the Constitution of the United States"), though he claimed familiarity with the contents of the Supreme Court rulings. Warren explained that, like other citizens, party members deserved equal justice under law, and asked how Eisenhower would have dealt with Communists. Eisenhower's reply—"I would kill the S.O.B.'s"—virtually lip-synched Mike Hammer.

Mickey Spillane's private detective was the hero of an astounding six of the top ten fictional best sellers of the decade of the 1950s: #3 *The Big Kill* (1951), #5 *My Gun Is Quick* (1950), #6 *One Lonely Night* (1951), #7 *The Long Wait* (1951), #8 *Vengeance Is Mine* (1950), and #9 *Kiss Me, Deadly* (1952). This catalogue does not count the most popular novel of all, *I, the Jury,* which had been published prior to the decade. By 1953 the New American Library had sold 17 million paperbacks of his first six novels, which meant that having Mike Hammer's creator Spillane on the firm's list of authors was like a license to print money. Here, at the murkier edges of popular sensibility, was one of the most stridently representative and sensationalist voices of the era. Hammer's hairy-chested heroics would have made such novels popular even if they had been devoid of any explicit politics, but the overt anti-Communism of such fiction engraved it with the signature of the period. Two decades earlier Hammer might have combatted only organized criminals spawned in the lower depths; two decades later the adversaries would have been a cabal of Third World terrorists. In the early 1950s, however, the Red Scare required his special skills. For the comrades and conspirators in *One Lonely Night,* for example, Hammer reserved kicks that could shatter bone on impact, bursts of lead from his .45, and the sadistic pleasures of strangulation.

In that novel, which sold more than 3 million copies, the detective seduces a millionaire's estranged granddaughter, whom boredom has driven to communism. At first, Hammer cannot fathom why Ethel Brighton, despite her early exposure to the attractions of capitalism, can embrace the twisted creed of Bolshevism. He suspects that she needs only the substitute of *his* embrace. Confident that his virility can transform her politics, he has her spend one night in his apartment, and concludes: "Now that she had a taste of life[,] maybe she'd go out and seek some different company for a change." He is wrong—or at least seems to be, and realizes that Ethel Brighton has continued to associate with the scum who comprise the Communist movement. So he strips and whips her. Eventually Hammer poses as a member of the Soviet intelligence apparatus; and since no one in this supposedly clandestine organization thinks of challenging his credentials, he considers these conspirators as "dumb as horse manure." These malignant dreamers of world conquest "had a jackal look of discontent and cowardice." When they are not merely credulous cretins, they are either vicious hypocrites or else clinically insane. The supreme villain in *One Lonely Night* is Oscar Deamer, who is both a Communist and a psychopath. Hammer tells this master criminal, just before choking him to death: "You were a Commie, Oscar, because you were batty. It was the only philosophy that would appeal to your crazy mind. It justified everything you did and you saw a chance of getting back at the world." The explanation that such fiction offers for the appeal of Communism is, apparently, insanity.

In destroying such motiveless, psychopathic malevolence, Hammer personified the rejection of liberalism. The cure for the plague of Communism would not be the diffusion of New Deal programs to relieve economic misery, or the extension of the Four Freedoms to amplify the meaning of an open society, or more resonant calls to lighten the burden of social injustice. The solution would be violent prophylaxis. After the detective has saved his naked fiancée from Bolshevik flagellants, he murders them all and then torches the abandoned building, thus making it impossible to recover the corpses of his foes. "I killed more people tonight than I have fingers on my hands," he later boasts. "I shot them in cold blood and enjoyed every minute of it. . . . They were Commies. . . . They were red sons-of-bitches who should have died long ago. . . . They never thought that there were people like us in this country. They figured us all to be soft as horse manure and just as stupid." Such violence is presented as redemptive and even sacrificial, finding its source—however preposterously—in Christian ethics. For the feat of rescuing his fiancée in *One Lonely Night* has enabled Hammer to understand "why my rottenness was tolerated and kept alive. . . . I lived only to kill the scum and lice. . . . I lived to kill so that others could live. . . . I was the evil that opposed other evil, leaving the good and the meek . . . to live and inherit the earth."

To appraise the literary significance of such crude fiction would be pointless. What needs underscoring is that, at least in the night-battles of the Cold War for which Mickey Spillane recruited more Americans than any other author, the procedural rules and legal guarantees that helped make a civil society worth defending were treated with savage contempt. Justice was imagined as coming from the barrel of a pistol, and cruelty was not confined to party headquarters but was exalted in the exploits of Mike Hammer. Because of the official limitations under which formal authority chafed, vigilante ruthlessness was the only effective antidote to unmitigated evil. The end appeared to justify the means, so that it is almost too obvious to insist upon the analogy between the stigma that Spillane's fiction described and the methods that McCarthyism employed. To be sure, the junior Senator from Wisconsin had no *political* rival, journalist Richard Rovere observed, in gaining "access to the dark places of the American mind.'' But lurking beneath the civility of so much of American life in the early 1950s was nightmarish territory that Spillane had already penetrated, a realm of subterranean turmoil that was ripe for a ''fighting Irish Marine [who] would give the shirt off his back to anyone who needs it—except a dirty, lying, stinking Communist. That guy,'' Senator Herman Welker (R-Idaho) announced, ''he'd kill.''

The wickedness ascribed to domestic Communism allowed Americans to indulge in forbidden desires of demolishing it outside the rules. Locked in ultimate combat with the domestic apostles of totalitarianism, the policy readjusted itself to bear greater resemblance to the foe outside. Insisting on the rigid distinction between ''Americanism'' and Communism, some ardent patriots risked paying the sincerest form of flattery. ''We are facing an implacable enemy whose avowed objective is world domination by whatever means and at whatever cost,'' one notable committee on foreign intelligence reported to President Eisenhower. Discussing the work of the Central Intelligence Agency, the committee explained that ''hitherto acceptable norms of human conduct do not apply. We must develop effective espionage and counterespionage services and must learn to subvert, sabotage and destroy our enemies by more clever, more sophisticated, and more effective means than those used against us.''

The rules of political conflict at home needed revision as well. To help expose the duplicitous intrigue of Communist infiltrators, the public could turn to the testimony of ex-communists and FBI agents. Their memoirs—Louis Budenz's *This Is My Story* (1947), Angela Calomiris's *Red Masquerade* (1950), Elizabeth Bentley's *Out of Bondage* (1951), Whittaker Chambers's *Witness* (1952), and Herbert Philbrick's *I Led Three Lives* (1952)—were serialized in popular magazines or adapted for the movies and television. Such testimony depicted Communists as primed to commit espionage, as pursuing the violent overthrow of the government, as capable of submitting to a harsh mental discipline. Budenz wrote that ''the ordinary American has no idea of the alien world . . . whose leadership works secretly in the shadows.'' Party operations ''cannot be conveyed to a normal American mind,'' which thus faced an unprecedented danger.

Since the Cold War consensus was grounded so deeply in faith in the FBI, skepticism about its methods and motives represented a threat that the Bureau itself hastened to counter. Though publication of Max Lowenthal's *Federal Bureau of Investigation* in 1950 could not be halted, the campaign to discredit the book revealed the limits of criticism that domestic anti-Communism tried to establish. Lowenthal, a lawyer with a long record of government service, was also a friend of President Truman's. He construed a powerful civil libertarian case against the Bureau. In a text of 460 pages and eighty-three pages of citations, *Federal Bureau of Investigation* "constituted a rigorously argued and documented brief . . . , a marshalling of all the evidence that had been excluded by the mythologizers of the FBI legend," according to Professor Richard Gid Powers, a historian of the Bureau. The general accuracy of the book could not be rebutted. But in an era in which criticism of Hoover was iconoclastic in the precise sense of the term, it was all too easy to impugn Lowenthal's patriotism. Indeed, a speech by George Dondero (R-Mich.) belongs in a sequel to Freud's *Studies in Hysteria*. Taking the floor of the House of Representatives in September 1950, two months before the book was to be published, Dondero pinned its author at the center of an ominously anti-American conspiracy:

> When he is caught the revelation will be a bigger shock to this nation than the exposé of Benedict Arnold. It must be done. The nation can take it. But it cannot win the war of survival with Russia if this man is allowed to continue his clever, diabolical scheme to undermine our national security.

Dondero considered the author more than an attorney; he was a movement. "Every person still in the Government who has had a Lowenthal endorsement," the Congressman warned, "should be identified and their [*sic*] loyalty determined."

HUAC investigators applied pressure too. They visited William Sloan, the publisher of *Federal Bureau of Investigation,* and subpoenaed the author himself. They even urged his attorney—former Senator Burton Wheeler—not to represent Lowenthal at the executive session, which was timed to coincide with Congressman Dondero's assault. HUAC's questions were designed to stigmatize Lowenthal as a devotee of unsavory leftist causes. The hostility of the interrogation was as patent as the thinness of the accusations, and the transcript of the hearings was made public exactly two days before the publication of the book. In Professor Robert K. Carr's opinion:

> That the Committee had any legitimate basis for questioning Lowenthal even in executive session is doubtful, in view of the questions actually put to him; that it had any justification for making public his testimony, beyond a desire to tar him as a person who had been investigated by the Un-American Activities Committee, is in no way apparent.

Even though the Bureau could not prevent publication of so sinister a threat to the republic, it also campaigned against the book by providing reviewers with boiler-plate condemnations of *Federal Bureau of Investigation*. To coincide with its publication, the Bureau distributed a reassuring *Reader's Digest* reprint entitled "Why I No Longer Fear the FBI" by Morris Ernst, co-counsel and national board member of the American Civil Liberties Union. Ernst was then secretly giving the Bureau reports of ACLU meetings as well as the names of ACLU members whom he considered sympathetic to Communism. The impact of such efforts to discredit Lowenthal's book is difficult to measure, however, in the cultural atmosphere of the Cold War. The volume found few readers—and even among these may not have changed many minds about the Bureau as a bulwark against subversion. When the danger of Communism loomed larger than the value of the Bill of Rights, any exposure of police methods as resembling those of the enemy was unwelcome. Widespread interest in the subject seemed dormant. Although *The Nation* devoted a full issue to an exposé of the FBI late in 1958, it was not until journalist Fred J. Cook enlarged his *Nation* material into a book six years later—accurately entitled *The FBI Nobody Knows*—that another assault appeared in print. In that fourteen-year interregnum, criticism of the command post of the domestic Cold War was silenced.

The FBI was especially quick to connect a commitment to racial justice with political subversion. Bureau attitudes were faithfully reflected in the Warner Brothers feature, *I Was a Communist for the FBI* (1951), which shows the party taking credit for race riots in Harlem and Detroit in 1943. "To bring about Communism in America," one of its leaders announces to his comrades, "we must incite riots." The blacks who have died in these outbreaks of violence, an FBI agent in the film explains, "never knew that their death warrants were signed in Moscow." The Bureau had difficulty imagining racial change as anything but troublesome, and interpreted ordinary decency as extraordinarily radical. *Parting the Waters* (1988), Taylor Branch's Pulitzer Prize-winning saga of the life and times of Martin Luther King, Jr., reported that "FBI agents spotted white Communists by their ease and politeness around Negroes, or by the simple social fact that they socialized with Negroes at all." Of course party members and fellow-travellers held no franchise in the civil rights struggle, but many were actively involved in the implementation of interracial ideals.

The struggle to implement the Fourteenth Amendment, which became conspicuous in the 1950s, aroused the suspicion of others. As early as

1942 the chairman of HUAC, Martin Dies (D-Texas), deplored "the fact that throughout the South today subversive elements are attempting to convince the Negro that he should be placed on social equality with white people, that now is the time for him to assert his rights." For Albert Canwell, who chaired the Washington State Legislative Fact-Finding Committee on Un-American Activities, any awareness of imperfections in American society was suspect: "If someone insists that there is discrimination against Negroes in this country, or that there is inequality of wealth, there is every reason to believe that person is a Communist." From the evidence that Communism was loathsome, some politicians thus inferred that anything loathsome was Communism.

Indeed, so insensitive were most white Americans to the ordeal of systematic bigotry, that segregationists were not entirely wrong in suspecting that a dedicated opposition to racial discrimination *was* often Communist-inspired. "Concern for such things as human rights for American blacks came, ironically, to be regarded as *prima facie* proof of a person's communist inclinations," journalist Nicholas von Hoffman wrote, "because so few non-Communists in positions of power and influence cared to do anything about the problems of caste and deprivation." Not even President Roosevelt had bothered to support an anti-lynching bill. But by 1961 his son James was lamenting that the various investigating committees

> have helped to create such a general atmosphere of fear that all social reformers—including advocates of racial justice—tend to be frightened into silence. When the committees succeed in equating social reform with Bolshevism, it is to be expected that some people will confuse the Fourteenth Amendment with *The Communist Manifesto*. To avoid being called Reds, they will be sure not to talk like integrationists.

Even though HUAC was willing to certify the National Association for the Advancement of Colored People as "a non-Communist organization" in late 1954, various official committees in southern states like Alabama, Arkansas, Florida, and Louisiana summoned "expert witnesses," preferably ex-Communists, to brand the NAACP as an instrument of the international conspiracy. In a few states such investigations led to the "outlawing" of the organization, and the attendant publicity may have helped stifle criticism of Jim Crow. It mattered little to segregationists that the largest black organization in the country was not a Communist front like the National Negro Congress—nor even the NAACP—but the

National Baptist Convention, and that the ratio of black churches to churchgoers was double that of whites. It was therefore natural for King and other ministers who formed the Southern Christian Leadership Conference in 1957 to advertise their piety to the black community. But the Cold War was also taken into account. To include the word "Christian" in the name of the organization was also to demonstrate that, though the SCLC was consecrated to civil rights, it was not Communist-inspired.

The highest appellate court in the country lacked such camouflage. For its appreciation of the egalitarian implications of the Fourteenth Amendment, the Supreme Court after 1954 was also accused of susceptibility to Communism—especially in the South, and especially as it moved to broaden the concept of political rights to include Communists. A footnote in *Brown v. Board of Education* (1954) had cited the most influential scholarly account ever written about race relations, Gunnar Myrdal's *An American Dilemma*, published a decade earlier; and the citation gave segregationists the opening that they craved (even if they did not need it). Right-wing and racist attacks on his book as Communist became common in the following decade. Myrdal was tagged a "notorious Swedish Communist," though he was an anti-Communist, and a "Red psychologist" and an "alien anthropologist," though he was an economist. He was often called "Dr. Karl Gunnar Myrdal," the full name that he never used, because the first name that his parents had given him was the same as Dr. Marx's. By such acrobatics Senator James O. Eastland (D-Miss.) was able to charge, after *Brown v. Board of Education,* that the Supreme Court had dared "to graft into the organic law of the land the teachings, preachings and social doctrines [of] Karl Marx."

As liberal impulses became suspect, as sensitivities to Constitutional safeguards were coarsened, the axis of postwar American politics spun toward the primitive, the intolerant, the paranoid. In 1952, for example, the Supreme Court upheld in *Carlson v. Landon* a lower court decision to hold five aliens without bail, while the question of their deportation was under review. None had been convicted of—or even charged with—any crime. Refusing to grant the aliens' bail, the district judge explained: "I am not going to turn these people loose if they are Communists, any more than I would turn loose a deadly germ in this community." Anti-Communism was expected to be visceral. Though George Kennan, the diplomat who devised the strategy of containment, had compared Communists to a "swarm of rats" whose abandonment of Western civilization was a "sacrilege" that "someday must be punished as all ignorant presumption and egotism must be punished," that was not good enough for James Burnham, an especially hard-boiled egghead:

Although George Kennan is unquestionably anti-Soviet and from a rational standpoint anti-Communist, nowhere in his published writings does one ever find expressed in the texture of his style a powerful emotion concerning Communism, a hatred of Communism. . . . The analysis and rejection, which are there, are always pale and abstract.

After essayist E. B. White did a *New Yorker* satire that suggested that, if Senator McCarthy had known of Thoreau, the Concord writer would have been denounced as a security risk, McCarthy's classiest defender, William F. Buckley, Jr., rebutted: "Thoreau *was*."

Perhaps in so remorseless a spirit, the Department of State hoped to deflect McCarthy's young minions—Roy M. Cohn and G. David Schine—by issuing a directive which prohibited from its overseas libraries all materials, including paintings, by "any controversial persons, Communists, fellow-travellers, et cetera." The vagueness of a phrase like "controversial persons" aroused such strong criticism that the International Information Administration eliminated the category, but that adhesive "et cetera" remained in effect. Yet not even the experts could agree on who the Communists and fellow-travellers were. HUAC's list of subversive organizations, for example, was five times longer than the Attorney General's list, which interdicted seventy-eight groups when it was first promulgated in 1948. The National Lawyers Guild was only on HUAC's list; and when McCarthy decided to go for the jugular during the 1954 Army hearings, he identified one former Guild member as Fred Fisher, a young Hale & Dorr associate of Army special counsel Joseph N. Welch of Boston. Had McCarthy stuck to the Attorney General's list, which had omitted the organization that McCarthy called "the legal arm of the Communist Party," Welch's rebuttal of June 9, 1954 would not have struck with such magnum-force: "Until this moment, Senator, I think I never really gauged your cruelty or your recklessness."

Welch's puckish valor in stabbing at McCarthy during the televised hearings became famous, especially in contrast to the silence of Eisenhower himself. It was a sign of the fragility of civil liberties that the Anti-Defamation League of B'nai B'rith chose to celebrate its fortieth anniversary in 1953 by giving a Democratic Legacy Award to the President—not because he had done so much to enlarge the definition of an open society, but because he had done so little. Bestowing such an award, the donors hoped, might quicken Eisenhower's interest in civil rights and liberties. He agreed to accept on national television and then, with all three networks covering the presentation, was suddenly inspired enough to ad lib some objections to McCarthyism. The President mentioned his own origins in Abilene, where "Wild Bill" Hickok had served as marshal. "Now that town had a code," Ike reminisced, "and I was raised as a boy to prize that code. It was—meet anyone face to face with whom you disagree. You could not sneak up on him from behind—do any damage to him—without suffering the penalty of an outraged citizenry. If you met him face to face and took the same risks he did, you could get away with almost anything, as long as the bullet was in the front." The frontier moral that Eisenhower applied was that, "in this country, if someone dislikes you or accuses you, he must come up in front. He cannot hide behind the shadow. He cannot assassinate you or your character from behind, without suffering the penalties of an outraged citizenry."

The President's point might have been a little too oblique. His own Administration continued to sanction the faceless and nameless accusations that he deplored, and the right not to be shot in the back—but only in front—had been carelessly omitted from the first ten amendments to the Constitution. The lesson of forthright courage that the President drew from Abilene was not widely adopted. The liberal anti-Communist journalist James Wechsler wrote that "our republic is haunted by two kinds of silence—the calculated reticence of those who have something to hide and the deepening timidity of others who have nervously concluded that it is safer to have nothing to say."

By the end of the 1950s some equilibrium was restored to the political system. The death of Secretary of State John Foster Dulles in 1959 probably made a difference. A former Wall Street lawyer and a leading Presbyterian, the embattled capitalism and Christianity that he personified were no longer seen as incompatible with less frosty diplomatic relations with the Soviet Union. The rambunctious visit of Nikita Khrushchev to the United States that same year made its leader more human and less demonic; and when it became necessary to explain to the Russians what made American society so praiseworthy, even rabid anti-Communists were compelled to highlight the civil liberties that they themselves had sought to curtail. The Bill of Rights that Richard M. Nixon claimed abroad was operating in the United States was not a document that the Vice President and his allies were seeking to reinforce when he was at home. Yet in an address that he delivered in Moscow in 1959, printed in full in both *Pravda* and *Izvestia*, Nixon noted that the material achievements of the American economy coincided with liberty, such as the freedom to criticize the President (a daily occurrence), freedom of worship and information, and freedom of movement: "Within our country we live and travel where we please. . . . We also travel freely abroad.'' Passports even of non-Communists like playwright Arthur Miller had been lifted in this era, nor did whites permit blacks to live where they pleased. Such misrepresentations were endemic to the global struggle, but the proclivity for self-righteousness did not go unchallenged in the 1960s.

Thanks to appellate court decisions that reinforced and extended the Bill of Rights, the obsessions of the Cold War began to recede. By the early 1960s, a shrinking number of Americans came to share J. Edgar Hoover's fixation with domestic subversion. Neither *A Study of Communism* (1962) nor *J. Edgar Hoover on Communism* (1969) matched the popular impact of his earlier best-seller, *Masters of Deceit* (1958). The burgeoning civil rights movement had disturbed him because of its vulnerability to Communist infiltration and control, but national attention was shifting to the problem of persistent racial discrimination. Attorney General Robert F. Kennedy, who had become Hoover's superior in 1961, challenged the racism that had long permeated the Bureau, which employed no black agents, except for the director's servants. Though Hoover resented pressure to eliminate the segregationist practices of the Bureau, the fight against bigotry was no longer ominous; it had become obligatory. By then the citadel of the domestic Cold War was finding it difficult to recruit new agents. Late in 1960 new agents' classes had to be postponed three times for lack of applicants, and the ranks of non-lawyers were quietly trolled for potential G-men. The Bureau's own clerical workers were supplying over a sixth of its recruits at the beginning of the 1960s. Nevertheless, the sexagenarian Hoover, fortified by daily vitamin injections in his office, still operated on Red Alert. Haunted by the vestigial phantoms of the 1950s, he analyzed the increasing ''Turbulence on Campus'' in a 1966 article, calling the party-supported Du Bois Clubs, named after the radical black intellectual, ''new blood for the vampire of international communism.'' The most frost-bitten of Cold Warriors served on the national board of The Boys Clubs of America, as did former Vice President Nixon, who found something pernicious in the Communist decision to name its youth organization so sonorously like The Boys Clubs.

Despite the ridicule with which this particular warning was greeted, Nixon did not entirely abandon the habit of inflating fears of domestic Communism. In 1965 he intervened in the New Jersey gubernatorial race because incumbent Richard Hughes defended the academic freedom of Rutgers University historian Eugene D. Genovese, a Marxist who had proclaimed that he ''welcome[d] the victory of the Viet Cong.'' But the

former Vice President was functioning in a more open political climate
than in the 1950s, and threats to academic freedom did not go unchallenged. Both the president and the board of governors of Rutgers defended Genovese, a non-Communist who openly advocated opinions that
had been concealed or soft-pedalled among radicals over a decade earlier.
And he was more difficult to dislodge. Genovese did not go into exile, as
did M. I. Finley, an earlier Rutgers historian of slavery, who had not been
permitted to contaminate the American classroom after taking the Fifth
Amendment in 1952. Later, as Sir Moses Finley, he taught ancient history at Cambridge University. Professor Genovese remained in academe,
and Governor Hughes was re-elected in a landslide despite Nixon's intervention. Later, while Genovese was teaching at the University of Roch-
ester, a group of graduating seniors walked out of the commencement
ceremony there when Nixon came to accept an honorary degree in 1966,
citing his earlier challenge to Genovese's academic freedom. Such a
protest would have been unimaginable in the 1950s.

In 1968 Nixon's running mate inadvertently ended the Cold War style
of rock-'em, sock-'em partisanship. Spiro T. Agnew called Senator Hubert
Humphrey, the Democratic standard-bearer, "squishy-soft on Communism." This smear against a sponsor of the Communist Control Act of
1954—and an indefatigable drum-major for military intervention in
Vietnam—was bizarre. So fully did this anti-patriotic accusation appear to
erase the cultivated impression of a "new Nixon" that Governor Agnew
was forced to back down. He pleaded ignorance of the ugly historical implications of such a charge. Agnew was strangely convincing, since he had
been a supermarket manager in 1953 and may never have learned what
McCarthyism represented. Without political advantage to be derived from
such woolly accusations, the party system itself seemed at last to regain
some equilibrium, as though recoiling from the excesses of the domestic
Cold War. For if the "natural" tendency of Bolshevism was the denial of
legitimacy to any political opposition—"We are all Chekists," Lenin had
once asserted to party comrades, affirming their complicity with the secret
police—the "natural" tendency of the American political system has been
the give-and-take of partisan bargaining, the compromises negotiated according to the accepted rules of a vigorous democracy. Jefferson's first
inaugural address had proclaimed that "we are all Republicans, we are all
Federalists." And the few Americans who were not might well have med-
itated on the virtues of such comity, on the advantages of forbearance, and
on the wisdom of his reassurance that "every difference of opinion is not
a difference of principle."

6

Equal Justice Under Law

The Supreme Court and Rights of the Accused, 1932–1991

DAVID J. BODENHAMER

When the Warren Court bound states to follow the criminal procedures of the Bill of Rights during the 1960s, commentators aptly
termed it a "due-process revolution." In decision after decision, the
justices overturned long-standing precedents by declaring that the various
provisions of the Fourth, Fifth, and Sixth Amendments applied to state
law enforcement practices. For the first time in United States history, the
rights of the accused became truly national. The guarantee of due process
for criminal defendants no longer depended upon accidents of geography.

Americans divided sharply over the decisions. Liberals who distrusted
exclusive local control of criminal justice applauded the new direction.
The Court's actions promised equal justice under law through national
protection for the rights of the accused. Conservatives cast a darker
interpretation on the changes: the revolution portended an increase in
crime and disorder by hampering the ability of local police and courts to
protect citizens and property. Also at issue was the threat to democratic
process and the federal system. Appointed judges had usurped the legislative function, conservatives argued, and their newly proclaimed power
threatened the constitutional balance between the states and the central
government.

By 1968 the Supreme Court stood at the storm center of national
politics in a way not seen since the sectional crisis of the late 1850s, and

the rights of the accused became a central issue in the presidential election. Republican nominee Richard Nixon and third-party candidate George Wallace campaigned on "law and order" themes, pledging to restore a conservative cast to the federal judiciary, especially the Supreme Court. Nixon's election and his subsequent appointment of Warren E. Burger as Chief Justice in 1969 redeemed that promise and foreshadowed an attempt to undo much of what the liberal Warren Court had accomplished.

But there was no counterrevolution in the rights of the accused. The Burger Court essentially continued and consolidated major Warren Court doctrines, even though it refused to extend them except in the area of capital punishment. One reason was because the Warren Court decisions were not as radical as critics maintained. In many instances, the logic of rights stemmed from cases that predated the 1960s. The decisions appeared more revolutionary because the majority justices abandoned the Court's traditional deference to the states and the legislative process and actively pursued its own solutions to these constitutional issues. Yet if the Burger court did not reverse the trend toward greater protection for the rights of the accused, the actions of the Rehnquist Court suggest that the justices now may be marking the end of the due-process revolution.

Until the mid-twentieth century, state constitutions were the primary source for the rights of the accused, and state courts were responsible for their enforcement. The U.S. Supreme Court had ruled repeatedly that Bill of Rights' guarantees applied only in violations of federal criminal law, a position that contrasted sharply with the Court's decision on the First Amendment. Here, early in the twentieth century, the justices extended federal protection against state interference to the freedoms of speech, religion, press, and assembly. These rights, the Court decided, were fundamental to liberty and applied to all citizens through the Fourteenth Amendment, adopted in 1868. The rights of the accused, on the other hand, were not so essential; freedom, the justices concluded, could exist under a wide variety of criminal procedures.

From the 1930s to the 1950s the Court slowly incorporated some rights of the accused into the Fourteenth Amendment's guarantee of due process to all citizens. The catalog of nationalized rights—provisions of the Bill of Rights binding on the states—was quite extensive by the end of the three decades, especially given the previous absence of such guarantees; but the list pales when compared to current practice. Fundamental rights included limited protection against illegal searches and seizures (Fourth Amendment) and coerced confessions (Fifth); public trial, impartial jury, and counsel (Sixth); and protection against cruel and unusual punishments (Eighth). Other rights considered central by later Courts were not included: prohibition of double jeopardy, protection against self-incrimination, and guarantee of jury trial, among others.

The nationalization of the Bill of Rights traveled an uncertain course prior to 1960 because the justices lacked a sure theoretical foundation for their decisions. There was no consensus on principles to guide interpretation of the amendments, in part because of the novelty of the idea that defendants' rights needed protection against state misconduct. Few judges doubted that injustice could—and did—occur in state criminal trials, but even many enlightened jurists accepted the traditional argument that classical federalism, with its curb of central power, offered the best security for individual liberty. Well into the twentieth century, courts accepted the states' authority in criminal matters and the primacy of state constitutions in guaranteeing the rights of the accused.

Powell v. Alabama (1932), the so-called Scottsboro case, first breached the jurisdictional wall separating state and federal authority in criminal procedure. In response to the inadequate representation provided to eight black youths who were sentenced to death for the alleged rape of two white girls, the U.S. Supreme Court ruled, 7–2, that the right to counsel was part of the due process clause of the Fourteenth Amendment and thus binding on the states. But this right was only similar to, not identical with, the same right guaranteed by the Sixth Amendment. The distinction permitted the Court to fashion a guide through the thicket of claims made by defendants anxious to secure federal protection for their rights. Five years later, in *Palko v. Connecticut* (1937), the justices decided that the Fourteenth Amendment required states to accept rights essential to a "scheme of ordered liberty." Rights received constitutional protection, Justice Benjamin Cardozo wrote for the majority, if their denial imposed "hardships so shocking that our polity will not endure it" or if the actions of government violated the "fundamental principles of liberty and justice which lie at the base of all our civil and political institutions."

In criminal matters, the guarantee of fair trial alone was fundamental to liberty. States could employ widely different procedures without denying fair treatment. The fair trial test meant that the Court would decide case-by-case which rights of the accused enjoyed constitutional protection. It also suggested that the values of individual judges would determine which state procedures created such hardships or so shocked the conscience that they denied fair treatment. Yet the test also provided a method for modernizing the Bill of Rights by inviting justices to extend liberties if modern conditions required it.

Some members of the Court accepted such judicial discretion as inescapable, but other justices distrusted any approach that allowed judges to substitute their personal notions of fairness for an objective standard. Chief among those who sought more definitive criteria was Justice Hugo Black. He urged his colleagues to acknowledge that the framers of the Fourteenth Amendment intended to incorporate the Bill of Rights into the due-process clause and to apply these rights as limits upon state action. This position, often called total incorporation, had considerable appeal. It was easy to express, simple to apply, and embraced a conviction that individual rights should not vary from state to state.

Total incorporation also promised to remove the Court from a doctrinal nightmare, namely, its recurrent assertion, first announced in *Hurtado v. California* (1884), that the Bill of Rights and Fourteenth Amendment carried different meanings even when the same right was at issue. Under the fair trial test, the justices frequently found themselves deciding that a right essential to fair proceedings under the Fourteenth Amendment's due-process clause—assistance of counsel, for instance—was not identical to the right guaranteed in federal trials by the Sixth Amendment. It was only a similar right. Otherwise, the framers of the Fourteenth Amendment would have repeated needlessly a right already granted. Total incorporation would allow the Court to escape the dilemma. But it also would radically change the nature of the federal system; and it was on these grounds that the Court engaged in a debate that shaped the rights of defendants for the next few decades.

The argument for total incorporation was unpersuasive to Justice Felix Frankfurter. The Fourteenth Amendment's due-process clause, he argued, called for "an exercise of judgment upon the whole course of the proceedings" to determine "whether they offend those canons of decency and fairness which express the notions of justice of English-speaking peoples" (*Malinski v. New York*, 1945). Due process incorporated fundamental values, one of which was fairness, and judges could dispassionately discover and apply these values to claims of injustice. Frankfurter also believed that imposing the Bill of Rights on the states would alter irrevocably the federal division of governmental power, a basic principle of American constitutionalism. And it would undermine popular government, which demanded judicial deference to the judgment of elected representatives. Even in the area of civil liberties, legislative actions should be respected unless they flagrantly defied the community's sense of values.

Procedural rights needed closer scrutiny, Frankfurter acknowledged in *McNabb v. United States* (1943), because "the history of liberty has largely been the history of observance of procedural safeguards." But here, too, the Court could require simply that states enforce fundamental principles of liberty and justice. It should intervene only when states denied or refused to enforce appropriate constitutional guarantees. Due process, after all, was not solely a federal standard. It was a concept that expressed local values arising from different historical and practical considerations. These divergent circumstances should be recognized insofar as they did not conflict with traditionally accepted Anglo-Saxon principles of justice.

The dispute between Black and Frankfurter was symptomatic of the Court's deep divisions in the 1940s and 1950s concerning nationalization of the Bill of Rights for criminal defendants. No one denied the importance of guaranteeing fair procedures. If anything, the rise of European and Asian police-states intensified the Court's sense of responsibility for careful evaluation of the administration of justice. But beyond a general concern for fairness in state trials, the justices could not agree on what their role should be. In case after case, the Court found itself deeply divided, first upholding a national standard and then, in similar circumstances, rejecting it as an infringement of state authority.

Notwithstanding its expressed reluctance to interfere with state procedures, the Court's adherence to the fair trial test led to small gains in nationalizing due process. The most important—and most controversial—decision was *Wolf v. Colorado* (1949), a case that raised questions about the Fourth Amendment's application to the states and its enforceability in state courts. At issue was the conviction of a Denver abortionist based on evidence seized after a warrantless search of his offices. In federal courts the exclusionary rule, adopted by the Supreme Court in *Weeks v. United States* (1912), would have prevented use of any illegally obtained evidence at trial. But under Colorado law the only test of admissibility was whether evidence was relevant and material. The question upon appeal was straightforward: did the Fourth Amendment's prohibition of unreasonable searches and seizures extend to states?

The Supreme Court affirmed Wolf's conviction. The due-process clause, wrote Justice Frankfurter, did not incorporate the Bill of Rights. But "security of one's privacy against arbitrary intrusion by the police—which is at the core of the Fourth Amendment—is basic to a free society." Under the fair trial test it was implicit in the scheme of ordered liberty and enforceable against states. Still, Wolf's conviction stood because the exclusionary rule was a judicially created guide that Congress could repeal. It was not a command of the Fourth Amendment and governed federal trials alone. States could reject the principle—and the vast majority did—without violating the Bill of Rights.

Wolf v. Colorado protected a right but denied a remedy. Even though the Fourth Amendment was a shield against warrantless searches and seizures, defendants in state courts could not bar evidence gained illegally. The illusory promise of the decision did not go unnoticed. "The Court," one justice wrote in a stinging dissent, "now allows what is indeed shabby business: lawlessness by officers of the law." Another justice concurred: "[The] version of the Fourth Amendment today held applicable to the States . . . is a pale and frayed carbon copy of the original."

During the 1950s the Court's continued reliance on the fair trial test led to much confusion regarding which criminal procedures were acceptable. Some state practices it permitted, others it rejected, but no clear standard emerged to guide local law enforcement. In 1952 the Court modified *Wolf* to exclude from state trials any illegal evidence gained by violent means. The facts in the case—forcible extraction of narcotic capsules from the defendant's stomach—shocked the justices. Therein lay the rationale for the decision. Yet over the next five years two similar instances of official misconduct produced dramatically different results. In 1954, the Court permitted the introduction of illegally seized evidence gained from repeated nonviolent but unauthorized police entries into a private home. The justices once again registered their concern: "Few police measures have come to our attention that more flagrantly, deliberately, and persistently violated" a citizen's rights. But a 5–4 majority found there was no physical coercion, so the evidence was admissible. Even this distinction was lost three years later when the Court upheld a conviction for involuntary manslaughter while intoxicated based upon a blood sample drawn without consent from an unconscious defendant.

The Court's decisions had produced only the most nebulous standards to guide law officers. Increasingly, it became more difficult to predict with certainty which actions of police, prosecutors, and judges were subject to constitutional limitations and which were not. The changing composition of the Court undoubtedly created some of the confusion: thirty men occupied seats on the bench from 1930 to 1960. So, too, did indecision elsewhere in the central government on issues touching the nationalization of rights. During World War II and the early part of the Cold War, both Congress and President hesitated to extend individual rights by statute or otherwise, because to do so might restrain the campaign against subversion and disloyalty. The nascent civil rights movement also led to unresolved tensions as southern whites raised the banner of state sovereignty in response to black demands for equal protection.

Whatever the reasons, continued adherence to the fair trial test exposed the Court to charges that defendants' rights depended on judges' personal reactions to the facts presented by each case. Such an ad hoc approach,

Chief Justice Warren cautioned in 1957, "is to build on shifting sands." It was also at odds with the Court's decisions on First Amendment freedoms. These rights applied fully and identically to central and state governments alike under the due process clause of the Fourteenth Amendment. Why should not the same standard govern the rights of the accused? *Palko v. Connecticut,* forbearer of the fair-trial doctrine, contained no "license to the judiciary to administer a watered-down subjective version of the individual guarantees of the Bill of Rights."

By the late 1950s, four justices—Warren, Black, Douglas, and Brennan—were ready to abandon the fair-trial approach to the Fourteenth Amendment. The 1960s witnessed their triumph. Too much had changed nationally to permit continuation of an interpretation that defined rights of the accused in terms of state boundaries. Prosecutors and police officers alike had grown weary of a tribunal in distant Washington deciding long after trial that state practices used to convict were at odds with the U.S. Constitution. Law schools and bar associations, too, desired more uniform standards. Increasingly, commentators and legal scholars questioned why the Fourth, Fifth, Sixth, and Eighth Amendments were not equally as fundamental to national citizenship as economic liberties or the freedom of speech and of the press, rights long since subject to national jurisdiction.

Suddenly, in a rush of Supreme Court cases during the 1960s and 1970s, the Bill of Rights became the national code of criminal procedure. Leading the due-process revolution was Chief Justice Earl Warren, a former California district prosecutor, attorney general, and governor whose appointment represented President Eisenhower's repayment of a political debt. Nothing marked Warren as a man of judicial temperament. He was instead an experienced politician; the judiciary scarcely figured in his pre-Court calculus of proper government. No wonder the conservative Eisenhower felt betrayed when Earl Warren led the Court through an extraordinarily controversial period, one that witnessed the triumph of judicial liberalism, the nationalization of the Bill of Rights, and an unprecedented expansion of the rights of criminal defendants.

Warren's tenure signaled a shift in judicial style from restraint to activism. As Chief Justice, he rejected the canons of judging that prescribed deference to legislative actions, respect for federalism and its diversity of state practice, and reliance upon neutral decision-making based upon narrow case facts rather than broad constitutional interpretation. His philosophy emerged from political experience. Warren specifically dismissed as "fantasy" the notion that justices should be impartial: "as the defender of the Constitution," he wrote, "the Court cannot be neutral." He also sought a broad role and active stance for the high bench: the "Court sits to decide cases, not to avoid decision." More important, cases must reach the right result, a condition defined by ethics, not legal procedures. Warren firmly believed the Constitution embodied moral truths which were essential to enlightened government. It was the Court's duty to apply these principles, even if doing so contravened the expressed wishes of the legislature, and to champion the individual, especially citizens without a meaningful political voice.

Nowhere was Warren's judicial philosophy more evident than in his attitude toward the Bill of Rights. The first ten amendments, he believed, protected the natural rights of man against arbitrary actions of government. It codified the sense of justice inherent in human nature and provided the basis for bringing American law into harmony with moral principles. "The pursuit of justice," he argued, "is not the vain pursuit of remote abstraction." It was an active search for a fundamental morality to guide daily life, led by an independent judiciary. This process implied "constant and creative application" of the catalog of rights, leaving "a document that will not have exactly the same meaning it had when we received it from our fathers," but one that would be better because it was "burnished by growing use."

By the 1960s the Court was ready to embrace Warren's activist stance. Acting with unprecedented boldness during the 1960s, the majority justices of the Warren Court promoted liberal policies they deemed essential to a just society. The reforms came so swiftly that many commentators proclaimed them revolutionary—and in a sense, they were. There was nothing new in the Court's method: conservative justices from 1890 to 1937 had often assumed power to make policy in defense of property rights. And the imposition of national standards on the states was a familiar constitutional refrain. What seemed fundamentally different was the vast range of issues addressed by the Court and the controversy its opinions stirred. There were sweeping decisions on the electoral process, on political representation, school desegregation, public support of religion, obscenity, and free speech, among others, each one greeted by widespread public debate, often accompanied by angry threats to reverse the Court's action. But no judicial reforms were as bold as, or ignited more protest than, the landmark cases involving criminal process.

Between 1961 and 1969 the Warren Court accomplished what previous courts had stoutly resisted: it applied virtually all of the procedural guarantees of the Bill of Rights to the states' administration of criminal justice. Adopting the strategy of selective incorporation, the justices explicitly defined the Fourteenth Amendment phrase, due process of law, to include most of the rights outlined in the Fourth, Fifth, and Sixth Amendments. The result was a nationalized Bill of Rights that dimmed the local character of justice by applying the same restraints to all criminal proceedings, both state and federal. The majority justices did not seek to diminish states' rights; they desired instead to elevate subminimal state practices to a higher national standard. But in the process, the Court reshaped the nature of federalism itself.

The first breakthrough occurred early in the decade as the Court extended the Fourth Amendment fully to the states. Previous to 1960 there were two exceptions to constitutional protection against unreasonable searches. First, prosecutors could use illegally gained evidence to secure a conviction. The Fourth Amendment prohibition of unreasonable searches applied equally to state and federal officials, but state courts were not required to adopt the federal exclusionary rule. Second, even federal courts, under the so-called silver platter doctrine, might permit the use of evidence obtained illegally by state officers in searches which involved neither federal participation nor federal direction. By 1961 the Court had removed both exceptions, initially discarding the silver platter doctrine and then applying the exclusionary rule to state criminal trials.

In *Mapp v. Ohio* (1961) the Court, 5–4, extended the federal exclusionary rule to state criminal procedure. To hold otherwise was to grant the rights under the Fourth Amendment but deny the remedy. Any other decision was also harmful to healthy federal-state relations. The lack of an exclusionary policy in many states only encouraged federal officers to disobey constitutional standards by delivering illegally seized evidence to local police and prosecutors. A common exclusionary rule would promote federal-state cooperation "by recognition of their now mutual obligation to respect the same fundamental criteria in their approach." The decision would not impede effective law enforcement, but if it did, the Constitution was more important. "Nothing can destroy a government more quickly," the majority concluded, "than its failure to observe its own laws, or worse, its disregard of the charter of its own existence."

The barrier against selective incorporation of the criminal safeguards of the Bill of Rights had fallen. The margin was slim, but the abandonment of the fair-trial interpretation of constitutional guarantees was unmistakable. Dissenting justices recognized the shift and in defeat raised an objection that accompanied subsequent advances in the due-process revolution: the Court had exceeded its authority. Justice Harlan, rapidly becoming the spokesman for his more conservative colleagues, bluntly stated his concern:

[T]his Court can increase respect for the Constitution only if it rig-
idly respects the limitations which the Constitution places upon it,
and respects as well the principles inherent in its own processes. In
the present case I think we exceed both, and that our voice becomes
only a voice of power, not reason.

The Court had acted uncharacteristically, although in a manner symbolic of future cases. Not only did the majority justices abruptly jettison
an interpretive posture that had guided decisions since 1937—and discard
an even earlier doctrinal separation of state and federal criminal power—
they openly fashioned the decision on their sense of a right result. No
matter how explained, the decision buttressed Justice Harlan's claim that
the majority "simply 'reached out' to overrule" *Wolf*. Liberal judicial
activists, despite their trenchant criticism of earlier attempts to legislate
social and economic policy from the bench, were in turn vulnerable to the
same charge.

The next year, 1962, the Court employed the same tactic in extending
the Eighth Amendment to the states. Under challenge was a section of the
California health and safety code which made a condition, narcotics
addiction, a misdemeanor punishable by fine and imprisonment. Again
the Court determined that the Fourteenth Amendment's due-process
clause incorporated a protection found in the Bill of Rights. The states too
were bound by the prohibition of cruel and unusual punishments. Equally
significant was the justices' willingness to go beyond the issues framed by
precedent. It was becoming apparent that an activist majority controlled
the Court, one intent on expanding the catalog of defendants' rights and
applying it uniformly across the nation.

This new direction became certain one year later when the Court unanimously declared that the Sixth Amendment right to counsel in criminal
cases applied to the states under the due process clause of the Fourteenth
Amendment. Reflecting upon *Gideon v. Wainwright* (1963) after his
retirement, former chief justice Warren viewed it as one of the most
important decisions made during his tenure. Few scholars would disagree. Its significance was two-fold: it extended an important federal
guarantee to state criminal defendants; and it marked the triumph of the
incorporationists over fair-trial advocates in determining the meaning of
the Bill of Rights.

The *Gideon* decision employed fair-trial rhetoric but only to ensure a
unanimous Court. The opinion clearly represented a major victory for
incorporationists. What made this conclusion inescapable were twenty-
three *amicus curiae,* or friend-of-the-court, briefs from state attorneys

general asking the justices to impose a uniform rule on state and federal courts alike. For more than two decades the prevailing fair-trial view had justified the case-by-case determination of due process and the resulting diversity of state practice as a necessary requirement of federalism. Now the states' chief lawyers wanted the Court to mandate the assistance of counsel in all serious criminal cases. Their assessment of the fair-trial approach to defendants' rights was damning. It had resulted only in "twenty years' accumulation of confusion and contradictions" that failed totally "as a beacon to guide trial judges."

The next year, 1964, the incorporationist majority added the Fifth Amendment protection against self-incrimination to the growing list of criminal procedures applied to the states through the Fourteenth Amendment. *Malloy v. Hogan,* decided 5–4, reversed another long-standing precedent: *Twining v. New Jersey* (1908) had determined the right against self-incrimination to be only a valued rule of evidence, not an essential part of due process. More important was the Court's explicit recognition of the theory of selective incorporation: rights found to be part of the due process clause of the Fourteenth Amendment were identical to corresponding guarantees of the Bill of Rights. "[I]t would be incongruous," Justice Brennan wrote for the majority, "to have different standards" for state and federal courts. The Fourteenth Amendment did not extend a "watered down, subjective version of the Bill of Rights" to the states.

The concept of identical meaning in criminal procedure marked a significant advance for advocates of selective incorporation. Justice Harlan recognized this shift and registered his disapproval. Brennan's opinion, he charged, had distorted the historical development of due process by pretending its guarantees were the same as rights listed in the first eight amendments. Even worse, the majority incorporationists had broken well-established bounds of judicial restraint. They had taken the Fourteenth Amendment's due-process clause as a "short-hand directive . . . to pick and choose among the [Bill of Rights] . . . and apply those chosen, freighted with their entire accompanying body of federal doctrine, to law enforcement in the States." The result damaged the federal system by establishing a national guide for problems best left to state discretion. "The Court's reference to a federal standard is, to put it bluntly, simply an excuse to substitute its own superficial assessment of the facts and state law for the careful and better informed conclusions of the state court."

Harlan's remarks went unheeded. The incorporationists now commanded a majority on the Court, thanks to new appointments to the bench. Eventual nationalization of defendants' rights seemed inevitable.

In a decision in 1963, the year previous to the *Malloy* decision, the Court had extended all federal standards on search and seizure to the actions of state law enforcement. Now, federal rules governed trial court decisions on issues regarding self-incrimination. The next year, 1965, in *Pointer v. Texas,* the Court ruled that "the Sixth Amendment right of an accused to confront the witnesses against him is a fundamental right and is made obligatory on the States by the Fourteenth Amendment."

The liberal majority had chosen a course of selectively incorporating the procedural guarantees of the Bill of Rights, but by what rationale? Although the incorporationist justices never advanced a systematic theory, Justice Goldberg's concurring opinion in *Pointer* offered an explanation. The fair-trial approach, rather than preserving federalism as its defenders maintained, had actually subverted healthy relations between the states and the central government because its case-by-case decisions invited "haphazard and unpredictable intrusions by the federal judiciary in state proceedings." Yet much more was at stake than the federal principle, even though it too, as Justice Harlan reminded his colleagues, was "constitutionally ordained." States might properly experiment in socioeconomic policy without harm to the nation, Goldberg asserted. This characteristic was a virtue of the federal system. But there could be no "power to experiment with the fundamental liberties of citizens." Diversity here was unacceptable because it failed to ensure equal justice.

A surprisingly muted public response greeted these early decisions. News coverage of the landmark cases was limited, and, except for the exclusionary rule, few commentators made the changes an issue for extended discussion. The civil rights movement, and the cases resulting from it, made far more dramatic claims on public attention. Especially telling was the lack of response by the states. Numerous national associations expressed and defended state interests before federal courts, yet their most significant intervention occurred in *Gideon v. Wainwright* in support of a national standard. Only state judges made any sustained criticism of the Court's decisions. Thirty-two of the fifty state supreme courts voiced disagreement with one or more of the nationalizing cases, usually *Mapp*. Even so, state courts implemented the new policies without comment in 95 percent of the applicable cases. Uniform rules, at least the ones announced by 1965, did not threaten the core of state power, and they removed much of the uncertainty that accompanied numerous appeals.

The scant public attention given to the nationalization of defendants' rights disappeared abruptly in 1966 when the Court tackled the politically controversial task of reforming the states' pretrial procedures. *Miranda v.*

Arizona ignited a firestorm of criticism. At issue was the admissibility of confessions obtained during police interrogations in which the suspect had not been told of his right to consult an attorney or to remain silent. There were several relevant precedents. The Court in 1936, in *Brown v. Mississippi,* held that a coerced confession brought about by police torture was a violation of the due process clause of the Fourteenth Amendment. More recently, *Escobedo v. Illinois* (1964) had invalidated con fessions gained as a result of extended police questioning without the suspect's attorney being present. The ruling in *Escobedo* especially—that police could not deny access to an attorney—pointed directly to the result announced in *Miranda*: the Fifth Amendment protection against self-incrimination extended to suspects under interrogation by the police.

Chief Justice Warren's opinion for the Court was a classic expression of his ethically based, result-oriented jurisprudence. The opinion first detailed the unfair and forbidding nature of police interrogations. Standard techniques described in police manuals—beatings, intimidation, psychological pressure, false statements, and denial of food and sleep—were morally reprehensible. These practices tricked or cajoled suspects from exercising their constitutional rights, leaving them dependent, isolated, abandoned, and vulnerable. This imbalance between interrogator and suspect did not belong in a democratic society. "The prosecutor under our system," he commented later, "is not paid to convict people [but to] protect the rights of people . . . and to see that when there is a violation of the law, it is vindicated by trial and prosecution under fair judicial standards." The presence of a lawyer and a protected right of silence created a more equal situation for the accused; thus, these conditions were essential to the constitutional conception of fairness.

By far the longest part of the opinion was a detailed code of police conduct, created and prescribed by the Court. The new rules quickly became familiar to anyone who watched crime dramas on television: the suspect must be informed that he has the right to remain silent; that anything he says can and will be used against him in court; that he has the right to have counsel present during questioning; and that if he could not afford an attorney, the court will appoint a lawyer to represent him. These privileges took effect from the first instance of police interrogation while the suspect was "in custody at the station or otherwise deprived of his freedom in any significant way." And the rights could be waived only "knowingly and intelligently," a condition presumed not to exist if lengthy questioning preceded the required warnings.

Policemen, prosecutors, commentators, and politicians were quick to denounce the *Miranda* warnings. Critics charged that recent Court decisions, culminating with *Escobedo* and *Miranda*, had "handcuffed" the police. This claim found a receptive audience among a majority of the general public worried about rising crime rates, urban riots, racial conflict, and the counterculture's challenge to middle-class values. Politicians eager to curry votes joined the chorus of protest. "Support your local police" became a familiar campaign slogan for candidates who sought electoral advantage in opposing the Court's reforms of pretrial procedure. The belief that the *Miranda* decision threatened public safety even acquired a certain legitimacy from members of the Supreme Court itself. "[I]n some unknown number of cases," Justice White warned in dissent, "the Court's rule will return a killer, a rapist or other criminal to the streets . . . to repeat his crime whenever it pleases him."

The police response to *Miranda* was predictable but exaggerated. Numerous studies have since demonstrated that the decision, like the ones in *Mapp* and *Escobedo,* did not restrain the police unduly and, in fact, had little effect on the disposition of most cases. The reason lay in the nature of police work. Much law enforcement necessarily occurs without supervision. Who was to determine whether policemen followed Court-mandated procedures in conducting investigations? Trial judges and prosecutors, the logical supervisors, often were elected officials sensitive to public demands to punish criminals. Suspects also were inadequate monitors because they willingly cooperated with the police, hoping to secure more lenient treatment. Neither did the presence of attorneys ensure compliance with the new rules. Access to an attorney, usually an overworked and underpaid public defender, merely speeded the plea bargaining that occurred already in an overwhelming number of cases.

At the time these things went unnoticed. What everyone recognized instead was the dramatic rise in crime and disorder. There was indeed a rapid growth in the incidence of reported crime, but the Supreme Court did not cause it. Rather, the baby boom generation had come of age. Young males, ages 15–24, traditionally account for most violations of law, and this group now comprised a larger-than-usual percentage of the nation's population. *Miranda* rules or not, there would be more crime. Police critics of the Court, frustrated by public demands to do something, simply found the Supreme Court a convenient scapegoat.

Although controversial, the *Miranda* decision—and to some extent the *Mapp* and *Escobedo* cases which preceded it—gradually brought needed improvements in police practices. Police procedures came more fully into public view, resulting in heightened awareness of official misconduct and greater expectations of professionalism. In response, many police departments raised standards for employment, adopted performance guidelines, and improved training and supervision. The Court's actions had begun to bear fruit, much in the manner desired by the majority justices who believed that hard work and respect for the law, not deception or law-breaking, were the requirements of effective law enforcement.

Significantly, the Court did not stand alone in its effort to reform pretrial criminal process. At the time of the *Miranda* decision, some state legislatures had already mandated stricter rules for custodial interrogation, and the subject was under study by several professional and governmental commissions. Federal and state bail-reform laws sought to end discrimination against the poor by greatly expanding a defendant's right to be released upon his own promise to appear in court voluntarily. The American Law Institute had completed a draft of a Model Code of Pre-Arraignment Procedure, and the newly created President's Commission on Law Enforcement and the Administration of Justice had as one of its goals the reform of criminal procedures. Ironically, the Court's *Miranda* decision slowed attempts to strengthen defendants' rights through legislation. Imposition of sweeping guidelines by the nation's highest bench had the obvious advantage of immediate and uniform application, but it also short-circuited the political process, a step which might have defused some of the issue's volatility.

The Court, ever aware of public criticism, did make concessions to ensure more widespread acceptance of its actions. Most important was its decision not to apply new rulings retroactively. Prisoners convicted under older, discredited procedures would not be granted new trials simply because the Court now found those policies unconstitutional. The justices acknowledged that applying rules to future cases alone might benefit some defendants, while denying equal treatment to prisoners convicted under abandoned procedures. But they admitted candidly that wholesale release of prisoners was politically unacceptable.

The Court also hesitated to restrict the police unduly. In 1966, the same year as the *Miranda* decision, it upheld the government's use of decoys, undercover agents, and hired informers to gain evidence of crime. The justices further approved the admissibility of information secured by wire-taps. The next year the Court accepted as constitutional a warrantless arrest in a narcotics case based upon the word of an informer whom the prosecution refused to identify in a pretrial hearing. And in a Fourth Amendment case the justices sustained the right of police "in hot pursuit" of a suspect to search a house and seize incriminating evidence without a warrant.

These moderating decisions failed to quiet the Court's critics, but mounting pressure did not deter the justices from making further reforms in state criminal procedures. *In re Gault* extended certain due-process requirements of the Bill of Rights to juvenile courts. Several important decisions incorporated the remaining Sixth Amendment guarantees—specifically, the rights to compulsory process, speedy trial, and trial by jury—into the due process clause of the Fourteenth Amendment, thus creating new restraints on state criminal process. The Court continued to insist that poverty should be no impediment to justice by requiring the state to furnish transcripts to indigent defendants. And it maintained its long-established position that confessions be truly voluntary.

The cases, in hindsight, hardly appear controversial, but at the time they departed significantly from the decades-old tradition which defined criminal justice as a local responsibility. *Duncan v. Louisiana* (1968), a jury trial case, underscored this departure. Earlier Courts had accepted state experimentation with any element of due process, including jury trial, unless the justices considered it essential to a scheme of ordered liberty. But Justice White's opinion for the majority in *Duncan* rejected theory and diversity in favor of history and uniformity: "state criminal processes are not imaginary and theoretical schemes but actual systems bearing virtually every characteristic of the common-law system that has been developed in England and this country." The issue was not whether a procedure is "fundamental to fairness in every criminal system that might be imagined but is fundamental in the context of the criminal processes maintained by the American states." Jury trials were essential to Anglo-American justice, and therefore the Sixth Amendment guarantee applied to the states.

These later cases brought only scattered protest. Evidently most people accepted the premise that the rights of the accused were national in scope and that the Supreme Court should oversee the criminal process. Far more controversial were decisions like *Miranda* which defined these rights by proscribing certain police practices. Several cases in 1967 brought especially bitter criticism from "law and order" advocates. The justices struck down a New York eavesdropping law under which police could obtain permission to tap or bug conversations without identifying the crime suspected or the evidence sought. The decision, based on the Fourth Amendment's prohibition of unreasonable searches, undermined similar laws in other states and, according to law enforcement officials, deprived them of yet another valuable crimefighting tool.

The charge that the Court was coddling criminals gained momentum when, on the same day, it extended the right to counsel to suspects in a police lineup. And in another case, *Katz v. United States* (1967), the justices reversed a gambler's conviction based on evidence gained by the warrantless bugging of a public telephone booth. The Fourth Amendment, Justice Marshall wrote, extended to persons, not places, thus abandoning the precedent which limited its protection only to physical spaces. Forgotten in the rush to criticize the Court were other decisions which endorsed law enforcement values, such as several 1968 cases upholding a police officer's right to stop and frisk a suspect, admittedly a personal search within the Fourth Amendment meaning, and even to seize evidence without a warrant, so long as the officer's actions were reasonable under the circumstances.

The activist justices could not long ignore this shift in support for their reform of criminal justice. But first, in 1969, the Warren Court completed its due process revolution by reversing, fittingly, the landmark case that had justified state experimentation with criminal procedures: *Palko v. Connecticut.* The issue, as it had been in 1937, was double jeopardy. The question: did the Fifth Amendment prohibition restrain the states? Again, the answer was yes. The majority opinion in *Benton v. Maryland* thoroughly rejected the premise that a denial of fundamental fairness rested on the total circumstances of a criminal proceeding, not simply on one element of it. Once the Court decides a particular guarantee is fundamental, then failure to honor that safeguard is a denial of due process. Equally important, these essential protections applied uniformly to all jurisdictions. The rights of the accused did not vary from state to state; they were truly national rights.

In a dual sense, the *Benton* case signaled the end of an era: it concluded the Warren Court's nationalization of the Bill of Rights, and it marked Earl Warren's retirement. The Chief Justice and his associates left an undeniable legacy. Never before had a group of judges championed so vigorously the rights of social outcasts—racial minorities, dissidents, the poor, and criminal defendants. Never before had the Court given such substantive meaning to the time-honored ethic of equal justice under law. No longer did the expression and application of rights depend so much on accidents of geography. In 1961 only eight of twenty-six provisions of the Bill of Rights restrained both federal and state governments; by 1969 nineteen guarantees had been incorporated into the Fourteenth Amendment.

Most of the safeguards nationalized under decisions of the Warren Court were rights of the accused. In a brief eight years, the liberal majority had revolutionized the concept of criminal due process. But the expansion of rights was highly controversial, especially among state and local officials charged with law enforcement. The 1968 election of a conservative law-and-order candidate, Richard Nixon, as President foreshadowed an attempt to undo much of what the liberal justices had accomplished. Now the question was, would the revolution hold?

The new Chief Justice, Warren Earl Burger, previously on the Court of Appeals for the District of Columbia, had little sympathy for the Court's due process revolution. His appointment redeemed candidate Nixon's pledge to restore a conservative cast to the nation's highest bench, especially when a few years later three other appointees replaced Warren Court justices. But contrary to expectations, there was no counterrevolution in the law governing defendants' rights. Upon Burger's retirement in 1986, the major criminal-procedure decisions of the Warren Court remained intact.

The lasting influence of the due-process revolution owed little to the new Chief Justice. Burger did not share his predecessor's concern for rights of the accused. He had often attacked the Court's procedural reforms while on the appellate bench, at one point claiming that recent decisions made guilt or innocence "irrelevant in the criminal trial as we flounder in a morass of artificial rules poorly conceived and often impossible of application." His announced goal was to limit the Court's rule-making intrusions into areas more properly reserved for the federal and state legislatures and to manage the Court's large caseload more efficiently.

Under Burger's leadership, the Court declined to expand further the rights of the accused. Instead, it was more tolerant of police behavior than the Warren Court had been. Symbolic of the change was the Court's treatment of the Fourth Amendment's requirement for a search warrant. The conservative majority denounced "mere hypertechnicality" in warrant affidavits and applied a much less restrictive interpretation to the probable-cause requirement for granting a search warrant; accepted a warrantless search as voluntary, based on all the circumstances of the case rather than on an individual's knowledgeable consent; and permitted illegally seized evidence to be presented to a grand jury even though it was inadmissible at trial. The justices also approved the "stop and frisk" practices of state and local police and allowed law officers broad latitude to search automobiles, even accepting in a narcotics case evidence seized from the car's passenger compartment without a warrant.

Not only did the Court lower the threshold requirements for a valid search, it redefined the exclusionary rule. The justices in 1974 characterized the rule as a "judicially created remedy designed to safeguard Fourth Amendment rights generally through its deterrent effect." It was not a "personal constitutional right," and its use presented "a question, not of rights but of remedies''—one that should be answered by weighing the costs of the rule against its benefits.

For a decade the Court invoked its new cost-benefit analysis cautiously, declining to apply it fully and directly to criminal prosecutions. But in 1984 the justices decided in *United States v. Leon* that evidence produced by an officer's reasonable or good-faith reliance on the validity of a search warrant was admissible in court, even if the warrant later proved defective. The ''good faith'' exception to the exclusionary rule rested explicitly on a balancing of the costs and benefits involved: using evidence captured innocently under a defective warrant exacted a small price from Fourth Amendment protection when compared to the substantial cost society would bear if an otherwise guilty defendant went free. Although the exception applied only to the small percentage of police searches conducted under a warrant, opponents of the decision worried that it invited a more casual approach to law enforcement. The concern was not misplaced. Since the 1960s, strict adherence to the rule had resulted in improved police work, with evidence excluded or prosecutions dropped in fewer than 2 percent of all cases because of Fourth Amendment violations.

The Burger Court shifted the direction of Fourth Amendment decisions, but it did not abandon entirely a concern for the rights of the accused. The justices declared unconstitutional a New York law permitting police to conduct a warrantless search of a private home in order to make a felony arrest. It also prohibited a warrantless search of an automobile luggage compartment and required law officers to show probable cause of crime to check driver's licenses and auto registrations, although a later case lowered this threshold to ''only a probability or substantial chance of criminal activity.'' More important, the new conservative majority left undisturbed the Warren Court's signal contribution on search and seizure issues, namely, that Fourth Amendment standards applied equally to state and federal jurisdictions.

In most other areas of criminal procedure, the Court maintained but did little to advance the rights of the accused that had been extended during the Warren era. Arguing that the law requires only a fair trial, not a perfect one, the Court upheld a conviction even though the police, when giving the required *Miranda* warnings, neglected to tell the defendant of his right to appointed counsel if he could not afford one. It also allowed admissions secured without the required warnings to be used to impeach the defendant's credibility, though not to obtain his conviction, if he took the stand on his own behalf. In Sixth Amendment cases the Court guaranteed the right to counsel to all trials that could lead to imprisonment, but following the lead of Congress in the Omnibus Crime Control Act of 1968, it refused to grant the protection to unindicted suspects in a police lineup. Similarly, the justices extended the guarantee of a jury trial to include all petty misdemeanors punishable by six months or longer imprisonment, yet allowed states to experiment with the size of juries and less than unanimous verdicts in non-capital cases.

Only in cases involving the death penalty did the Burger Court move beyond the Warren Court's conception of defendants' rights. All federal and state courts in the 1960s accepted capital punishment as constitutional, but late in the decade there was obvious judicial concern over its implementation. In 1968 the Supreme Court prohibited states from excluding opponents of executions from service as jurors in capital cases, although the justices otherwise refused to label the death penalty as cruel and unusual punishment. The Court of Appeals for the Fourth Circuit ruled in 1970 that the death penalty for rape was excessive, a position supported by recommendations from the National Commission on Reform of Federal Criminal Laws and the Model Penal Code. One year later the California Supreme Court decided, 6–1, that the death penalty violated the state's constitutional injunction against cruel or unusual punishments.

The next year, 1972, in *Furman v. Georgia,* a 5–4 majority of the Supreme Court set aside the death penalty for three black defendants, two convicted of rape and one of murder. There was no majority opinion: each of the five concurring justices reached the decision by separate routes. Only Justices Marshall and Brennan concluded that the death penalty was cruel and unusual punishment within the meaning of the Eighth Amendment. Justices Douglas, Stewart, and White objected on more limited grounds: the death penalty was arbitrary and capricious punishment; it discriminated against the poor, blacks, and other groups at the margins of society; and it failed to deter violent crime.

Although the decision did not hold the death penalty unconstitutional, it nullified the capital laws of thirty-nine states. It also forecast a new interpretation for the Eighth Amendment. All nine justices agreed that the death penalty was morally repugnant, and they concurred that the amendment must be interpreted flexibly and in light of contemporary values. For executions to be constitutional, the Court implied, they must be administered consistently and fairly, without discriminatory intent or effect. Sentencing juries must be given objective standards to guide their choice of life or death. Above all, the punishment must be rational and reliable.

Significantly, the decision reflected the influence of the Warren Court's result-oriented view of criminal justice. Punishment by death was qualitatively different from any other sanction: the penalty was unique; mistakes were irreversible. The decision to execute required not only strict adherence to objective and reliable rules but also strong assurance that it was proper in light of the crime, the defendant, and the patterns of punishment for similar crimes. At least in capital cases, equal justice joined fair procedure as a requirement of due process.

Guided by these standards, numerous states adopted mandatory death sentences for certain crimes, while other states established special post-trial hearings to determine whether to impose the death penalty. Reflecting a worldwide trend, states also reduced the number of capital crimes. The object of these reforms was to avoid arbitrary or capricious punishment; and in 1976, in *Gregg v. Georgia,* the Court, while declining to outlaw executions, accepted the two-stage process for capital cases, with guilt determined first and punishment fixed later. To pass constitutional muster, the justices implied, courts must apply capital punishment equally yet fit the penalty to the circumstances of individual cases.

By the 1980s the inherent contradiction between equal justice and individual treatment became unacceptable to a majority of the justices. Although the Court intended the *Gregg* decision to make the process of punishment more rational, the effect was to involve the Court more deeply in the supervision of capital convictions. Every inmate on death row sought a high court review, often repeatedly on different issues. Both state prosecutors and the general public viewed the years required to settle an appeal as a denial of justice, not a necessary delay to ensure fairness. Wearied by the issue, the Court retreated. Unable to accept the proposition that death was by definition cruel and unusual punishment, the justices abandoned the quest for reliability and settled instead for assurance that the process was not wholly arbitrary.

But by what standards would the justices determine arbitrariness? In *McCleskey v. Kemp* (1987), evidence from 2,000 Georgia murder cases between 1973 and 1979 revealed that race was significant in a jury's decision to impose capital punishment. Blacks convicted of killing whites were five times more likely to receive the death penalty than were white murderers. The Court, now led by conservative Chief Justice William Rehnquist, narrowly concluded that these figures made no difference. The decision reaffirmed a need for discretion in fitting the sentence to the circumstances of the crime. Racial bias may be a reason for setting aside a death sentence, but each defendant would have to prove that it affected his case.

Appeals in capital cases commanded less of the Court's attention during the last half of the 1980s. And decisions in this area became decidedly more favorable to the state. In *Tison v. Arizona* (1987), for example, the justices accepted as constitutional those statutes allowing capital punishment for anyone convicted of a felony in which a death occurred, whether or not they actually participated in the killing. And in 1991 the Court sharply limited the number of federal appeals that death row inmates could make. One result was a steady increase in the number of executions. By 1990 there were more than 2,700 inmates on death row, most of them black men, and executions averaged twenty-five per year. Yet there were few demands for the justices to reconsider their course.

In other areas of criminal procedure, the Rehnquist Court generally declined to extend the rights of the accused beyond the limits established in earlier cases, and in some instances it restricted protections already granted. Law officers gained greater latitude in applying the *Miranda* rule when, in *Colorado v. Connelly* (1986), the justices adopted a less strict standard to determine whether or not a confession was truly voluntary. Police cannot fail to give the required *Miranda* warnings and must stop all questioning if a suspect demands a lawyer, but they can use non-threatening tactics, such as pretending to sympathize with the suspect, to secure a valid confession. The Court also concluded in 1991 that illegal confessions would not necessarily taint a conviction if other evidence exists to prove the defendant's guilt. Clearly, these cases were far removed in spirit and effect from the decisions of the Warren Court two decades earlier.

One of the more interesting developments of the 1980s was the effort to reestablish state bills of rights as primary guardians of individual rights. Justice William Brennan, in an influential 1977 article, called for states to create broader guarantees than the increasingly conservative United States Supreme Court would allow under the Bill of Rights. Some state courts responded to this call. The Wisconsin court required that interpreters be provided at state expense for defendants who do not understand English. And the Michigan court concluded that a suspect should have an opportunity to request counsel at identification proceedings, a right not granted by the Supreme Court. In other instances—Mississippi, for example—the state's highest bench declined to accept the good-faith exception to the exclusionary rule as part of state constitutional law.

Yet it is doubtful that these cases represent a revival of the states' traditional role in maintaining the standards of criminal due process. State legislatures have passed tougher laws in response to increased public fear of crime; most of these statutes reject more expansive views of defendants' rights. Voters in numerous states have ratified amendments to their constitutions depriving individuals of procedural rights they previously enjoyed. Connecticut in 1972 reduced the size of the criminal jury to as few as six persons in non-capital cases; Florida in 1982 retreated from a more liberal exclusionary rule to the one mandated by federal decisions; and numerous states permitted the police to practice preventive detention, that is, to hold suspects in custody for a period of time without charging them with a crime. This trend continued into the 1990s, in part because lawyers, most of them trained since 1960, have little experience in arguing state constitutional law. The constitutional tradition that flourished for over 150 years may well have atrophied during the last several decades.

Even with the more conservative judicial stance during recent years, the legacy of the Warren Court remains substantially intact. The rights of the accused are now truly national, no longer dependent upon accidents of geography for their expression. Court decisions in large measure have redressed the imbalance of power that inevitably occurs in criminal proceedings when the state accuses an individual of wrongdoing. In restraining the hand of government, the Warren Court refused to heed ill-founded fears of disorder, and honored instead the older American tradition of limiting power to promote liberty. The Court led by Chief Justice Burger did not abandon the new understanding of rights, despite widespread political demands to reverse the most controversial decisions. The justices concerned themselves more with finding the practical meaning of these safeguards in individual cases than with rejecting either in whole or in part the advances of earlier Courts.

It is too early to know what modifications or new interpretations the Supreme Court in the 1990s will make in the rights of criminal defendants. But almost certainly the due process revolution is over. Under the leadership of Chief Justice William Rehnquist the Court has more often favored the prosecution than the defense. This trend will undoubtedly continue. And it will gain sustenance from legitimate concerns about continuing threats to public safety, including a startling increase in the rate of violent crime. But to date, the legacy of the Warren Court is secure. The justices have not abandoned their role to oversee the criminal process or to ensure equal justice, nor are they likely to do so, and for good reason. The nineteenth-century constitutional order is past; it cannot be recreated. Constitutional safeguards gain meaning from experience, and now a large part of our experience includes the due process revolution of the 1960s, and the new legal world it formed.

7

Balancing Acts

The Supreme Court and the Bill of Rights, 1965–1991

PAUL L. MURPHY

*T*he contours of the Bill of Rights have changed dramatically during the last twenty-five years, a period that witnessed the transition from the liberal Supreme Court of Earl Warren to the more conservative Courts of Warren Burger and William Rehnquist. The Court in these years not only saw a change in membership to more conservative justices but also a developing resonance with an increasingly conservative American public. However, this judicial shift to the right should not be exaggerated. During the last quarter century, the Court has generally stayed close to the center when deciding questions involving civil liberties or civil rights, balancing conservative and liberal pressures well in a number of areas, and even pushing far ahead of the Warren Court in some areas, particularly women's rights. Let's look at the record.

The mid-1960s saw the passage by Congress of the Civil Rights Act of 1964, and the Voting Rights Act of 1965. Both were based upon a principle that the Constitution was "color blind." Even NAACP attorneys as late as the mid-1960s were arguing that racial considerations should not be factored into public policy considerations. An individual's advancement should be based on his or her merit, not on skin color. But by the late 1960s, growing discontent in the black community made the color-blind principle seem antiquated and inadequate. By 1964, for example, only 2 percent of the black students in the Deep South attended schools with white students, and southern politicians boasted of their success in frustrating the implementation of the mandate of *Brown v. Board of Education*. This had led, among other things to black anger, and in turn, to black power and black nationalism. The spokesmen for black power frequently ridiculed the earlier leaders of the civil rights movement as Uncle Toms and accommodationists. This was true, despite the fact that Martin Luther King, Jr., in his last book, was himself calling for a second phase of the civil rights movement, and a new open advocacy of black self-interest. The potential for black power rose after the passage of the 1965 Voting Rights Act, which enfranchised millions of blacks who had not been able to vote. No longer limited to the world of rhetoric, black power had a new political power dimension which was difficult to ignore.

What this meant in practice was that color blindness was replaced by color consciousness, a policy which sought to bring about, by compulsion, what the color-blind policy should have brought about, if implemented in good faith. One important dimension of this was the Elementary and Secondary Education Act of 1965. This measure, for the first time, provided massive federal funding for public, and even private, schools with the act further providing that to qualify for such money, schools had to desegregate. This new, more aggressive approach, which was embraced by the federal government in the late 1960s, came to be known as affirmative action. It has had its critics and defenders ever since, both off and on the Supreme Court. Indeed, the affirmative action rulings, both in the educational and in the employment area, have been among the most explosive and divisive issues, as far as public opinion has been concerned, in virtually any area the Court has entered in the last twenty years.

The cases take a variety of forms, but most are familiar. Beginning around 1967, the Department of Health, Education, and Welfare (HEW) began demanding that colleges and universities develop comprehensive plans directed toward increasing the enrollment of blacks, Chicanos, Native Americans, and other racial and cultural minorities. HEW also demanded affirmative action plans to increase the percentage of female and minority group faculty members and to raise both the rank and salaries of such individuals. It sought also to equalize funds and opportunities for male and female students in athletic programs, vocational education, and dormitory facilities. The penalty for noncompliance was the loss of lucrative federal contracts for research, building funds, and scholarships, which for many universities could amount to millions of dollars. Colleges and universities then scrambled to put together programs, initially including even quotas for minority students, to avoid losing their federal funding.

The *DeFunis* case at the University of Washington in 1974 dramatized the issue, and to a degree it reinforced the critics, who saw this whole approach as reverse discrimination based upon race, incompatible with the Fourteenth Amendment's equal protection clause. DeFunis was a white male, who was passed over for entrance to the University's law school in favor of 36 minority students, all of whom had lower test scores than his. It is not fair, his attorneys argued, to discriminate against a white male, in order to make restitution for prior racial discrimination which he had no part in perpetrating. But, by the time the case reached the Supreme Court, DeFunis had reapplied for the next year's class and had been accepted, thereby mooting the case. The Court issued opinions, nonetheless, including one by Justice William O. Douglas which strongly suggested the racial bias inherent in testing.

It remained for the Court, in the 1978 *Bakke* case, to rule upon the issues. There the Court backed away from minority quotas, holding them unconstitutional, but split sharply on the place of race in admissions, the majority holding that race could be a factor therein, if used to secure a more diversified student body. The ruling seemed to support the proposition that the majority could be asked to disadvantage itself in some ways to compensate minorities for previous injustices.

Affirmative action has also been extended in the job area. There the Court ruled in the 1970s that employer programs, which assisted blacks to rise in companies, or later in police forces, were defensible, as were programs "setting aside" a certain percentage of public works funds for minority business enterprises. Indeed, in the 1980 *Fullilove v. Klutznick* case, the Court indicated that alleviation and remediation of past societal discrimination was a legitimate goal, and race was a permissible classification to use in remedying the present effects of past discrimination. So despite the Reagan Justice Department's assaults on affirmative action, the policy is still with us, even if in a somewhat curtailed way.

But if ending more overt forms of race discrimination was a central concern, a second such concern pushed its way into the public arena during the 1970s and 1980s. This was gender discrimination. Here the pattern was complex, but in some ways, reasonably consistent. Much has been written, and many tears have been shed, over the ultimately unsuccessful Equal Rights Amendment (ERA), which had been passed by Congress in March 1972, but after a bitter struggle finally failed of ratification. In many ways, this was not where the action was for women, legally and constitutionally. That action was in the courts which, through case law, brought about many of the ends which the ERA was designed to achieve. As early as 1966, a three-judge panel from the Fifth Circuit

Court of Appeals struck down an Alabama law barring women from jury duty. Five years later, in *Reed v. Reed*, a case from Idaho, the Court for the first time in American history invalidated a state law because it discriminated against women. Idaho had a statute which provided that men should be estate administrators. But the Court ruled that when the state provides dissimilar treatment for men and women, its actions are suspect, and in this case, indefensible.

The 1970s saw a flurry of gender rulings, all turning on questions of sex discrimination. In *Roe v. Wade* (1973) the Court, speaking through Justice Harry Blackmun, struck at the then uneven patchwork of state abortion laws, laws which generally made abortions criminal. In operation, the system worked only for affluent women, who could afford to go to permissive states if they needed abortion services. The Court found the system inequitable and sought to set forth a uniform national standard which would both protect the pregnant woman's right to a viable choice, and protect the fetus. The state, it ruled, cannot prohibit voluntary abortions during the first trimester of a pregnancy. It may regulate procedures thereafter, and during the last ten weeks it may prohibit abortions, except where the life of the mother is endangered. The ruling was an attempt to balance a conditional right of privacy for women contemplating abortions, with an even more conditional right of the state to protect the fetus as a prospective person. Feminists cheered this new right of women to control their bodies. But self-designated Pro-Life groups quickly denounced the rulings, thereby setting up a national controversy which has raged ever since, with Pro-Choice advocates defending the Court, and their opponents fighting to overturn the ruling and return abortion law once again to the state.

In the same year, 1973, in *Frontiero v. Richardson*, the Court ruled that as long as male members of the armed services received dependents' benefits automatically, the government could not require females to prove that they provided more than half their husband's support in order to qualify for such benefits. Four Justices used the occasion to state that all laws that involved classification by sex should be regarded as "inherently suspect."

My favorite case, in this long string of cases expanding women's rights, is *Craig v. Boren* (1976). Oklahoma had passed a law allowing young women to buy beer at 18, while young men had to wait until 21. The suggested basis for the discrimination was that "beered up" boys, between the ages of 18 and 21, were a danger on the highways. The Court, in invalidating the law, argued that sex classification could only be condoned if it served an important government objective. Further, its enforcement had to be clearly related to the achievement of that objective. In another case which favored women, *Kahn v. Shevan* (1974), the Court upheld a Florida state law granting widows a $500 annual exemption on their property taxes, but not widowers. This was a reasonable classification, argued the Court, based on the reasonable distinction that in a prior day it had been harder for women to gain employment, and this was a legitimate compensation for past reality.

All case law did not provide victories for women, however. In 1974, in *Geduldig v. Aiello,* the Court held that women could not collect disability pay for absences from work caused by pregnancy. It was not a legitimate disability demanding compensation. In *Personnel Administrator of Massachusetts v. Feeney* (1979), the Court upheld a state law giving absolute preference to veterans in civil service employment, acknowledging at the time that the policy had a devastating effect on women, but arguing that the law itself had no discriminatory intent. On the other hand, the Court ruled in 1986, in *Meritor Savings Bank v. Vinson,* that Title VII of the 1964 Civil Rights Act, which barred sex discrimination in the workplace, also protected female employees against sexual harassment on the job.

One of the most interesting Bill of Rights issues of the 1980s entailed women and pornography. Early in the decade, feminist leaders launched an assault on the nation's six to eight billion dollar pornography industry. Their antipornography campaign operated on the plausible assumption that pornography debased women and put them at risk of exploitation, humiliation, and violence, by portraying them as pliant sex objects. Pornography, in other words, was an assault on the civil rights of women and a threat to their safety and integrity. The result was the drafting of model ordinances for cities which sought to provide legal remedies through injunctive relief, and monetary damages through judicial or special administrative proceedings. Such an ordinance was passed by the Minneapolis city council, but vetoed by the mayor. However, the Indianapolis ordinance was signed, after receiving strong support from the conservative moral right wing of the community. Civil liberties activists promptly rushed out the First Amendment's free speech and free press clauses, thereby stemming the tide, but hardly silencing the issue or its advocates, who, at the very least, wanted some lines drawn. First Amendment values, feminists argued back, do not preclude other forms of regulation. Surely, they argued, the government's interest in reducing sexual violence and subordination is not less substantial than the interests underlying other First Amendment restrictions. To date, they have lost in the courts. The Indianapolis case is central. There, in *American Booksellers*

Association v. Hudnut (1984), U.S. District Judge Sarah Barker struck down the ordinance. Conceding that "depictions of subordination tend to perpetuate subordination, and that the subordinate state of women in turn leads to affront, lower pay at work, insult and injury at home, battery and rape on the streets," she nonetheless rejected the ordinance on the grounds that "the government should not become a censor and director of which thoughts are good for people." This certainly did not kill the campaign. In fact, it steeled the determination of its leaders to continue the crusade. They especially seek to push the Supreme Court to take seriously and to respond to the importance of a woman's point of view on matters which so clearly affect half our population.

The other side of First Amendment free-speech law is political speech, an area of significant activity in this period. The famous case of *New York Times v. Sullivan* (1964) had opened up the 1960s to broad-scale freedom of political expression, particularly protecting the right to criticize public officials by shielding the critics from harassing libel suits. The case involved an advertisement in the *Times*, placed there by the followers of Martin Luther King, Jr., for which the *Times* had been sued under Alabama libel law for half a million dollars, because the advertisement indirectly criticized Alabama officials. The Court exonerated the *Times* and went on to state that "debate on public issues should be uninhibited, robust, and wide-open." In subsequent cases, the Court broadened this exemption from libel actions, or from its threat, to include "public figures" as well as "public officials."

As the civil rights movement subsequently became far more militant, and as the antiwar movement grew in volume and insistence, and as antiwar protestors became more frustrated and more emotionally outraged, the question of speech became one of what lawyers call "speech plus"—speech, plus picketing; speech, plus sit-ins; speech, plus marching; speech, plus forms of symbolic expression. This entailed two distinct considerations. The first involved the content of the speech; the second shifted to its circumstances. As to content, questions were raised as to what the speaker, or picketer, or demonstrator, attempting to convey ideas through symbolic representation, was calling for. Was this advocacy of the duty, necessity, or propriety of violence, sabotage, or terrorism? This is difficult, said the Court. If the purpose is to accomplish industrial, or political reform, such speech is protected, as long as it advocates such violent action in the abstract. Only the incitement of imminent lawless behavior was punishable, the Court ruled in the key *Brandenburg v. Ohio* case in 1969. It thereby greatly broadened the permissible limits of what, at times, could be extreme demands.

As to expressing such demands symbolically, the Court would not protect burning draft cards (*United States v. O'Brien*, 1968). It would protect children quietly wearing black arm bands to school to protest the Vietnam War (*Tinker v. Des Moines School District*, 1969). It would protect a young man parading around the Los Angeles Court House wearing a jacket with the words "Fuck the Draft" clearly visible (*Cohen v. California, 1971*). And it would protect flag burning as symbolic protest, before, and even after, Congress had passed legislation banning such a practice.

But circumstances were relevant. Here the Court over a period of time, developed what came to be known as the Time, Place, Manner distinction. Certainly no individual or group had the right to picket in such a way as to block entrances to a building, or to stop traffic at a busy intersection during rush hour. There was also doubt as to whether a person could express himself or herself in a manner sufficiently inflammatory to elicit violent retaliation. Yet the latter was not easy, and when the American Civil Liberties Union defended the right of hate-spewing Nazis to march through the highly Jewish city of Skokie, Illinois, it found itself the target of bitter criticism; several thousand ACLU members even resigned from the organization in protest over the Skokie case.

Nonetheless, it can be fairly said that by 1970 the permissible limits of political expression were such that the street-corner speaker could hold forth with virtually no legal inhibitions. But, from a political standpoint, this fact marked the end of a battle of earlier days, because, by the 1970s, the street-corner speaker's constituency was largely getting its information in its living room through the media. So protecting the street-corner speaker was a largely irrelevant response to the conditions of modern communication. The public forum was more clearly CBS or ABC. Thus, such a forum did not represent an electric street corner. In any event, the First Amendment did not provide easy access. Money did.

Here, Watergate intervenes in important constitutional ways; from a Bill of Rights standpoint, it was a disturbing intervention, in that it fit an ongoing pattern of Nixonian suppression of information, and of efforts to deceive the public. Nixon's frequent calls for "law and order," and for an end to student strikes, protest marches, and radical agitation, were supported by his unsuccessful effort to ban the publication of the Pentagon Papers—documents which revealed the origin and development of the policies pursued in Vietnam. Further, the Nixon administration had also instigated a program of internal wire tapping, executive espionage, and a war against subversives, all designed to discredit and silence criticism of executive actions. But the charges which brought down the

Nixon presidency were largely ones of corrupting the political process; they focused especially upon the extent to which economic power and money were a major contributing aspect of that development. Constitutionally, Watergate produced a broad public reaction which led to a series of judicial and legislative restrictions on presidential power. Pertinent was the Freedom of Information Act, which was strengthened in the 1970s and became an indispensable source for citizens seeking to gain information about government behavior. Significant also were the revelations of excess spending by the Committee to Re-Elect the President (CREEP), which led Congress to pass a Federal Election Campaign Act in 1974 designed to curtail both excessive campaign contributions and excessive campaign spending. The assumption behind the measure was the clear connection between money and voting, and the view that it was desirable to equalize the relative financial resources of candidates competing for public office.

The Supreme Court also entered the process. In a series of holdings in the early 1970s, it ruled that the owners of private property or private businesses could effectively determine who might use that property for extending their political views. This was true, whether the situation involved distributing handbills in a private shopping mall, or getting one's message into areas of the commercial media. The latter would obviously entail greater penetration and hence influence, but would entail far more expenditure.

The case of *Buckley v. Valeo* (1976) proved a turning point. In it the Court ruled that all limits on expenditures by candidates were a violation of the First Amendment. The spending of money in a campaign, the Court contended, constituted a form of expression, since it bought space or time in public forums to get ideas across. Limiting expenditures, therefore, limited speech by restricting the number of issues explored, the depth of their discussion, and the scope of the audience made aware of them. The overall implication was that the more money spent on a campaign the richer the information made available to the public. Justice Byron White dissented sharply. "The argument that money is speech, and limiting the flow of money to the speaker violates the First Amendment," he contended, "proves entirely too much." Expenditure ceilings reinforce the contribution limits and help eradicate the hazard of corruption. Without limits on total expenditures, campaign costs will inevitably escalate, creating an incentive to accept unlawful contributions. Moreover, the corrupt use of money by candidates is as much to be feared as the corrosive influence of large contributions. The expenditure limits could play a substantial role in preventing unethical practices. And he went on to contend that it is important to restore public confidence in federal elections.

White's concerns did not prevail, however, and indeed, the Court went on two years later to rule, in *First National Bank of Boston v. Bellotti* (1978), that business corporations could not be limited by state law from contributing money freely to influence elections. They had a First Amendment right to spend money in campaigns involving popular referenda. The inherent worth of the speech in terms of its capacity for informing the public, Justice Lewis Powell argued, does not depend upon the identity of its sources, whether corporation, association, union, or individual. In 1981, and again in 1985, the Court condoned the virtually unlimited spending of Political Action Committees (PACS), which the Justices again argued were entitled to full First Amendment protection.

Many Americans have been troubled by this development; $250 million was spent during the 1988 campaign, and more than that on the 1990 House and Senate races. Further, the results were not pretty, at least in terms of getting the hard core and important issues before the voters. To many Americans this represented the decline of American democracy, as the nation moved toward a form of demagogic exploitation. Individuals and groups with access to the vast sums now essential in American politics manipulated powerful images to their electoral advantage, in hopes of "selling" their candidates to the voters. All too often what occurred was the general substitution of irrelevant emotional appeals for free and open debate on the issues. Many candidates did everything they could to avoid unstructured or uncontrolled forms of exposure, since these interfered with the message and the image projected in their advertisements. They avoided debates and worked from prepackaged and often somewhat misleading "position" statements. The troubling result was that more than half the eligible population failed to vote at all. And why not? Why vote for sound bytes and media images? As Stephen Carter has argued: "[E]xpression rights are intended to promote free discussion of public policy; not to permit special interests to manipulate that discussion or prevent it from taking place."

Thus, calls for regulation of elections, for limited terms, and for curtailing excessive campaign spending have reached the sympathetic ears of many American voters. Proponents of regulation believe that the doctrine that "money is speech" hinders free public debate in two ways: unequal resources give some a special advantage in influencing the outcome of elections, and concentrated wealth reduces variety in the marketplace of political ideas. If government can move to equalize political power through reapportionment, then surely it can move to regulate electoral expenses as a way of according equal respect for the basic liberties of the person in a constitutional democracy.

With more than a touch of irony, 1989 saw a tribute to the positive social value of American free speech. It came from the peoples of Eastern Europe, and, for a while, from as far away as Tiananmen Square in the People's Republic of China. Maybe it is time to polish up our own professed value system, particularly when other people have so much respect for it.

This raises a further First Amendment question: Does the media really connive with those with the most money? Or does it attempt to present a more balanced view of the news, and enrich the public's knowledge of a range of issues in a campaign? I fear the answer is that from a constitutional standpoint the media does not worry too much about that. During the 1970s and 1980s the media was worrying about two things: constraints on publication and circulation, and constraints on the right of the press or other media representatives to be free in their news-gathering activities.

In the former instance the Court was split and flip-flopped. In 1976, reporters in Nebraska were kept out of a courtroom by a judge's gag order, on the argument that newspaper publicity created a serious danger to a fair trial for an accused mass murderer. The Court upheld the order (*Nebraska Press Association v. Stuart,* 1976), but made clear that in future cases a series of specific threats to a fair trial would have to exist before reporters could be barred. Three years later, in *Gannett Co. v. DePasquale* (1979), a badly divided Court rejected a publisher's attack on a court order closing the courtroom to the press and public during a pretrial hearing on the suppression of evidence. Justice Potter Stewart hardly mentioned the First Amendment, but concentrated on the limitations of the Sixth Amendment right to a public trial. However, Justice Powell in dissent argued that public confidence in the fairness and efficacy of the criminal justice system depended on receiving accurate information about its working, information that the press provides. In the following year, in *Richmond Newspapers, Inc. v. Virginia* (1980), the Court adopted Powell's reasoning. Chief Justice Warren Burger acknowledged that the First Amendment extended clear protection to the press against exclusion from criminal trials, and refused to allow the exclusion of the press as a lower court had ordered.

Reporters' rights to protect the confidentiality of their sources was also an issue of the 1970s, as courts and grand juries increasingly subpoenaed reporters to testify in criminal cases, thus forcing them into the uncomfortable choice of either betraying the confidence of their sources, or possibly going to jail on contempt charges. In *Branzburg v. Hayes* (1972), reporters argued that they should not be forced to testify unless the government could make a substantial case that they possessed important information that was not available from any other source. The Court rejected that claim by a vote of 5–4, the majority holding that law enforcement was more important than any freedom of news gathering. Again Justice Powell's opinion was influential, urging that the ruling should not be ironclad. There were times, he argued, when the balance ought to be struck in favor of the press. But that decision should be left up to the judges in individual cases.

The access issue has been even more troublingly repressive in the area of access to government information. It has long been argued that the major purpose of the First Amendment has been to facilitate the process of self-government, and that can best take place when all material relating to the operations of government is made available to the public. Yes, but not in the case of national security, government officials argue. There are times when the government must manage the news. This raises troubling current issues, for citizens and media representatives alike.

When the government announced its guidelines for reporting on the war in the Persian Gulf, it sounded very much like the press arrangements for Grenada and Panama. This entailed carefully controlled information prepared by the government, and released at its discretion. Reporters now can accompany military units only in government-approved "pools" and must submit all reports for security review before filing them with their news agencies. They cannot interview anyone without prior approval. The American Civil Liberties Union has already gone on record as believing that this censorship of press reports is unconstitutional. Not only does it violate the First Amendment rights of the news media, but it also jeopardizes the right of citizens to know what their government is doing and to get fair and honest reports of that government's behavior.

There are other First Amendment issues which have kept the courts busy in recent years. The whole question of freedom of cultural expression has seen a range of questions adjudicated, from keeping certain books in school libraries—one group sought to ban the *Wizard of Oz* because the witches allegedly represent a form of satanism—to keeping 2 Live Crew on the concert stage. The art world, both locally and nationally, rallied when Cincinnati officials set out after those who brought and presented a Robert Mapplethorpe photographic exhibit, which they alleged contained obscene works. This exhibit, and others which had support from the National Endowment for the Arts, brought forth congressional condemnation of the NEA for underwriting obscenity, and heightened the threat of cutting off NEA funds. In an Indiana case the Court recently rejected the argument that nude dancing is a form of protected expression. And the forces of morality have expressed the strong need to ban Madonna's latest rock video. Inevitably the courts find themselves called in and asked to strike some balance between the integrity of individual expression and the rights of the community to maintain standards of decency. The result is often brickbats from the losing constituency.

Balancing—a different kind of balancing—has fallen to the courts in the area of religious freedom. Here the liberal view of a high wall of separation, a view which led to the prayer rulings of the 1960s, has been challenged by a more conservative view known as accommodationism, or sometimes called non-preferentialism. Its advocates hold, generally, that the government should support religion, as long as it supports all religions. The Court steered a careful course between the two. In the case of *Lemon v. Kurtzman* (1971), the Court set forth a three-pronged test, which has come to govern all subsequent establishment-clause cases. Public religious practice and the support of religious programs was valid and did not violate separation of church and state if: (1) it was not coercive; (2) it had a clear secular purpose; and (3) it did not entangle church and state. For example, in the *Lemon* case, Rhode Island provided supplementary salary payments to parochial school instructors who taught secular subjects. Pennsylvania purchased secular educational services from parochial schools for its public schools. Both plans specifically prohibited payment for religious education and required use of state-approved texts for secular subjects. But the Court struck down both. Each entailed too much entanglement. Further, neither met the further test of not advancing religion in the process. Separationists cheered. Accommodationists grumbled, though they would have their day. In 1983 (*Lynch v. Donnelly*) and 1989 (*Court of Allegheny v. A.C.L.U. of Greater Pittsburgh Chapter*), the Court condoned public Christmas displays on public property which included crèche scenes. Once more, balance and line drawing occurred with a divided Court.

Such moral judgment-calls, as with so many First Amendment issues, fluctuate as the times, local communities, and local mores come into play. One thing is for sure. In none of these areas will the Supreme Court run out of business soon, as it must try to strike the delicate balance which both sides can live with.

8

"A Republic, If You Can Keep It"

Liberty and Public Life in the Age of Glasnost

JAMES W. CAREY

*T*here is a story from the Constitutional Convention, probably apoc-
ryphal, that sets the overall theme of this essay. Benjamin Franklin,
then 84, was the oldest delegate to the convention. A citizen of Philadelphia and a well-known public figure, Franklin each day at the conclusion of deliberations was asked by those gathered outside Independence
Hall: "Mr. Franklin, do we have a government and if so what kind is it?"
And each day Franklin answered, "We have no government as yet." On
the ultimate day as he exited the convention and was asked the predictable
question, he answered, or so the story goes: "We have a government; a
republic, if you can keep it." If you can keep it!

Franklin's remark reminds us that republican forms of government
were and still are odd and aberrant occurrences in history. The natural
state of humankind is domination; submission is the natural, our natural
condition. Political communities founded on civic ties rather than blood
relations or bureaucratic rule are rare creatures of history; they have a
definite beginning, a point of origin in historical time, and, therefore,
they presumably have an end. The suspicion that public liberty is aberrant
in nature, that dominion is our natural existence, was one obstacle Franklin and the Founding Fathers had to overcome. Their reading of history

convinced them that the last republic vanished some 1800 years earlier, when Caesar crossed the Rubicon in defiance of an edict of the Roman Senate. The founders, then, were acting against history and against nature in willing a republic into existence. Constitution-writing was an attempt to lay a foundation, to create, in the words of Bruce Smith, whose analysis I am closely following, a public space in which the two critical republican roles, citizen and patriot, might exist. Citizenship is a term of space; one is a citizen in relationship to one's contemporaries with whom one occupies the same space. Patriot is a term of time, a relationship to one's patrimony and posterity. A patriot is a lover of place; not my country right or wrong, but a lover of what happened in this particular place and might happen yet again.

The foundation of a political society, a republic, unites it in space and time. The art of political creation is to lay a foundation that will make citizens into patriots and patriots into citizens. Only when that is achieved will it be possible to prevent republican government from lurching back into domination; only then will it be possible to deliver republican government, public life, against all the vicissitudes of history, down unchangeable to posterity.

The typical way in which the Constitution and the Bill of Rights is discussed these days is as a legal document: the province of lawyers, a nest of juridically derived meanings, an instrument to adjust and avoid disputes, to advance and promote interests, to protect and enhance rights. In fact, for most people these days, the sole meaning of the First Amendment is that it means "rights." We are a people who have rights. We do not constitute ourselves as a people in any other sense, except in outbreaks of militant nationalism. Behind this rights-based image of the First Amendment is a powerful organizing symbol, that of the dissident and the dissenter. This side of the First Amendment, the Emersonian side according to a recent book by Steven Shiffrin, appeals to the individualism, the rebelliousness, and the antinomian, nonconformist spirit within, to a greater or lesser degree, all of us.

When a legalist view of the Bill of Rights prevails, the various cases decided by the courts are arrayed under the correct clauses such that we have interminable surveys of those cases that fall under the speech clause, the assembly clause, the religion clause, and we are brought up to date as to whither stand our rights. The construal of the Constitution and the Bill of Rights as a legal document, an enumeration of rights, a means of settling or at least anesthetizing disputes, is a tradition and view I deeply cherish and cannot imagine living without. This view is reinvented in each period of dissent and rebellion against onerous and illegitimate demands and duties. But the powerful imperialism of the "rights tradition" has smothered all other meanings of our founding documents, even in those periods and among those people who have no quarrel with the legitimacy of authority. The assertion of rights has become a mere tropism, as automatic as a plant turning toward light. In the biological world, however, tropisms get organisms in trouble when the environment radically changes. We now often act as if the Constitution were a suicide pact, as if it had been written on Masada rather than in Philadelphia. We act as if democracy will perpetuate itself automatically if we only pay due regard for the law and rights. It is as if our ancestors had succeeded in setting up a machine that, in the words of John Dewey, "solved the problem of perpetual motion in politics."

The historian Louis Hartz once cracked that "law has flourished on the corpse of philosophy in America." He meant, of course, that the law threatens to absorb the entire culture. Thus, the very meaning of speech, never mind the First Amendment, is increasingly defined, as Lee Bollinger has argued, by the notion of extremist speech, as for example in the famous Skokie case. But to allow the margin to define the center, the periphery to impose its meaning on the core, however valuable the peripheral meanings, is to evacuate the entire culture of republicanism under the pretense of saving it.

But this is not the whole story. The law is more than cases. The law is also, and in the first instance, a narrative: a set of stories about who we are and from whence we came and where we would like to go. As Mary Ann Glendon has put it, the law employs certain symbols and projects visions about a people; about, in short, what we were and are and yet might be again. In this view, the Bill of Rights is less a legal document than a political document. It is a constitution. To be redundant about it, it constitutes us as a people. A constitution is something besides the imposition of law. It is an act and foundation through which a people constitute themselves as a political community. It embodies hopes and aspirations. It is an injunction as to how we might live together as a people, peacefully and argumentatively but civilly and progressively. The audacious statement, so audacious we could not write it today except in nationalist tones, which opens the Constitution, "We the people," signifies a common and republican culture that cuts across and modifies all our vast and individual differences. Under this reading, merely legal rights guarantee little if in daily life the actual give and take of ideas, facts, and experiences is aborted by isolation, mutual suspicion, abuse, fear, and hatred. Or to put it in words similar to John Dewey's of fifty years ago, we have come to think of the First Amendment as a law, something external and institutional. We have to acquire it, however, as something personal, as something that is but a commonplace of living. And to help us do that we should look to what in this context must seem like rather odd and out-of-the-way places, namely, the countries of Eastern Europe.

The most dramatic event of recent times is the collapse of the totalitarian governments of most of Eastern Europe or, better, the emergence of a free public life in most of the states of the old Warsaw Pact. For the past year or more American journalists and intellectuals have been traveling east in order to teach these newly liberated peoples the practical arts of writing a First Amendment, managing a modern newspaper or television station or, more elementary yet, writing and editing Western-style journalism. We regularly assume these days that we have something to export to the peoples of Eastern Europe. We are less open to the thought that we might have something to learn from them, that they might teach us something about democracy and civic culture. This curious astigmatism results from the fact that we assume that the liberation of Eastern Europe resulted from something we did on their behalf and not from the internal dynamics of their own efforts. We explain these complex political changes in terms of broadcasting signals drifting over the Iron Curtain infecting a previously immune population with a desire for western consumer goods and ideas of freedom current in America. There is something, though not much, to this notion but it avoids the conclusion that flatters us less, namely, that the liberation of Eastern Europe resulted from what Poles, Czechs, and others did for themselves, and not primarily because of what we represent or what we inadvertently did for them.

How did they pull off this particular miracle? The image of totalitarianism that dominates our imagination—Orwell's *1984*—allows no room for what happened. Of all the depredations visited on the citizens of Airstrip One, it is not the censorship or the wall posters or the presence of Big Brother or the ubiquitous television screen or the surveillance or the reeducation of the informer children—all of which Orwell helped become the totems of totalitarianism—that stays with one the longest. Rather, it is the silence, the absence of talk, the loss of memory, the pitiless destruction of the private and public world you cannot forget. The novel begins and ends wordlessly: Winston squirreled in an out-of-sight corner writing words in his prized notebook; Winston staring at the telescreen in the Chestnut Tree Cafe. Rebellion begins with writing and ends in silence. There is cant and there is interrogation; there are furtive, stolen glances, and there are hurried coded messages. There is simply no conversation except in the pubs and the hidden room, and very little of it there. No danger Winston faces is quite as unnerving as that of starting a conversation; nothing more demoralizing than Julia's vacant memory.

We can happily ignore the coercion, social control, and domination, for we are by and large, on those terms at least, happily free of it. Not so the endless and endlessly repetitive news, the reduction of all thought to cliché, and the pervasive presence of bureaucracy: news, cliché, bureaucracy and, finally, silence are all too familiar and much more unnerving than the technology and the terror. The destruction of mind, the deracination of character, the invasion of the private, the diremption of the public, appear within but exist without the totalitarian and technological apparatus which sustains the fiction.

Orwell's *1984* is a prophetic book and valuable in that regard for what it tells us to guard against. But it is not good prophecy. In Eastern Europe there was, in fact, enormous resistance to the powers of the state and, more importantly, the will for the creation of a free public life despite totalitarian coercion. Eastern Europeans managed to create, however fragile it is now, whatever its prospects may be, a civic life of a distinctly republican kind, and central to that creation was the art of memory.

Milan Kundera pays testimony to that art when, at the opening of his novel, *The Book of Laughter and Forgetting,* he says that "the struggle of man against power is the struggle of memory against forgetting." Similarly, the workers at the shipyard in Gdansk inscribed a tombstone dedicated to their fallen comrades in Solidarity with the words of Milosz: "The poet remembers." Both examples pay testimony to the heroic acts of imaginative memory that have been engaged in over the last forty-five years, acts that formed the basis, the foundation, of a free public life.

The best known, and perhaps the most heroic, was that of Aleksandr Solzhenitsyn. In early February 1945 Solzhenitsyn was arrested on the East Prussian front as a political criminal on the evidence of unflattering remarks he had made about Stalin and Soviet literature in letters to a friend. During the next twelve years he endured interrogations, prisons, labor camps, and exile, and was "rehabilitated" in 1957.

He had always wanted to be a writer but prior to his arrest he could never find a subject, his subject. Once in prison his dilemma was resolved: he had to retain and make unforgettable the experience through which he was living and to transmit the meaning of that experience to posterity. But how does one write in prison? No writing paper or pens or pencils, no typewriters or VDTs. As a result, he recovered, as have so many others, the most primitive form of writing: he wrote without setting anything down on paper, learning to compose any time, anywhere—"on forced marches over the frigid steppe, in thundering foundries, in crowded barracks." As he puts it in his autobiography, *The Oak and the Calf:* "As a soldier falls asleep as soon as he sits down on the ground, as a dog's own fur is the stove that keeps him warm in the cold, so I instinctively became adjusted to writing everywhere." He converted his experience into verse, stored the compositions in memory, and, when finally released from the gulag, the words came forth as prose and poetry in a memorable series of books. The following lines from "God Keep Me from Going Mad" recall the tenacity and purpose of the effort:

> Yes, tight is the circle around us, tautly drawn,
> But my verses will burst their bonds and freely roam
> And I can guard, perhaps, beyond their reach,
> In rhythmic harmony this hard-won gift of speech.
> And then they can grope my body in vain—
> "Here I am. All yours. Look hard. Not a line . . .
> Our indestructible memory, by wonder divine,
> Is beyond the reach of your butcher's hands!"

Many similar episodes could be cited. For example, Nadezhda Mandelstam's recounting of how she and friends met to commit to memory the literature being destroyed by the O.G.U.P. She recalls in her memoirs how, when she was working in a punitive factory, she used the rhythms of mechanical looms to help her remember the lines of poems as she rushed back and forth between them, the entire scene reminiscent of the conclusion of Ray Bradbury's *Fahrenheit 451.* The point is this: the act of creating a public sphere in the Soviet Union and Eastern Europe did not begin with Western broadcasts floating across the Iron Curtain. It began in acts of recovery and the tenacious storage in memory of the experience through which people were living. It was only this that allowed people to maintain a desire for normal life or a memory of what normal life was and yet might be again.

This resistance everywhere required dealing with censorship. In 1984 *The Blackbook of Polish Censorship* was published after having been smuggled out of Poland in 1977. As Stanislaw Baranczak has commented about it:

> Everybody who read the documents was genuinely struck by the extent and meticulous elaboration of the censor's guidelines and reports. The documents proved that censorship had literally every kind of publication under its control, from wedding invitations, to

circus posters, to obscure quarterlies dealing with Mediterranean archaeology.

Here are samples of the guidelines from the censorship book:

All information concerning the participation of representatives of Israel in congresses, international conferences, or performances organized by Poland should be cleared. . . .

Information on direct threats to life or health caused by industry or chemical agents used in agriculture, or threats to the natural environment in Poland, should be eliminated from works on environmental protection.

No information concerning Poland's export of meat to the USSR should be permitted.

All criticism of Marxism should be eliminated from religious publications. . . . All material critical of the religious situation in countries of the socialist community should be eliminated. No material concerning the hippie movement in Poland may be permitted for publication if it expresses approval or tolerance. Nationwide data on increases in alcoholism should not be permitted for publication.

Among the more ingenious ways of circumventing censorship, as recounted by Baranczak, was that of Stefan Kisielewski, who wrote his most outrageous statements precisely so that they would be censored, thereby making their way into classified bulletins and brought to the attention of the political elite. Perhaps the most distinguished body of literature written under censorship is the genre of prison letters. Such letters were composed under the direct control of the secret police, forced to obey rigid guidelines—no more than four pages, no foreign words or expressions, precise margins, nothing crossed out, no references to anything but family matters. Nonetheless, Vaclav Havel's *Letters to Olga* is one of the great political documents of our time and, as Baranczak correctly says, one of the great articulations of human freedom. While inquiring about the health of his wife and children, while commenting on his own health and state of mind, his once-a-week four page letters added up to an entire philosophy of freedom.

By devices large and small—writing between the lines; creating novels about historical events that were disguised commentaries on contemporary affairs; strengthening the arts of memory; "flying" universities; public lectures in private apartments; choosing internal migration and "writing for the desk drawers"; reviewing Nazi-era films as if they were products of state socialism; circumlocution and densely coded messages

—through such devices East European writers constituted the basis of a free public life. Again, Stanislaw Baranczak:

> Poland, as an ironic result of decades of constant indoctrination, persecution of free speech, and official backing of obedient quasi-writers and quasi-artists . . . despite all this, or perhaps because of it, the phenomenon of independent culture . . . has been able not only to survive and develop but also to secure its position successfully.

The pivotal year was 1976, when the full power of the regime's monopoly of publication was recognized, and it became "necessary to go from weak and futile protests against abuses of censorship to creating a network of publishing and circulation which would remain outside the regime's control." Emboldened, given courage by an older generation of artists and writers, a number of younger people were willing

> to take the risk of serving as underground printers, editors, distributors, and so on. For the first time in postwar history, all the links of the chain of communication fell into place: there was someone to write for the independent circuit, someone to manage the process of independent publishing, and someone to read independent publications [and thus to form a market for them].

What began in clandestine speech spread to writing and then printing and latterly to yet more vulnerable media such as cinema and theatre.

Despite living under regimes almost as repressive as that described by Orwell, East Europeans, in country after country, managed to create a free public life. They had no help from the press; in fact, the press was their enemy. They created a life which, albeit submerged and clandestine, was one in which public discourse, argument, and debate was preserved, maintained, and developed. The entire episode speaks to the importance of human memory; the sheer stupidity, incompetence, and destructiveness of censorship; the critical need for vital independent traditions of art; and, despite the bedazzling advances in technology in our time, the need for the simplest practices: to speak clearly and effectively, to write with passion and directness, and to retain culture by the unaided powers of the mind. It was not by accident that only in the later stages of the revolution did film, broadcasting, and photography become agents of change, for these media require concentrated capital, rely upon skills not easily concealed, and are more vulnerable to state interference. With one exception; as one Czech put it: "Xerox was the best dissident for many years."

East Europeans did not have a public life; they simply acted as if they had one. Jonathan Schell has written of this "as if" philosophy in his introduction to Adam Michnik's *Letters from Prison*. Michnik helped devise an opposition strategy that could address itself to "independent public opinion rather than totalitarian power." In explaining this approach, Schell writes:

> Its simple but radical guiding principle was to start doing things you think should be done and to start being what you think society should become. Do you believe in freedom of speech? Then speak freely. Do you love truth? Then tell it. Do you believe in the open society? Then act in the open. Do you believe in a decent and humane society? Then act decently and humanely.

Vaclav Havel explained a similar strategy (or is it a philosophy?) in *Letters to Olga:*

> It is I who must begin. One thing about it, however, is interesting: once I begin—that is once I try—here and now, right where I am, not excusing myself by saying that things would be easier elsewhere, without grand speeches and ostentatious gestures, but all the more persistently—to live in harmony with the voice of "Being," as I understand it within myself—as soon as I begin that, I suddenly discover, to my surprise, that I am neither the only one, nor the first, nor the most important one to have set out upon that road. . . . Whether all is really lost or not depends entirely on whether or not I am lost.

It is time to leave the broad savannah of Eastern Europe for the village of America. It is dangerous to compare the struggle for freedom in Poland, for example, with its maintenance in an already free society, but it is equally dangerous to assume that the Polish experience has nothing to teach us. Of course, their new-found way of life is very fragile indeed, about where it was in 1914. But our way of life is very fragile too. They had to win a free public life from a repressive state; we have to win one from the media consultants and our own ingrained habits of living. Our task may be the more difficult even if without comparable risks. But let me put a grace note to this, courtesy of the sociologist Richard Flacks. Flacks recounts how a member of Solidarity had told him that the movement had come about because Polish workers had been able to learn from the experiences in Poland in 1956, 1967, 1971, and 1975. That is, they were able to conserve and pass on political experience. Flacks was dumbfounded, given his feeling that American students were unable to learn from earlier generations of student protestors—for example, those in Berkeley in 1964. How could it be, he wondered, that workers in Poland could learn lessons of the past when information was totally controlled by the state, and where the state systematically erased the memories of past protest? The state in our presumptively free society does none of those things, yet we are, in Joseph Featherstone's acid phrase, the "United States of Amnesia." Flack's Polish respondent replied that because the Polish people do not believe they have trustworthy mass media it never enters their mind to rely on the official media, or any public media, to transmit any useful information. "We have had to create our own frameworks of communication and memory."

These independent frameworks of communication and memory were assumed to exist by the framers of the Constitution and the Bill of Rights, and such frameworks were thought to be worth protecting and enhancing. The documents assume, in short, a set of personal dispositions, and the existence of certain social conditions. We now are faced with the task of recreating, by deliberate and determined endeavor, the forms of political life which in our origins two hundred years ago were largely the product of a fortunate combination of persons and circumstances.

We value, or so we say, the First Amendment because it contributes, in Thomas Emerson's formulation, four things to our common life. It is a method of assuring our own self-fulfillment; it is a means of attaining the truth; it is a method of securing participation of members of society in political decision-making; and it is a means of maintaining a balance between stability and change.

It is the third of Emerson's clauses, the clumsily expressed notion of political participation, that is critical here. If we think of the First Amendment against the background of recent East European experience, the interrelation among its parts becomes clearer. While the First Amendment contains four clauses—religion, speech, press, and assembly—one must think of them less as separate clauses and more as a compact way of describing a political society. In other words the amendment is not a casual and loose consolidation of high-minded principles. It was an attempt to define the nature of public life as it existed at the time or as the founders hoped it would exist. To put it in an artlessly simple way, the amendment says that people are free to gather together without the intrusion of the state or its representatives. Once gathered, they are free to speak to one another openly and fully. They are further free to write down what they have to say and to share it beyond the immediate place of utterance.

But where does freedom of religion fit into this? Of all the freedoms of public life for the eighteenth century, freedom of religion was, perhaps, the most difficult liberty for Americans to adjust to. Compared with other forms of speech, religious heresy was the one most likely to be viewed as both a personal and a community assault. From the banishment of heretics to the hanging of witches, religious persecution often could count on popular sanction. And yet, the intricate relationship of public freedoms also was evident to Americans in the colonies. The First Amendment was designed to resolve the dilemma. As such, free speech and free press were a little like bargains struck with the Devil. No one could be excluded from the public realm on the basis of their religion, the one basis upon which people were likely to exclude one another. In turn that clause has allowed us to open up progressively the public realm, to make it more broadly inclusive, to reduce the barriers to entrance based on the secondary criteria of class, race, and gender.

The interconnections among the clauses of the First Amendment would be clearer if some of the draft language often attributed to Madison had been adopted. The language of progressive verbs, rather than nouns, would allow us to see the interrelations among assembling, speaking, and writing. It would show more clearly the injunction in the First Amendment to create a conversational society: a society of people who speak to one another, who converse. Other words might do: a society of argument, disputation, or debate, for example. But I believe we must begin from the primacy of conversation. It implies social arrangements less hierarchical and more egalitarian than its alternatives. While people often dry up and shy away from the fierceness of argument, disputation, and debate, and while those forms of talk often bring to the surface the meanness and aggressiveness which is our second nature, conversation implies the most natural and unforced, unthreatening, and most satisfying of arrangements.

Under this conception of the First Amendment, the press, whether conceived of as a technology or an institution or simply as a recording device, is largely an extension and amplification, an "outering" of conversation. But the conversation is ours to conduct with one another and its amplification merely extends its reach. A press independent of the conversation of the culture, or existing in the absence of such a conversation, is likely to be, in practical terms, whatever the value of the right the press represents, a menace to public life and an effective politics. The idea of the press as a mass medium, independent of, disarticulated from, the conversation of the culture inherently contradicts the goal of creating an active remembering public. Public memory can be recorded by but cannot be transmitted through the press as an institution. The First Amendment, to repeat, constitutes us a society of conversationalists, of people who talk to one another, who resolve disputes with one another through talk. This is the foundation of the public realm, the inner meaning of the First Amendment, and the example the people of Eastern Europe were quite inadvertently trying to teach us.

The "public" is the God term of the press, the term without which the press does not make any sense. Insofar as the press is grounded, it is grounded in the public. The press justifies itself in the name of the public. It exists, or so it is said, to inform the public, to serve as the extended eyes and ears of the public. The press is the guardian of the public interest and protects the public's right to know. The canons of the press originate in and flow from the relationship of the press to the public.

While the Constitution and the Bill of Rights are silent on the matter, the public is the deepest and most fundamental concept of the entire liberal tradition. Liberal society is formed around the notion of a virtuous public. For John Locke, to be a member of the public was to accept a calling.

This notion of a public, a conversational public, has been pretty much evacuated in our time. Public life started to evaporate with the emergence of the public opinion industry and the apparatus of polling. Polling [the word, interestingly enough, derived from the old synonym for voting] was an attempt to simulate public opinion in order to prevent an authentic public opinion from forming. With the rise of the polling industry, intellectual work on the public went into eclipse. In political theory, the public was replaced by the interest group as the object of analysis; soon enough, interest groups displaced the public as the key political actors. But interest groups, by definition, operate in the private sector, behind the scenes, and their relationship to public life is essentially propagandistic and manipulative. In interest-group theory the public ceases to have a real existence. It fades into a statistical artifact: an audience whose opinions count only insofar as individuals refract the pressure of mass publicity. In short, while the word "public" continues in our language as an ancient memory and pious hope, the public as a feature and factor of real politics disappears.

The strongest advocate of a diminished and vanishing public was, oddly enough, a distinguished journalist, Walter Lippmann, who on the surface seemed to lament its passing. His conclusions were hard-won in experience as a result of his participation, as Woodrow Wilson's aide, in the negotiations that led to the Treaty of Versailles. In *Public Opinion* (1922) and in a number of other books and articles, Lippmann concluded, whether dourly or eagerly it is not always easy to tell, that it was impossible to have an informed public opinion and that the public cannot master events. Voters, he thought, were inherently incompetent to direct public affairs. "They arrive in the middle of the third act, and they leave before the last curtain. They stay just long enough to decide who is the hero and who is the villain." Lippmann adds: "I set no great store on what can be done by public opinion or the actions of citizens . . . ; the common interest in life largely eludes public opinion entirely and can be managed only by a specialized class." Lippmann's only hope was that the weight could be taken off the shoulders of citizens, the burdens of citizenship lifted, by recognizing that the average man or woman had neither the capacity nor interest nor competence to direct society.

Political mastery could come only from a class of experts, a new order of samurai, who would mold the public mind and character; men and women dedicated to making democracy work for us whether we like it or not. He concludes:

> The burden of carrying on the work of the world, of inventing,
> creating, executing, of attempting justice and formulating laws and
> moral codes, of dealing with technique and substance, lies not upon
> the public and not upon government even, but on those who are rea-
> sonably concerned as agents in the affair. When problems arise, the
> ideal is settlement by the particular interest involved. They alone
> truly know what the problem is.

In short, Lippmann, in a backhanded defense of the press, dissolved the public theoretically as a prelude to dissolving it practically and, in the spot the public occupied in democratic theory and our understanding of the press, he inserted interest groups and the cadres of experts in their employ.

Lippmann's solution was not that of the commissars and no one should be confused about that. However, his overvaluing of experts and interest groups reduced the public to a phantom and set the stage for our present situation and dilemma. Citizens now are primarily, if not exclusively, the objects rather than the subjects of politics. The First Amendment is primarily a possession of the press and of the interest groups with whom the press engages in both combat and accommodation. Towards that combat citizens stand largely as spectators and ratifiers. In truth, the conversation of the culture has been taken outside the public realm and into private spaces.

However artlessly and awkwardly, I want to contrast the situation just described with the requirements of republican life. Republics require conversation, often cacophonous conversation, for they should be noisy places. That conversation has to be informed, of course, and the press has a role in supplying that information. But the kind of information required can only be generated by public conversation; there is simply no substitute for it. We have virtually no idea what it is we need to know until we start talking to someone. Conversation focuses our attention; it engages us, and in the wake of conversation we have need not only of the press but the library. From this view of the First Amendment, the task of the press is to encourage the conversation of the culture—not to preempt it or substitute for it or to supply it with information as a seer from afar. Rather, the press maintains and enhances the conversation of the culture, becomes one voice in that conversation, amplifies the conversation outward, and helps it along by bringing forward the information that the conversation itself demands.

President John F. Kennedy said in 1962:

> Most of us are conditioned [a telling word] for many years to have a particular viewpoint: Republican or Democrat, Liberal or Conservative or Moderate. The fact of the matter is that most of the problems that we now face are technical problems, administrative problems. They require sophisticated judgments which do not lend themselves to the kinds of social movements that involve the citizenry and which stir the country. They deal with problems that are beyond the circumspection of most men.

Kennedy had read his Lippmann. But pretty much the same thing was said to the shipyard workers at Gdansk who formed Solidarity: These affairs are beyond you; you're not technically qualified to judge. Let us take care of these matters; you are simply interfering with the normal processes of government.

The important thing about public conversation is that, in an old saw of E. M. Forster, we don't know what we think until we hear what we say. Conversation not only forms opinion; it also forms memory. We remember best the things that we say, the things that we say in response to someone else with whom we are engaged. Talk is the surest guide to remembering and knowing what we think. To take in information passively guarantees that we will remember little and know less, except for a trace of the passion of the moment. And soon we have no interest in information or knowledge at all. If we insist on public conversation as the essence of democratic life, we will come, as Christopher Lasch has recently put it, "to defend democracy, not as the most efficient form of government but as the most educational one, the one that extends the circle of debate as widely as possible and thus asks us all to articulate our views, to put them at risk, and to cultivate the virtues of clarity of thought, of eloquence and sound judgment.''

A press which encourages the conversation of its culture is the equivalent of an extended town meeting. However, if the press sees its role as limited to informing whomever happens to turn up at the end of the communication channel, it explicitly abandons its role as an agency for carrying on the conversation of the culture. Having embraced certain of Lippmann's notions, the press no longer serves to cultivate certain vital habits: the ability to follow an argument, grasp the point of view of another, expand the boundaries of understanding, decide the alternative purposes that might be pursued. A free press is a necessary condition of a free public life, but it is not the same thing as a free public life. If I am right in contending that we should value the press to the precise degree that it sustains public life, that it helps keep the conversation going among us; and that we devalue the press to the degree it seeks to inform us and turn us into silent spectators, then there are two diremptions of the central meaning of the First Amendment against which we must be on guard. The first is the tendency of the press to treat us like a client, a group with a childlike dependency and an eight-year-old mind incapable of functioning at all without our daily dose of the news. The historian John Lukacs has pointed out that one of the things that astonished Europeans about America in the nineteenth century was that we regularly overestimated the intelligence of ordinary men and women. These Europeans felt America expected more from its people than they could deliver. That, of course, was a mistake, but it is infinitely preferable to its opposite, namely, the systematic underestimation of the intelligence of people. Such an underestimation is the contemporary mistake made not only by the press but by all our major institutions—education, government, and business.

Second, the press endangers us when it disarms us, when it convinces us that just by sitting at home watching the news or spending an hour with the newspaper, we are actually participating in the affairs which govern our lives. At least the people of Eastern Europe never swallowed that. Sociologists Paul Lazarsfeld and Robert Merton coined the awkward but apt phrase ''narcotizing dysfunction'' to describe the condition in which participation in the media becomes confused with participation in public life.

Paul L. Murphy noted that the decision in the libel case *New York Times v. Sullivan*, and in many parallel cases, was an attempt by the Supreme Court to create a robust society of debate. We have, he concluded, secured freedom of speech for the street-corner orator. Unfortunately, the constituency of that orator is no longer on the corner, listening; it is at home watching television. However, if one looks at voting statistics and other evidence of political participation, or examines the knowledge people have of public affairs, or the declining attention to news on television or in print, one must conclude that the political constituency has disappeared altogether. Out there there is no there there. The press has a great interest in the restoration of this constituency if only to assure its own financial survival. But that constituency will be found neither on the street corner nor in the audience until it has some reason to be either place. Since there is no public life, there is no longer a public conversation in which to participate, and, because there is no conversation, there is no reason to be better informed and hence no need for information.

Or, to take another example: At a minimum the press has to actively lead the fight to reform the financing of political campaigns. Until the structure of campaigning changes, there is little hope of much by way of robust debate. Because we cannot control campaign financing, there is a growing movement to put term limitations on elected officials. That is, by and large, not a particularly helpful idea, but it should be understood as a substitute for the reform of campaign financing. When we learned a few years ago that the chances of staying in Congress were infinitely better than the chances of a Soviet official retaining his seat in the Politburo, we realized how sclerotic our politics had become. Without reform of campaign financing, there is no possibility of public debate. However, newspapers and television, particularly the latter, have no interest in campaign reform for they are the financial beneficiaries of a system which clogs the public mind, chokes the public voice, and keeps the legislature full of winningly familiar and compliant coconspirators in the diremption of the public realm. The situation would not be so parlous if our legislatures and political parties were themselves driven by debate. Then, even if we did not get a chance to discuss the issues, we could at least have the pleasure of watching someone else do it. We could thereby form our imaginations off public argument. Debate is no longer any part of campaigning, despite the ersatz confrontations arranged every four years by the networks and the League of Women Voters. By rule the cameras on the floor of Congress can only focus on the speaker of the moment, lest the dirty little secret get out that Congressional debate occurs without Congressional listeners: the words are spoken only for the Congressional Record and the chance viewer back home who stumbles across C-Span. Contrast that with the British House of Commons, also courtesy of C-Span, where one can actually see the benches, hear the debate, and form an opinion by selecting among carefully nuanced positions one that more or less matches one's own.

That is all pretty dour as prognosis, so let's balance it with three hopeful examples—one, of what an individual can do, a second of what a newspaper can do, and a third of what a public institution can do.

The individual story originally appeared in the *Philadelphia Inquirer* on February 4, 1989. "An era ends for a voice in education," the *Inquirer* headline said, and then it went on as follows:

The prose was always simple and direct. Listen to an excerpt from the *Oakes Newsletter* of March 1984: "High schools face enormous problems. Thousands of ill prepared students [this was 1984] are disinterested in their courses. Poor attendance. Cut classes. Students have difficulties concentrating on their studies because of struggling with problems at home such as alcoholism, abusive adults, and poverty or face hurdles such as pregnancy or drug dependence. High schools must endeavor to cope with all of these problems while pushing, cajoling, and encouraging pupils to learn."

Helen Oakes described her newsletter from its beginnings nineteen years ago as "an independent monthly dedicated to improving public education." Every month—quarterly for the last few years—Oakes carefully researched an important educational issue and then presented her findings to the readership of her little periodical.

But Oakes, 64, announced last week that her January newsletter, on the problems of new teachers and the looming teacher shortage, would be her last.

With that decision, what some have described as a one-of-a-kind record of an urban school system's struggles and evolution came to an end. The circulation of the *Oakes Newsletter* was a mere 2,300. Her readers passed it from hand to hand. She would send copies to the Mayor, City Council, School Board members, other influential people, regardless of whether they subscribed. She only had 600 paid subscriptions at $10.00 per year, and her work was underwritten by the Alfred and Mary Douty Foundation. Over nearly two decades, there have been 156 newsletters, each four pages long, each written in the same low-key explanatory style even at the height of the school district's financial, education, and labor troubles.

As she is leaving her work, one citizen of Philadelphia, Happy Fernandez, who helped found the Parents Union in 1972 during a time of escalating labor strikes, says: "The *Oakes Newsletter* was invaluable. I was coming from a neighborhood organization that had never looked at the issues of the whole system. A number of the newsletters helped us understand the budget dynamics that were the driving force behind the strikes. We gobbled up the stuff like the Bible and would wait for each new issue to come out."

To its credit the *Inquirer,* when she retired, said:

Most public officials know only two ways of communicating: emotional displays in public and conspiratorial whispers in private. As a result, the public's real need for discourse that is open and rational is rarely served. One of the few exceptions is Helen Oakes, who instead of adding decibel level to the traditional cacophony of the school scene, or wheeling and dealing behind the scenes, set her thoughts down on paper in a personal letter that she sends out eight times a year.

This tiny story of Helen Oakes tells us more about the value of Freedom of the Press than a year's worth of issues of the *New York Times.* In fact the major reason for defending freedom of the press for the *New York Times* is to insure that we can defend and enhance that freedom in the case of people like Helen Oakes.

A second example concerns a newspaper as related in a recent essay by Jay Rosen of New York University. What follows is a condensed version of Rosen's description. Columbus, Georgia, a city of 175,000 in southwestern Georgia, has, like many American cities, experienced significant growth in recent years. And that growth has caused all sorts of problems. The local paper, the *Columbus Ledger-Enquirer,* commissioned a poll of area residents to seek their opinion on what the city needed to do. They also received about 85 questionnaires from influential citizens. On the basis of these two sources of information, the paper published a report entitled "Columbus—Beyond 2000" in daily installments in the spring of 1989. The report identified key issues in the city, including transportation bottlenecks, low wages, the lack of night life, a faltering school system, and the perceived dominance of a local elite in city politics. The editor recalled that, after the series was published, the paper sat back and waited for someone to do something—but no one did. So the editor, the late Jack Swift, decided to leap across the chasm that normally separates journalism from its community.

At the newspaper's expense, he planned a town meeting to turn up the public heat on local government. Members of the newspaper staff were trained in the art of moderating public discussion by the Kettering Foundation in Ohio. A six-hour meeting in December 1988 drew 300 people from a variety of income levels and social standings. Off the momentum of that meeting, Swift organized a barbecue at his home for 75 prominent citizens, again from diverse backgrounds. The result was a loosely organized citizen's movement calling itself United Beyond 2000, after the newspaper series. It included a steering committee, and a variety of task forces to address specific issues such as recreation, child care, teenagers, and race relations. As it expanded, the citizens' movement remained a concern of the newspaper but it was not its creature. United Beyond 2000 devolved into a coordinating mechanism for civic groups and their leaders, a path of entry for citizens whose civic involvement was ordinarily low, and a signal to government that public opinion was organized and active.

The newspaper supported the movement with a community bulletin board featuring letters from readers and a series of articles on the region's problems, focusing particularly on the lack of a clear agenda at different levels of local and regional government. The editor did not merely deal with current problems. Employing the metaphor of the tribal fire, he noted that newspapers should share history, celebrate heroes, reinforce common values, retell legends. Among the legends they retold was the story of a 1912 lynching of a black youth by a white mob in Columbus. No one was convicted and it passed out of local history. He resurrected it as "The Incident at Wynn's Hill," written and researched by a reporter whose ancestors were among the city's founders.

This entire episode illustrates, as Jay Rosen insightfully argues, how journalism might, as one of its central functions, expand the definition of public time, the temporal framework within which discussion takes place and we consider our collective history. As Rosen says, "In a racially mixed Southern city, to re-install a lynching in the community's collective memory"—and to do it for some reason other than inducing collective guilt—"is a decidedly political act, an extension of 'public time' backward to include a troubled and forgotten past."

The experiment by the *Columbus Ledger-Enquirer* raises a number of troubling issues for professional journalists and, rather unfortunately, it has been rationalized by the owner of the paper, the Knight-Ridder Company, as an exercise in romance and profitability. However, such issues need not detain us. The lesson of the episode is the example of a newspaper attempting, without becoming a simple-minded community booster, to reconceive its public function and to assist in the reemergence of a public conversation about the public interest.

A final example from McLean County, Illinois. The county seat at Bloomington was concerned about the cohesion of the community with the arrival of a new Chrysler/Mitsubishi manufacturing plant and the many new residents that followed in its wake. How could the transformed community be brought together and equipped with a common memory and vocabulary so that the newcomers could talk to the "oldcomers" in creating an authentic civic culture? The county Historical Society undertook this task by first identifying six groups that collectively constituted the history of the community: Yankees, Irish, African-Americans, Anabaptists, Germans, and Upland Southerners. The society considered doing an oral history of these groups but finally rejected it as an exercise in, to use their splendid phrase, the "strip-mining of memory." Instead, they created a remarkable series of events the centerpiece of which was a living museum in which people in the community were asked to exhibit and portray the histories of their own families: to dramatize the history of McLean County by dramatizing family history, by simply talking about and displaying the artifacts which sedimented that history and brought the past of the community to life.

Public life stands for a form of politics in which, in Jefferson's phrase, "we could all be participators in the government of our affairs." Political equality in its most primitive mode probably meant simply the right to be seen and heard. When one or a few dominate the life of a people, the others, denied the ability to be seen and heard, despair of public joy and go in search of private pleasure. Only when citizens can speak and act with some promise that their fellows will see and hear and remember will the passions grow which are true and lasting. And, therefore, unless we can create or restore what de Tocqueville called the "little republics within the frame of the larger republic," within political parties and trade unions, within local communities and workplaces, within places that can aggregate public opinion and sustain public discourse, political objects must remain indefinite and transient and political action short-lived and ineffective.

As we celebrate the two hundredth anniversary of the Bill of Rights, we find ourselves in the wake of the War in the Persian Gulf at another pivotal moment in our history. Everyone is busily trying to assess the coverage of the war and the legality and efficacy of the censorship and pool arrangements of the American military. We are so busy discussing that First Amendment problem that we forget and ignore the real problem. The War in the Gulf, not in specifics but as an emanation of our foreign and domestic policy, should have been discussed in 1988 and again in 1990. In those political campaigns, among the silliest and most tragic in our history, there was no conversation or debate anywhere: not in the press, not among the candidates, not among the people. We had an opportunity then to discuss whether, in the wake of the end of the Cold War, it might not be time to end the long period of liberal internationalism that dates back to Woodrow Wilson, and the domination of the National Security state that dates back, at least, to World War II. We missed the opportunity to conduct that conversation of the culture, and we may not get another one any time soon.

"What a nation is, is essential. What it does can only express what it is," according to William Pfaff. What the United States does on the international stage is of some consequence. But our enduring success lies in the quality of our civilization and, in particular, of our political society. Our success in the postwar years lay in the creation of a vital and energetic society, attempting, at least, to extend social justice and engage the imagination of the young. Foreign relations rightly dominated our attention during the period now ending. The true test the United States now confronts, the national challenge, is within.

We must turn to the task of creating a public realm in which a free people can assemble, speak their minds, and then write or tape or otherwise record the extended conversation so that others, out of sight, might see it. If the established press wants to aid this process, so much the better. But if, in love with profits, and tied to corporate interests, the press decides to sit out public life, we shall simply have to create a space for citizens and patriots by ourselves. Like the peoples of Eastern Europe, we will have to constitute a free public life, whatever the odds. That was the message of Franklin at the close of the Constitutional Convention: a republic, if you can keep it.

The Constitution
of the
United States of America

PREAMBLE

We the People of the United States, in order to form a more perfect Union, establish justice, insure domestic tranquility, provide for the common defense, promote the general welfare, and secure the blessings of liberty to ourselves and our posterity, do ordain and establish this Constitution for the United States of America.

ARTICLE I

Section 1. All legislative powers herein granted shall be vested in a Congress of the United States, which shall consist of a Senate and House of Representatives.

Section 2. The House of Representatives shall be composed of members chosen every second year by the people of the several States, and the electors in each State shall have the qualifications requisite for electors of the most numerous branch of the State Legislature.

No person shall be a Representative who shall not have attained to the age of twenty-five years, and been seven years a citizen of the United States, and who shall not, when elected, be an inhabitant of that State in which he shall be chosen.

Representatives and direct taxes shall be apportioned among the several States which may be included within this Union, according to their respective numbers, which shall be determined by adding to the whole number of free persons, including those bound to service for a term of years, and excluding Indians not taxed, three-fifths of all other persons. The actual enumeration shall be made within three years after the first meeting of the Congress of the United States, and within every subsequent term of ten years, in such manner as they shall by law direct. The number of representatives shall not exceed one for every thirty thousand, but each State shall have at least one Representative; and until such enumeration shall be made, the State of New Hampshire shall be entitled to choose three, Massachusetts eight, Rhode Island and Providence Plantations one, Connecticut five, New York six, New Jersey four, Pennsylvania eight, Delaware one, Maryland six, Virginia ten, North Carolina five, South Carolina five, and Georgia three.

When vacancies happen in the representation from any State, the executive authority thereof shall issue writs of election to fill such vacancies.

The House of Representatives shall choose their Speaker and other officers; and shall have the sole power of impeachment.

Section 3. The Senate of the United States shall be composed of two Senators from Each State, chosen by the legislature thereof, for six years and each Senator shall have one vote.

Immediately after they shall be assembled in consequence of the first election, they shall be divided as equally as may be into three classes. The seats of the Senators of the first class shall be vacated at the expiration of the second year, of the second class at the expiration of the fourth year, and of the third class at the expiration of the sixth year, so that one-third may be chosen every second year; and if vacancies happen by resignation, or otherwise, during the recess of the legislature of any State, the executive thereof may make temporary appointments until the next meeting of the legislature, which shall then fill such vacancies.

No person shall be a Senator who shall not have attained to the age of thirty years, and been nine years a citizen of the United States, and who shall not, when elected, be an inhabitant of that State for which he shall be chosen.

The Vice President of the United States shall be President of the Senate, but shall have no vote, unless they be equally divided.

The Senate shall choose their other officers, and also a President pro tempore, in the absence of the Vice President, or when he shall exercise the office of President of the United States.

The Senate shall have the sole power to try all impeachments. When sitting for that purpose, they shall be on oath or affirmation. When the President of the United States is tried, the Chief Justice shall preside; and no person shall be convicted without the concurrence of two thirds of the members present.

Judgment in cases of impeachment shall not extend further than to removal from office, and disqualification to hold and enjoy any office of honor, trust or profit under the United States: but the party convicted shall nevertheless be liable and subject to indictment, trial, judgment and punishment, according to law.

Section 4. The times, places and manner of holding elections for Senators and Representatives, shall be prescribed in each State by the legislature thereof; but the Congress may at any time by law make or alter such regulations, except as to the places of choosing Senators.

The Congress shall assemble at least once in every year, and such meeting shall be on the first Monday in December, unless they shall by law appoint a different day.

Section 5. Each House shall be the judge of the elections, returns and qualifications of its own members, and a majority of each shall constitute a quorum to do business; but a smaller number may adjourn from day to day, and may be authorized to compel the attendance of absent members, in such manner, and under such penalties as each House may provide.

Each House may determine the rules of its proceedings, punish its members for disorderly behaviour, and, with the concurrence of two-thirds, expel a member.

Each House shall keep a journal of its proceedings, and from time to time publish the same, excepting such parts as may in their judgment require secrecy; and the yeas and the nays of the members of either house on any question shall, at the desire of one-fifth of those present, be entered on the journal.

Neither House, during the session of Congress, shall, without the consent of the other, adjourn for more than three days, nor to any other place than that in which the two Houses shall be sitting.

Section 6. The Senators and Representatives shall receive a compensation for their services to be ascertained by law, and paid out of the Treasury of the United States. They shall in all cases, except treason, felony and breach of the peace, be privileged from arrest during their attendance at the session of their respective Houses, and in going to and returning from the same; and for any speech or debate in either House, they shall not be questioned in any other place.

No Senator or Representative shall, during the time for which he was elected, be appointed to any civil office under the authority of the United States, which shall have been created, or the emoluments whereof shall have been increased during such time; and no person holding any office under the United States, shall be a member of either House during his continuance in office.

Section 7. All bills for raising revenues shall originate in the House of Representatives; but the Senate may propose or concur with amendments as on other bills.

Every bill which shall have passed the House of Representatives and the Senate, shall, before it becomes a law, be presented to the President of the United States; if he approves he shall sign it, but if not he shall return it, with his objections to that House in which it shall have originated, who shall enter the objections at large on their journal, and proceed to reconsider it. If after such reconsideration two thirds of that House shall agree to pass the bill, it shall be sent, together with the objections, to the other House, by which it shall likewise be reconsidered, and if approved by two thirds of that House, it shall become a law. But in all such cases the votes of both Houses shall be determined by yeas and nays, and the names of the persons voting for and against the bill shall be entered on the journal of each House respectively. If any bill shall not be returned by the President within ten days (Sundays excepted) after it shall have been presented to him, the same shall be a law, in like manner as if he had signed it, unless the Congress by their adjournment prevent its return, in which case it shall not be a law.

Every order, resolution, or vote to which the concurrence of the Senate and House of Representatives may be necessary (except on a question of adjournment) shall be presented to the President of the United States; and before the same shall take effect, shall be approved by him, or being disapproved by him, shall be repassed by two thirds of the Senate and House of Representatives, according to the rules and limitations prescribed in the case of a bill.

Section 8. The Congress shall have power to lay and collect taxes, duties, imposts and excises, to pay the debts and provide for the common defense and general welfare of the United States; but all duties, imposts and excises shall be uniform throughout the United States;

To borrow money on the credit of the United States;

To regulate commerce with foreign nations, and among the several States, and with the Indian tribes;

To establish a uniform rule of naturalization, and uniform laws on the subject of bankruptcies throughout the United States;

To coin money, regulate the value thereof, and of foreign coin, and fix the standard of weights and measures;

To provide for the punishment of counterfeiting the securities and current coin of the United States;

To establish post offices and post roads;

To promote the progress of science and useful arts, by securing for limited times to authors and inventors the exclusive right to their respective writings and discoveries;

To constitute tribunals inferior to the Supreme Court;

To define and punish piracies and felonies committed on the high seas, and offenses against the law of nations;

To declare war, grant letters of marque and reprisal, and make rules concerning captures on land and water;

To raise and support armies, but no appropriation of money to that use shall be for a longer term than two years;

To provide and maintain a navy;

To make rules for the government and regulation of the land and naval forces;

To provide for calling forth the militia to execute the laws of the Union, suppress insurrections and repel invasions;

To provide for organizing, arming, and disciplining the militia, and for governing such part of them as may be employed in the service of the United States, reserving to the States respectively, the appointment of the officers, and the authority of training the militia according to the discipline prescribed by Congress;

To exercise exclusive legislation in all cases whatsoever, over such district (not exceeding ten miles square) as may, by cession of particular States, and the acceptance of Congress, become the seat of the Government of the United States, and to exercise like authority over all places purchased by the consent of the legislature of the State in which the same shall be, for the erection of forts, magazines, arsenals, dock-yards, and other needful buildings;—And

To make all laws which shall be necessary and proper for carrying into execution the foregoing powers, and all other powers vested by this Constitution in the Government of the United States, or in any department or officer thereof.

Section 9. The migration or importation of such persons as any of the States now existing shall think proper to admit, shall not be prohibited by the Congress prior to the year one thousand eight hundred and eight, but a tax or duty may be imposed on such importation, not exceeding ten dollars for each person.

The privilege of the writ of habeas corpus shall not be suspended, unless when in cases of rebellion or invasion the public safety may require it.

No bill of attainder or ex post facto law shall be passed.

No capitation, or other direct, tax shall be laid, unless in proportion to the census or enumeration herein before directed to be taken.

No tax or duty shall be laid on articles exported from any State.

No preference shall be given by any regulation of commerce or revenue to the ports of one State over those of another; nor shall vessels bound to, or from, one State, be obliged to enter, clear, or pay duties in another.

No money shall be drawn from the Treasury, but in consequence of appropriations made by law; and a regular statement and account of the receipts and expenditures of all public money shall be published from time to time.

No title of nobility shall be granted by the United States: And no person holding any office of profit or trust under them, shall, without the consent of the Congress, accept of any present, emolument, office, or title, of any kind whatever, from any King, Prince, or foreign State.

Section 10. No State shall enter into any treaty, alliance, or confederation; grant letters of marque and reprisal; coin money; emit bills of credit; make any thing but gold and silver coin a tender in payment of debts; pass any bill of attainder, ex post facto law, or law impairing the obligation of contracts, or grant any title of nobility.

No State shall, without the consent of the Congress, lay any imposts or duties on imports or exports, except what may be absolutely necessary for executing its inspection laws; and the net produce of all duties and imposts, laid by any state on imports or exports, shall be for the use of the Treasury of the United States; and all such laws shall be subject to the revision and control of the Congress.

No State shall, without the consent of Congress, lay any duty of tonnage, keep troops, or ships of war in time of peace, enter into any agreement or compact with another State, or with a foreign power, or engage in war, unless actually invaded, or in such imminent danger as will not admit of delay.

ARTICLE II

Section 1. The executive power shall be vested in a President of the United States of America. He shall hold his office during the term of four years, and together with the Vice President, chosen for the same term, be elected, as follows:

Each State, shall appoint, in such manner as the legislature thereof may direct, a number of electors, equal to the whole number of Senators and Representatives to which the State may be entitled in the Congress; but no Senator or Representative, or person holding an office of trust or profit under the United States, shall be appointed an elector.

The electors shall meet in their respective States, and vote by ballot for two persons, of whom one at least shall not be an inhabitant of the same State with themselves. And they shall make a list of all the persons voted for, and of the number of votes for each; which list they shall sign and certify, and transmit sealed to the seat of the Government of the United States, directed to the President of the Senate. The President of the Senate shall, in the presence of the Senate and House of Representatives, open all the certificates, and the votes shall then be counted. The person having the greatest number of votes shall be the President, if such number be a majority of the whole number of electors appointed; and if there be more than one who have such majority, and have an equal number of votes, then the House of Representatives shall immediately choose by ballot one of them for President; and if no person have a majority, then from the five highest on the list the said House shall in like manner choose the President. But in choosing the President, the votes shall be taken by States, the representation from each State having one vote; a quorum for this purpose shall consist of a member or members from two thirds of the States, and a majority of all the States shall be necessary to a choice. In every case, after the choice of the President, the person having the greatest number of votes of the electors shall be the Vice President. But if there should remain two or more who have equal votes, the Senate shall choose from them by ballot the Vice President.

The Congress may determine the time of choosing the electors, and the day on which they shall give their votes; which day shall be the same throughout the United States.

No person except a natural born citizen, or a citizen of the United States, at the time of the adoption of this Constitution, shall be eligible to the office of President; neither shall any person be eligible to that office who shall not have attained to the age of thirty-five years, and been fourteen years a resident within the United States.

In case of the removal of the President from office, or of his death, resignation, or inability to discharge the powers and duties of the said office, the same shall devolve on the Vice President, and the Congress may by law provide for the case of removal, death, resignation, or inability, both of the President and Vice President, declaring what officer shall then act as President, and such officer shall act accordingly, until the disability be removed, or a President be elected.

The President shall, at stated times, receive for his services, a compensation, which shall neither be increased nor diminished during the period for which he shall have been elected, and he shall not receive within that period any other emolument from the United States, or any of them.

Before he enter on the execution of his office, he shall take the following oath or affirmation:—"I do solemnly swear (or affirm) that I will faithfully execute the office of President of the United States, and will to the best of my ability, preserve, protect and defend the Constitution of the United States."

Section 2. The President shall be Commander in Chief of the Army and Navy of the United States, and of the militia of the several States, when called into the actual service of the United States; he may require the opinion, in writing, of the principal officer in each of the executive departments, upon any subject relating to the duties of their respective offices, and he shall have power to grant reprieves and pardons for offenses against the United States, except in cases of impeachment.

He shall have power, by and with the advice and consent of the Senate, to make treaties, provided two thirds of the Senators present concur; and he shall nominate, and by and with the advice and consent of the Senate, shall appoint ambassadors, other public ministers and consuls, Judges of the Supreme Court, and all other officers of the United States, whose appointments are not herein otherwise provided for, and which shall be established by law; but the Congress may by law vest the appointment of such inferior officers, as they think proper, in the President alone, in the courts of law, or in the heads of departments.

The President shall have power to fill up all vacancies that may happen during the recess of the Senate, by granting commissions which shall expire at the end of their next session.

Section 4. The President, Vice President and all civil officers of the United States, shall be removed from office on impeachment for, and conviction of, treason, bribery, or other high crimes and misdemeanors.

ARTICLE III

Section 1. The judicial power of the United States, shall be vested in one Supreme Court, and in such inferior courts as the Congress may from time to time ordain and establish. The judges, both of the Supreme and inferior Courts, shall hold their offices during good behaviour, and shall, at stated times, receive for their services, a compensation, which shall not be diminished during their continuance in office.

Section 2. The judicial power shall extend to all cases, in law and equity, arising under this Constitution, the laws of the United States, and treaties made, or which shall be made, under their authority;—to all cases of admiralty and maritime jurisdiction;—to controversies to which the United States shall be a party;—to controversies between two or more States;—between a State and citizens of another State;—between citizens of different States;—between citizens of the same State claiming lands under grants of different States, and between a State, or citizens thereof, and foreign States, citizens or subjects.

In all cases affecting ambassadors, other public ministers and consuls, and those in which a State shall be a party, the Supreme Court shall have original jurisdiction. In all the other cases before mentioned, the Supreme Court shall have appellate jurisdiction, both as to law and fact, with such exceptions, and under such regulations as the Congress shall make.

The trial of all crimes, except in cases of impeachment, shall be by jury; and such trial shall be held in the State where the said crimes shall have been committed; but when not committed within any State, the trial shall be at such place or places as the Congress may by law have directed.

Section 3. Treason against the United States, shall consist only in levying war against them, or in adhering to their enemies, giving them aid and comfort. No person shall be convicted of treason unless on the testimony of two witnesses to the same overt act, or on confession in open court.

The Congress shall have power to declare the punishment of treason, but no attainder of treason shall work corruption of blood, or forfeiture except during the life of the person attainted.

ARTICLE IV

Section 1. Full faith and credit shall be given in each State to the public acts, records, and judicial proceedings of every other State. And the Congress may by general laws prescribe the manner in which such acts, records, and proceedings shall be proved, and the effect thereof.

Section 2. The citizens of each State shall be entitled to all privileges and immunities of citizens in the several States.

A person charged in any State with treason, felony, or other crime, who shall flee from justice, and be found in another State, shall on demand of the executive authority of the State from which he fled, be delivered up, to be removed to the State having jurisdiction of the crime.

No person held to service or labour in one State, under the laws thereof, escaping into another, shall, in consequence of any law or regulation therein, be discharged from such service or labour, but shall be delivered up on claim of the party to whom such service or labour may be due.

Section 3. New States may be admitted by the Congress into this Union; but no new State shall be formed or erected within the jurisdiction of any other State; nor any State be formed by the junction of two or more States, or parts of States, without the consent of the legislatures of the states concerned as well as of the Congress.

The Congress shall have power to dispose of and make all needful rules and regulations respecting the Territory or other property belonging to the United States; and nothing in this Constitution shall be so construed as to prejudice any claims of the United States, or of any particular State.

Section 4. The United States shall guarantee to every State in this Union a republican form of Government, and shall protect each of them against invasion; and on application of the legislature, or of the executive (when the legislature cannot be convened) against domestic violence.

ARTICLE V

The Congress, whenever two thirds of both Houses shall deem it necessary, shall propose amendments to this Constitution, or on the application of the legislatures of two thirds of the several States, shall call a convention for proposing amendments, which, in either case, shall be valid to all intents and purposes, as part of this Constitution, when ratified by the legislatures of three fourths of the several States, or by conventions in three fourths thereof, as the one or the other mode of ratification may be proposed by the Congress; provided that no amendment which may be made prior to the year one thousand eight hundred and eight shall in any manner affect the first and fourth clauses in the Ninth Section of the First Article; and that no State, without its consent, shall be deprived of its equal suffrage in the Senate.

ARTICLE VI

All debts contracted and engagements entered into, before the adoption of this Constitution, shall be as valid against the United States under this Constitution, as under the Confederation.

This Constitution, and the laws of the United States which shall be made in pursuance thereof; and all treaties made, or which shall be made, under the authority of the United States, shall be the supreme law of the land; and the judges in every State shall be bound thereby, any thing in the Constitution or laws of any State to the contrary notwithstanding.

The Senators and Representatives before mentioned, and the members of the several State legislatures, and all executive and judicial officers, both of the United States and of the several States, shall be bound by oath or affirmation, to support this Constitution; but no religious test shall ever be required as a qualification to any office or public trust under the United States.

ARTICLE VII

The ratification of the conventions of nine States shall be sufficient for the establishment of this Constitution between the States so ratifying the same.

Done in convention by the unanimous consent of the States present the seventeenth day of September in the year of our Lord one thousand seven hundred and eighty seven and of the independence of the United States of America the twelfth. In witness whereof we have hereunto subscribed our names.

Go. WASHINGTON—*Presid't.*
and deputy from Virginia

Attest WILLIAM JACKSON *Secretary*

New Hampshire

John Langdon   Nicolas Gilman

Massachusetts

Nathaniel Gorham   Rufus King

Connecticut

Wm. Saml. Johnson   Roger Sherman

New York

Alexander Hamilton

New Jersey

Wil: Livingston   Wm. Paterson
David Brearly   Jona: Dayton

Pennsylvania

B. Franklin   Thos. FitzSimons
Thomas Mifflin   Jared Ingersoll

Robt Morris   James Wilson
Geo. Clymer   Gouv Morris

Delaware

Geo: Read   Richard Bassett
Gunning Bedfordjun   Jaco: Broom
John Dickinson

Maryland

James McHenry   Danl Carroll
Dan of St. Thos. Jenifer

Virginia

John Blair—   James Madison Jr.

North Carolina

Wm. Blount   Hu Williamson
Richard Dobbs Spaight

South Carolina

J. Rutledge   Charles Pinckney
Charles Cotesworth Pinckney   Pierce Butler

Georgia

William Few   Abr Baldwin

Amendments

ARTICLE I

Congress shall make no law respecting an establishment of religion, or prohibiting the free exercise thereof; or abridging the freedom of speech, or of the press; or the right of the people peaceably to assemble, and to petition the Government for a redress of grievances.

ARTICLE II

A well regulated militia, being necessary to the security of a free State, the right of the people to keep and bear arms, shall not be infringed.

ARTICLE III

No soldier shall, in time of peace be quartered in any house, without the consent of the owner, nor in time of war, but in a manner to be prescribed by law.

ARTICLE IV

The right of the people to be secure in their persons, houses, papers, and effects, against unreasonable searches and seizures, shall not be violated, and no warrants shall issue, but upon probable cause, supported by oath or affirmation, and particularly describing the place to be searched, and the persons or things to be seized.

ARTICLE V

No person shall be held to answer for a capital, or otherwise infamous crime, unless on a presentment or indictment of a Grand Jury, except in cases arising in the land or naval forces, or in the militia, when in actual service in time of war or public danger; nor shall any person be subject for the same offense to be twice put in jeopardy of life or limb; nor shall be compelled in any criminal case to be a witness against himself, nor be deprived of life, liberty, or property, without due process of law; nor shall private property be taken for public use, without just compensation.

ARTICLE VI

In all criminal prosecutions the accused shall enjoy the right to a speedy and public trial, by an impartial jury of the State and district wherein the crime shall have been committed, which district shall have been previously ascertained by law, and to be informed of the nature and cause of the accusation; to be confronted with the witnesses against him; to have compulsory process for obtaining witnesses in his favor, and to have the assistance of counsel for his defense.

ARTICLE VII

In suits at common law, where the value in controversy shall exceed twenty dollars, the right of trial by jury shall be preserved, and no fact tried by a jury, shall be otherwise reexamined in any Court of the United States, than according to the rules of the common law.

ARTICLE VIII

Excessive bail shall not be required, nor excessive fines imposed, nor cruel and unusual punishments inflicted.

ARTICLE IX

The enumeration in the Constitution, of certain rights, shall not be construed to deny or disparage others retained by the people.

ARTICLE X

The powers not delegated to the United States by the Constitution, nor prohibited by it to the States, are reserved to the States respectively, or to the people.

ARTICLE XI

The judicial power of the United States shall not be construed to extend to any suit in law or equity, commenced or prosecuted against one of the United States by citizens of another State, or by citizens or subjects of any foreign State.

ARTICLE XII

The electors shall meet in their respective States, and vote by ballot for President and Vice President, one of whom, at least, shall not be an inhabitant of the same State with themselves; they shall name in their ballots the person voted for as President, and in distinct ballots the person voted for as Vice President, and they shall make distinct lists of all persons voted for as President, and of all persons voted for as Vice President, and of the number of votes for each, which lists they shall sign and certify, and transmit sealed to the seat of the government of the United States, directed to the President of the Senate;—The President of the Senate shall, in the presence of the Senate and House of Representatives, open all the certificates and the votes shall then be counted;—The person having the greatest number of votes for President, shall be the President, if such number be a majority of the whole number of electors appointed; and if no person have such majority, then from the persons having the highest numbers not exceeding three on the list of those voted for as President, the House of Representatives shall choose immediately, by ballot, the President. But in choosing the President, the votes shall be taken by States, the representation from each State having one vote; a quorum for this purpose shall consist of a member or members from two-thirds of the States, and a majority of all the States shall be necessary to a choice. And if the House of Representatives shall not choose a President whenever the right of choice shall devolve upon them, before the fourth day of March next following, then the Vice President shall act as President, as in the case of the death or other constitutional disability of the President.—The person having the greatest number of votes as

Vice President, shall be the Vice President, if such number be a majority of the whole number of electors appointed, and if no person have a majority, then from the two highest numbers on the list, the Senate shall choose the Vice President; a quorum for the purpose shall consist of two-thirds of the whole number of Senators, and a majority of the whole number shall be necessary to a choice. But no person constitutionally ineligible to the office of President shall be eligible to that of Vice President of the United States.

ARTICLE XIII

Section 1. Neither slavery nor involuntary servitude, except as a punishment for crime whereof the party shall have been duly convicted, shall exist within the United States, or any place subject to their jurisdiction.

Section 2. Congress shall have power to enforce this article by appropriate legislation.

ARTICLE XIV

Section 1. All persons born or naturalized in the United States, and subject to the jurisdiction thereof, are citizens of the United States and of the State wherein they reside. No State shall make or enforce any law which shall abridge the privileges or immunities of citizens of the United States; nor shall any State deprive any person of life, liberty, or property, without due process of law; nor deny to any person within its jurisdiction the equal protection of the laws.

Section 2. Representatives shall be apportioned among the several States according to their respective numbers, counting the whole number of persons in each State, excluding Indians not taxed. But when the right to vote at any election for the choice of electors of President and Vice President of the United States, Representatives in Congress, the executive and judicial officers of a State, or the members of the legislature thereof, is denied to any of the male inhabitants of such State, being twenty-one years of age, and citizens of the United States, or in any way abridged, except for participation in rebellion, or other crime, the basis of representation therein shall be reduced in the proportion which the number of such male citizens shall bear to the whole number of male citizens twenty-one years of age in such State.

Section 3. No person shall be a Senator or Representative in Congress, or elector of President and Vice President, or hold any office, civil or military, under the United States, or under any State, who, having previously taken an oath, as a member of Congress, or as an officer of the

United States, or as a member of any State legislature, or as an executive or judicial officer of any State, to support the Constitution of the United States, shall have engaged in insurrection or rebellion against the same, or given aid or comfort to the enemies thereof. But Congress may by a vote of two-thirds of each house, remove such disability.

Section 4. The validity of the public debt of the United States, authorized by law, including debts incurred for payment of pensions and bounties for services in suppressing insurrection or rebellion, shall not be questioned. But neither the United States nor any State shall assume or pay any debt or obligation incurred in aid of insurrection or rebellion against the United States, or any claim for the loss or emancipation of any slave; but all such debts, obligations and claims shall be held illegal and void.

Section 5. The Congress shall have power to enforce, by appropriate legislation, the provisions of this article.

ARTICLE XV

Section 1. The right of citizens of the United States to vote shall not be denied or abridged by the United States or by any State on account of race, color, or previous condition of servitude.

Section 2. The Congress shall have power to enforce this article by appropriate legislation.

ARTICLE XVI

The Congress shall have power to lay and collect taxes on incomes, from whatever source derived, without apportionment among the several States, and without regard to any census or enumeration.

ARTICLE XVII

Section 1. The Senate of the United States shall be composed of two Senators from each State, elected by the people thereof, for six years; and each Senator shall have one vote. The electors in each State shall have the qualifications requisite for electors of the most numerous branch of the State legislatures.

Section 2. When vacancies happen in the representation of any State in the Senate, the executive authority of such State shall issue writs of election to fill such vacancies: *Provided*, That the legislature of any State may empower the executive thereof to make temporary appointments until the people fill the vacancies by election as the legislature may direct.

Section 3. This amendment shall not be so construed as to affect the election or term of any Senator chosen before it becomes valid as part of the Constitution.

ARTICLE XVIII

Section 1. After one year from the ratification of this article the manufacture, sale, or transportation of intoxicating liquors within, the importation thereof into, or the exportation thereof from the United States and all territory subject to the jurisdiction thereof for beverage purposes is hereby prohibited.

Section 2. The Congress and the several States shall have concurrent power to enforce this article by appropriate legislation.

Section 3. This article shall be inoperative unless it shall have been ratified as an amendment to the Constitution by the legislatures of the several States, as provided in the Constitution, within seven years from the date of the submission hereof to the States by the Congress.

ARTICLE XIX

Section 1. The right of citizens of the United States to vote shall not be denied or abridged by the United States or by any State on account of sex.

Section 2. Congress shall have power to enforce this article by appropriate legislation.

ARTICLE XX

Section 1. The terms of the President and Vice President shall end at noon on the 20th day of January, and the terms of Senators and Representatives at noon on the 3d day of January, of the years in which such terms would have ended if this article had not been ratified; and the terms of their successors shall then begin.

Section 2. The Congress shall assemble at least once in every year, and such meeting shall begin at noon on the 3d day of January, unless they shall by law appoint a different day.

Section 3. If, at the time fixed for the beginning of the term of the President, the President elect shall have died, the Vice President elect shall become President. If a President shall not have been chosen before the time fixed for the beginning of his term, or if the President elect shall have failed to qualify, then the Vice President elect shall act as President until a President shall have qualified; and the Congress may by law provide for the case wherein neither a President elect nor a Vice President elect shall have qualified, declaring who shall then act as President, or the manner in which one who is to act shall be selected, and such person shall act accordingly until a President or Vice President shall have qualified.

Section 4. The Congress may by law provide for the case of the death of any of the persons from whom the House of Representatives may choose a President whenever the right of choice shall have devolved upon them, and for the case of the death of any of the persons from whom the Senate may choose a Vice President whenever the right of choice shall have devolved upon them.

Section 5. Sections 1 and 2 shall take effect on the 15th day of October following the ratification of this article.

Section 6. This article shall be inoperative unless it shall have been ratified as an amendment to the Constitution by the legislatures of three-fourths of the several States within seven years from the date of its submission.

Article XXI

Section 1. The eighteenth article of amendment to the Constitution of the United States is hereby repealed.

Section 2. The transportation or importation into any State, Territory, or possession of the United States for delivery or use therein of intoxicating liquors, in violation of the laws thereof, is hereby prohibited.

Section 3. This article shall be inoperative unless it shall have been ratified as an amendment to the Constitution by conventions in the several States, as provided in the Constitution, within seven years from the date of the submission hereof to the States by the Congress.

Article XXII

Section 1. No person shall be elected to the office of the President more than twice, and no person who has held the office of President, or acted as President, for more than two years of a term to which some other person was elected President shall be elected to the office of the President more than once. But this article shall not apply to any person holding the office of President when this article was proposed by the Congress, and shall not prevent any person who may be holding the office of President, or acting as President, during the term within which this article becomes operative from holding the office of President or acting as President during the remainder of such term.

Section 2. This article shall be inoperative unless it shall have been ratified as an amendment to the Constitution by the legislatures of three-fourths of the several States within seven years from the date of its submission to the States by the Congress.

ARTICLE XXIII

Section 1. The District constituting the seat of Government of the United States shall appoint in such manner as the Congress may direct:

A number of electors of President and Vice President equal to the whole number of Senators and Representatives in Congress to which the District would be entitled if it were a State, but in no event more than the least populous State; they shall be in addition to those appointed by the States, but they shall be considered, for the purposes of the election of President and Vice President, to be electors appointed by a State; and they shall meet in the District and perform such duties as provided by the twelfth article of amendment.

Section 2. The Congress shall have the power to enforce this article by appropriate legislation.

ARTICLE XXIV

Section 1. The right of citizens of the United States to vote in any primary or other election for President or Vice President, for electors for President or Vice President, or for Senator or Representative in Congress, shall not be denied or abridged by the United States or any State by reason of failure to pay any poll tax or other tax.

Section 2. The Congress shall have the power to enforce this article by appropriate legislation.

ARTICLE XXV

Section 1. In case of the removal of the President from office or of his death or resignation, the Vice President shall become President.

Section 2. Whenever there is a vacancy in the office of the Vice President, the President shall nominate a Vice President who shall take office upon confirmation by a majority vote of both Houses of Congress.

Section 3. Whenever the President transmits to the President pro tempore of the Senate and the Speaker of the House of Representatives his written declaration that he is unable to discharge the powers and duties of his office, and until he transmits to them a written declaration to the contrary, such powers and duties shall be discharged by the Vice President as Acting President.

Section 4. Whenever the Vice President and a majority of either the principal officers of the executive departments or of such other body as

Congress may by law provide, transmit to the President pro tempore of the Senate and the Speaker of the House of Representatives their written declaration that the President is unable to discharge the powers and duties of his office, the Vice President shall immediately assume the powers and duties of the office as Acting President.

Thereafter, when the President transmits to the President pro tempore of the Senate and the Speaker of the House of Representatives his written declaration that no inability exists, he shall resume the powers and duties of his office unless the Vice President and a majority of either the principal officers of the executive department or of such other body as Congress may by law provide, transmit within four days to the President pro tempore of the Senate and the Speaker of the House of Representatives their written declaration that the President is unable to discharge the powers and duties of his office. Thereupon Congress shall decide the issue, assembling within forty-eight hours for that purpose if not in session. If the Congress, within twenty-one days after Congress is required to assemble, determines by two-thirds vote of both Houses that the President is unable to discharge the powers and duties of his office, the Vice President shall continue to discharge the same as Acting President; otherwise, the President shall resume the powers and duties of his office.

ARTICLE XXVI

Section 1. The right of citizens of the United States who are 18 years of age or older, to vote shall not be denied or abridged by the United States or by any State on account of age.

Section 2. The Congress shall have the power to enforce this article by appropriate legislation.

Chronology

The Bill of Rights and American Law

1215   A group of rebellious English barons forced King John to agree to the Magna Carta, a ''great charter'' that placed limits on royal power and symbolized the rule of law.

1354   ''Due process of law'' appeared in an English statute for the first time.

1639   The Fundamental Orders of Connecticut, drafted largely by the Reverend Thomas Hooker of Hartford, became the modern world's first written constitution.

1641   The Massachusetts Body of Liberties provided a series of constitutional safeguards regarding due process of law and the protection of personal freedom.

1648   The Massachusetts General Laws and Liberties offered a more comprehensive codification of liberties than its predecessor, the Massachusetts Body of Liberties.

1689   The English Bill of Rights limited royal prerogatives and ratified parliamentary supremacy. It also endorsed several of the principles (such as freedom of petition and freedom of assembly) later embodied in the American Bill of Rights.

1701   The Pennsylvania Charter of Privileges, an important antecedent of the Bill of Rights, included several clauses promoting the "Enjoyment of Civil Liberties."

1735   In the landmark John Peter Zenger trial, the printer of the *New York Weekly Journal* was acquitted of seditious libel.

1765–69 William Blackstone's *Commentaries on the Laws of England,* published in Oxford, provided Americans with a convenient reference source on British common law. For more than a century, Blackstone's work had a profound influence on American jurisprudence and constitutional law.

1776   The Declaration of Independence was adopted by the Continental Congress in Philadelphia.

       Virginia's constitutional convention adopted a Declaration of Rights.

1781   Four years after they received Congressional approval, the Articles of Confederation were ratified, creating "The United States of America."

1786   The Virginia Statute for Religious Freedom endorsed the principle of separation of church and state, later embodied in the establishment clause of the First Amendment.

1787   At the Constitutional Convention in Philadelphia, a resolution by Elbridge Gerry and George Mason calling for the inclusion of a bill of rights in the new federal Constitution was rejected unanimously.

1788   Ratification of the United States Constitution

1789   The Bill of Rights received Congressional approval.

1791   Ratification of the Bill of Rights

1793   The first Fugitive Slave Act was enacted by Congress. The Act allowed any slaveholder or his "agent or attorney" to bring an alleged runaway before a federal judge or local magistrate and prove title to the slave by offering a written affidavit or oral testimony.

1798   The Alien and Sedition Acts, four federal statutes that curtailed the civil liberties of aliens and political dissenters, were enacted by a Federalist-controlled Congress and signed into law by President John Adams.

The Virginia and Kentucky Resolutions declared the Alien and Sedition Acts to be unconstitutional. Thomas Jefferson drafted the nine Kentucky Resolutions, and James Madison drafted the more moderate Virginia Resolutions.

Ratification of the Eleventh Amendment, which proclaims that "the judicial power of the United States shall not be construed to extend to any suit in law or equity, commenced or prosecuted against one of the United States by citizens of another state, or by citizens or subjects of a foreign State."

Calder v. Bull, 3 Dallas 386. Supreme Court Justice Samuel Chase issued his "vested rights" interpretation of American contract law and private property rights.

1803   *Marbury v. Madison*, 1 Cranch 137. Establishing the Supreme Court's right of judicial review, Chief Justice John Marshall and the Court unanimously declared an act of Congress (the Judiciary Act of 1789) unconstitutional.

1804   Ratification of the Twelfth Amendment, which refined the Electoral College system established in Article 11 of the Constitution. Under the Twelfth Amendment, electors vote for President and Vice-President in separate ballots; if no candidate receives a majority, the Presidential election is determined by a vote in the House of Representatives (each state delegation casts one vote), and the Vice Presidential election is determined by a vote of the Senate.

1807   The Abolition of the Slave Trade Act outlawed American involvement in the international slave trade.

1811   *Dennis v. Leclerc*, 1 Mart. (O.S.) 297. A Louisiana state court rejected an editor's claim that the First Amendment gave him the right to publish a letter without the author's consent.

1815   *Terrett v. Taylor*, 9 Cranch 43. The Supreme Court disallowed the confiscation of Episcopal glebe lands by the State of Virginia. This clarified the property redistribution implications of the Virginia Statute for Religious Freedom.

1816   *Martin v. Hunter's Lessee*, 1 Wheaton 304. The Supreme Court overruled a decision of the Virginia Court of Appeals and affirmed the principle that the Supreme Court's appellate jurisdiction extends to the state courts.

1819   *McCulloch v. Maryland*, 4 Wheaton 316. In a case involving Congress's right to incorporate a state bank, Chief Justice John Marshall and the Supreme Court endorsed the doctrine of "implied powers," which became a touchstone of broad constructionist interpretations of American Constitutional law.

1824   *Gibbons v. Ogden*, 9 Wheaton 1. In a case involving the regulation of steamship companies, the Supreme Court issued a nationalistic interpretation of the commerce clause that challenged the constitutionality of state-created monopolies.

1833   *Barron v. Baltimore*, 7 Peters 243. In a case involving the Fifth Amendment, the Supreme Court ruled unanimously that the Bill of Rights does not apply to the actions of state governments.

1838   *Commonwealth v. Kneeland*, Thacher Cr. Cas. 346. Chief Justice Lemuel Shaw and the Massachusetts Supreme Court upheld a state law against blasphemy.

1842   *Prigg v. Pennsylvania*, 16 Peters (U.S.), 539. The Supreme Court upheld the Fugitive Slave Act of 1793 and invalidated Pennsylvania's personal liberty law.

1850   The second Fugitive Slave Act was adopted as part of the Compromise of 1850, a series of measures designed to bring "finality" to the debate over slavery in the territories.

1857   *Dred Scott v. Sandford*, 19 How. 393. Chief Justice Roger Taney and the Supreme Court temporarily invalidated the concept of black citizenship and declared the Missouri Compromise of 1820 to be unconstitutional. Relying on the concept of substantive due process, the Court ruled that Congress could not prohibit slaveowners from taking their slaves into federal territories.

1859   *Ableman v. Booth*, 21 Howard 506. The Supreme Court sustained the 1850 Fugitive Slave Act.

1862   The Emancipation Proclamation, issued by President Abraham Lincoln on September 22, 1862, following the Union victory at Antietam, freed the slaves of all Confederate slaveowners, unless the owners publicly renounced the rebellion prior to January 1, 1863. The Proclamation also encouraged gradual emancipation in the slaveholding states of the Union.

1865   Ratification of the Thirteenth Amendment, which abolished slavery and involuntary servitude in the United States.

1866   *Ex Parte Milligan*, 4 Wallace 2. The Supreme Court placed severe restrictions on the power of the President to suspend habeas corpus or to substitute military for civilian courts.

The Civil Rights Act of 1866 was enacted into law over President Andrew Johnson's veto. Providing enforcement legislation for the Thirteenth Amendment, the Act conferred citizenship on African-Americans.

1868   Ratification of the Fourteenth Amendment, which declares: "No State shall make or enforce any law which shall abridge the privileges or immunities of citizens of the United States; nor shall any State deprive any person of life, liberty, or property without due process of law; nor deny to any person within its jurisdiction equal protection of the laws."

1870   Ratification of the Fifteenth Amendment, which declares: "The right of citizens of the United States to vote shall not be denied or abridged by the United States or by any State on account of race, color, or previous condition of servitude."

The Civil Rights Act of 1870 (also known as the first Enforcement Act) provided enforcement legislation for the Fourteenth and Fifteenth Amendments.

1871   The Second Enforcement Act put Congressional elections under the control of federal courts and officers.

The Third Enforcement Act (also known as the Ku Klux Act) empowered the president to suspend habeas corpus and to declare martial law in areas threatened by a Ku Klux Klan-style conspiracy.

1873   *United States v. Susan B. Anthony*, 24 F. Cas. (14459) 829. Rejecting the applicability of the privileges and immunities clause of the Fourteenth Amendment, the Supreme Court denied that citizenship implied suffrage. The Court did not recognize the right of women's suffrage.

The Slaughterhouse Cases, 16 Wallace 36. In the first case involving an interpretation of the Fourteenth Amendment, the Supreme Court upheld a Louisiana law granting a monopoly to a New Orleans slaughterhouse company. The Court offered a severely restrictive interpretation of the privileges and immunities and equal protection clauses of the Fourteenth Amendment.

Bradwell v. Illinois, 16 Wallace 130. In this early Fourteenth Amendment sex discrimination case, the Supreme Court sustained an Illinois state ruling that effectively denied Myra Bradwell's admission to the state bar. The Illinois Supreme Court had refused to admit female attorneys.

1875   The Civil Rights Act of 1875 declared that all citizens, regardless of race, have an equal right to enjoy access to transportation facilities, to hotels and inns, and to theaters and places of public amusement.

1876   *United States v. Reese*, 92 U.S. 214. In upholding the right of a Kentucky official to disfranchise a black voter, the Supreme Court severely weakened the Fifteenth Amendment and the Enforcement Act of 1870.

1878   *Reynolds v. United States*, 98 U.S. 145. Distinguishing between religious action and religious belief, the Supreme Court ruled that the government can restrict the former but not the latter.

1879   *Strauder v. West Virginia*, 100 U.S. 303. Citing the due process and equal protection clauses of the Fourteenth Amendment, the Supreme Court disallowed a jury selection system that blatantly and systematically excluded potential jurors on the basis of race.

1882   Congress enacted the Chinese Exclusion Act, overriding the veto of President Chester A. Arthur.

1883   *Civil Rights Cases*, 109 U.S. 3. Arguing that the Fourteenth Amendment did not prohibit racial discrimination by private individuals, the Supreme Court invalidated most of the 1875 Civil Rights Act.

1884   *Hurtado v. California*, 110 U.S. 516. The Supreme Court rejected the notion that the due process clause of the Fourteenth Amendment requires state governments to provide the accused with the protections of the Fifth Amendment.

1886   *Presser v. Illinois*, 6 S.C.R. 585. Rejecting the doctrine of incorporation, the Supreme Court held that the Second Amendment's declaration of "the right to bear arms" applied only to the federal government.

Boyd v. United States, 116 U.S. 616. In declaring an 1874 federal importation law unconstitutional, the Supreme Court rendered its first important decision in the areas of search and seizure and self-incrimination. The Court ruled that the law violated the Fourth and Fifth Amendments.

Yick Wo v. Hopkins, 118 U.S. 356. Invoking the equal protection clause of the Fourteenth Amendment, the Supreme Court unanimously struck down a San Francisco ordinance that implicitly discriminated against Chinese laundry owners.

1894   The Civil Rights Repeal Act of 1894 invalidated the Enforcement Acts of 1871.

1896   *Plessy v. Ferguson*, 163 U.S. 537. The Supreme Court held that a Louisiana separate coach law did not violate the equal protection clause of the Fourteenth Amendment. The Court established the "separate but equal" doctrine which became a canon of American law.

1898   *United States v. Wong Kim Ark*, 169 U.S. 649. In affirming the U.S. citizenship of Wong Kim Ark, the Supreme Court invalidated part of the Chinese Exclusion Act of 1882.

        Williams v. Mississippi, 170 U.S. 213. In a case involving a black man sentenced to death by an all-white jury, the Supreme Court unanimously upheld the constitutionality of the 1890 Mississippi state constitution. Despite evidence that the constitution promoted racial discrimination, the Court denied that the State of Mississippi had violated the equal protection clause of the Fourteenth Amendment.

1905   *Lochner v. New York*, 198 U.S. 45. Following the doctrine of substantive due process, the Supreme Court struck down a New York law regulating the work hours and working conditions of bakers.

1908   *Muller v. Oregon*, 208 U.S. 412. Influenced by Louis Brandeis's "sociological" brief, the Supreme Court upheld an Oregon law limiting a woman's work day to ten hours.

        Twining v. New Jersey, 211 U.S. 78. By a vote of 8–1, the Supreme Court rejected the argument that the Fifth Amendment right against self-incrimination was a fundamental right incorporated into state law through the privileges and immunities and due process clauses of the Fourteenth Amendment. Justice John Marshall Harlan was the lone dissenter.

1911   *Bailey v. Alabama*, 219 U.S. 219. Citing the Thirteenth Amendment's prohibition of involuntary servitude, the Supreme Court invalidated an Alabama contract law that legalized peonage.

1913   Ratification of the Sixteenth Amendment, which empowers Congress to collect federal income tax.

Ratification of the Seventeenth Amendment, which provides for the direct election of United States Senators.

1914   *Weeks v. United States*, 232 U.S. 383. Reinforcing the power of the Fourth Amendment, the Supreme Court unanimously endorsed the ''exclusionary rule'' in federal trials. Evidence gathered in an unlawful search and seizure was ruled to be inadmissible in federal court.

1915   *Guinn v. United States*, 238 U.S. 347. In the NAACP's first successful appearance before the Supreme Court, Oklahoma's ''grandfather clause'' disfranchisement law was declared unconstitutional.

1917   Congress passed the Selective Service Act.

1918   Congress passed the Espionage Act and the Sedition Act, which placed severe restrictions on antiwar activities.

1919   *Schenck v. United States*, 249 U.S. 47. The Supreme Court unanimously upheld Schenck's conviction under the 1918 Espionage Act. Justice Oliver Wendell Holmes, Jr., judged Schenck's distribution of antidraft pamphlets in terms of the ''clear and present danger'' test, which later became the standard test in First Amendment cases.

Abrams et al. v. United States, 250 U.S. 616. With Justices Holmes and Brandeis dissenting, the Supreme Court upheld Abrams's conviction under the 1918 Sedition Act. Reversing his judgment in the Schenck case, Holmes added the ''imminent harm'' corollary to the ''clear and present'' danger test.

Ratification of the Eighteenth Amendment, which required the national prohibition of alcoholic beverages.

1920   Harvard Law School Professor Zechariah Chafee, Jr., published his classic work, *Freedom of Speech.*

The American Civil Liberties Union was founded in New York by Roger Baldwin, Felix Frankfurter, Jane Addams, Norman Thomas, and other leading civil libertarians.

Ratification of the Nineteenth Amendment, which states: "The right of citizens of the United States to vote shall not be denied or abridged by the United States or by any State on account of sex."

1922   *United States v. Lanza*, 260 U.S. 377. Refining the rule against double jeopardy, the Supreme Court sustained the constitutionality of a second trial when the two trials involve state and federal prosecutions. Conviction or acquittal in a state court does not provide immunity to federal prosecution for the same crime.

1923   *Moore v. Dempsey*, 261 U.S. 86. Citing the absence of due process the Supreme Court overturned the murder convictions of five black men from Phillips County, Arkansas.

Adkins v. Children's Hospital, 261 U.S. 525. By a vote of 5–3, the Supreme Court struck down a federally mandated minimum wage law for women and children working in the District of Columbia.

Meyer v. Nebraska, 262 U.S. 390. Citing the Fourteenth Amendment, the Supreme Court struck down a Nebraska law outlawing the teaching of the German language.

1925   *Pierce v. Society of Sisters*, 268 U.S. 510. The Supreme Court struck down an Oregon compulsory public school attendance law.

Gitlow v. New York, 268 U.S. 652. In sustaining a New York criminal anarchy statute, the Supreme Court ruled that the free-speech clause of the First Amendment applies to state government action.

State of Tennessee v. John T. Scopes, 289 SW 363. Despite the courtroom heroics of defense attorney Clarence Darrow, a jury in Dayton, Tennessee found John T. Scopes guilty of violating the Butler Act, which prohibited the teaching of Darwinian theory in the public schools of Tennessee. The state supreme court reversed Scopes's conviction on a technicality, but upheld the constitutionality of the Butler Act.

1927   *Nixon v. Herndon*, 273 U.S. 536. The Supreme Court ruled in favor of Nixon, a black man who was disqualified from voting in a Texas Democratic Party primary because of his race. The Court sustained Nixon's claim that he had been denied equal protection of the law as guaranteed by the Fourteenth Amendment.

Whitney v. California, 274 U.S. 353. Although the Supreme Court upheld the conviction of an IWW member accused of having violated a state syndicalist law, Justice Louis Brandeis's concurring opinion included a ringing defense of the principle of free speech.

1928   *Olmstead v. United States*, 277 U.S. 438. The Supreme Court exempted federal wiretaps (which did not involve forcible trespass) from the Fourth Amendment prohibition of unreasonable searches and seizures.

1931   *Stromberg v. California*, 283 U.S. 359. The Supreme Court struck down a "red flag" statute that denied freedom of expression to radical political dissenters.

Near v. Minnesota, 283 U.S. 697. In striking down a Minnesota law that allowed state officials to prohibit the publication of false charges against public officials, the Supreme Court held that "prior restraint" press censorship is unconstitutional.

1932   *Powell v. Alabama*, 287 U.S. 45. A majority of the Supreme Court held that criminal defendants in state felony cases have a Constitutional right to counsel. The defendant Ozie Powell was one of the nine Alabama "Scottsboro boys."

1933   Ratification of the Twentieth Amendment, which changed the beginning and ending dates of Presidential, Vice Presidential, Senatorial, and Congressional terms, and reorganized the process of succession in the event of a President's death.

Ratification of the Twenty-First Amendment, which repealed the Eighteenth (National Prohibition) Amendment.

1935   *Norris v. Alabama*, 294 U.S. 587. In a second landmark decision involving the Scottsboro case, the Supreme Court, citing the equal protection clause of the Fourteenth Amendment, overturned the conviction of Clarence Norris by a state court system that systematically excluded black jurors.

Grovey v. Townsend, 295 U.S. 45. Ruling that the Fifteenth Amendment did not apply to the procedures of the Texas Democratic Party, the Supreme Court upheld the constitutionality of the white primary system. By privatizing the party primary, Texas Democrats avoided the state action problem cited in *Nixon v. Herndon* (1927) and *Nixon v. Condon* (1932).

Grosjean v. American Press Co., 297 U.S. 233. In a case involving nine Louisiana newspaper publishers, the Supreme Court ruled that a state license tax on newspaper advertisement revenues represented an unconstitutional infringement of the First and Fourteenth Amendments.

1936   *Brown v. Mississippi*, 297 U.S. 278. A unanimous Supreme Court held that a coerced confession was inadmissible as evidence in a state court because it violated the due process clause of the Fourteenth Amendment. Speaking for the Court, Chief Justice Charles Evans Hughes declared: ''The rack and torture chamber may not be substituted for the witness stand.''

1937   *De Jonge v. Oregon*, 299 U.S. 353. The Supreme Court upheld the right of the Communist Party to sponsor a meeting in which ''neither criminal syndicalism nor any unlawful conduct was taught or advocated.'' The Oregon Criminal Syndicalism Law outlawed sponsorship by any organization known to advocate the violent overthrow of the government.

Palko v. Connecticut, 302 U.S. 319. Upholding a state law that allowed a second trial in criminal cases, the Supreme Court ruled that the incorporation of federal trial rights in state law via the Fourteenth Amendment is appropriate but must be handled on a case-by-case basis. In *Palko* the Court held that the federal protection against double jeopardy does not extend to state courts.

1938   The House of Representatives created a Special Committee on Un-American Activities, under the chairmanship of Texas congressman Martin Dies.

United States v. Carolene Products Company, 304 U.S. 144. In upholding a 1923 federal ban on interstate shipments of adulterated milk, the Supreme Court offered a new doctrine of judicial restraint. Footnote #4 of Justice Harlan Fiske Stone's opinion presented a set of legislative categories designed to help the Court decide when judicial review was in order.

1939   *United States v. Miller*, 59 S.C.R. 816. The Supreme Court unanimously upheld the constitutionality of the National Firearms Act of 1934, which restricted the use of concealed weapons.

Hague v. Congress of Industrial Organizations, 307 U.S. 496. The Supreme Court invalidated a Jersey City, New Jersey ordinance designed to inhabit the activities of organized labor. The defendant in the case was the infamous city boss, Mayor Frank "I am the law" Hague.

1940   *Chambers v. Florida*, 309 U.S. 227. Citing the due process clause of the Fourteenth Amendment, the Supreme Court overturned a conviction based on a forced confession.

Thornhill v. Alabama, 310 U.S. 68. The Supreme Court struck down a sweeping anti-picketing statute.

Cantwell v. Connecticut, 310 U.S. 296. In a case involving the solicitation rights of Jehovah's Witnesses, the Supreme Court invalidated a Connecticut antisolicitation statute that inhibited the free exercise of religion. The Court declared that the free exercise clause of the First Amendment applied to state law through the due process clause of the Fourteenth Amendment, and that the First Amendment protected religious actions as well as religious beliefs.

Minersville School District v. Gobitis, 310 U.S. 586. With one dissenting vote, the Supreme Court upheld a state law requiring a daily flag salute in public schools. Gobitis, a Jehovah's Witness, claimed that the compulsory salute violated his religious beliefs.

Congress passed the Alien Registration Act, commonly known as the Smith Act. The act was used to prosecute members of the Communist Party of the United States, most notably in *Dennis v. United States* (1951); it required aliens living in the United States to register with the government, report annually, submit to fingerprinting, and carry identification cards. The act also provided for deportation of aliens linked to "subversive organizations."

1941   *United States v. Classic*, 313 U.S. 299. In a significant departure from *Grovey v. Townsend* (1935), the Supreme Court held that the electoral practices of the Louisiana Democratic Party constituted state action.

Chaplinsky v. New Hampshire, 315 U.S. 568. Using the logic of the clear and present danger doctrine, the Supreme Court endorsed a "fighting words" exception to the First Amendment's guaranty of free expression.

1943   *McNabb v. United States*, 318 U.S. 332. The Supreme Court ruled that a statement obtained from a suspect detained illegally or unnecessarily by federal officers was inadmissible as evidence in federal court. Clarified in the 1957 *Mallory v. United States* decision, the Court's dictum was later known as the "McNabb-Mallory Rule."

West Virginia State Board of Education v. Barnette, 319 U.S. 624. Reversing its 1940 *Gobitis* decision, the Supreme Court struck down a compulsory flag salute statute.

1944   *Hirabayashi v. United States*, 320 U.S. 81. Despite the due process clause of the Fifth Amendment, the Supreme Court upheld the wartime internment of Japanese-Americans.

Smith v. Allwright, 321 U.S. 649. Overruling *Grovey v. Townsend* (1935), the Supreme Court held that the Texas white primary system violated the Fifteenth Amendment.

Korematsu v. United States, 323 U.S. 214. The Supreme Court reaffirmed the 1943 Hirabayashi decision.

Thomas v. Collins, 323 U.S. 516. Abandoning the traditional presumption of constitutionality, the Supreme Court ruled that a Texas antilabor statute violated the free speech clause of the First Amendment.

1947   *Everson v. Board of Education*, 330 U.S. 1. While upholding the principle of separation of church and state, the Supreme Court refused to prohibit the use of public taxpayer-supported transportation by parochial school students.

Adamson v. California, 332 U.S. 46. A divided Supreme Court rejected Justice Hugo Black's argument that the due process clause of the Fourteenth Amendment requires the total incorporation of the Bill of Rights.

President Harry Truman established a federal Loyalty Program by issuing Executive Order 9835. The program mandated investigations of federal government employees, and of applicants for federal employment.

1948 *McCollum v. Board of Education*, 333 U.S. 203. The Supreme Court disallowed an Illinois public school program that gave students "released time" for religious instruction on school grounds.

Shelley v. Kraemer, 334 U.S. 1. The Supreme Court prohibited judicial enforcement of restrictive residential covenants, ruling that state involvement in such covenants violates the Fourteenth Amendment.

The Universal Declaration of Human Rights was adopted by the General Assembly of the United Nations.

1949 *Wolf v. Colorado*, 338 U.S. 25. The Supreme Court held that the Fourth Amendment's basic protection against unreasonable searches applied to state law through the Fourteenth Amendment, but that the enforcement corollary of the Fourth Amendment, the "exclusionary rule," did not. This doctrine of partial incorporation was overruled in *Mapp v. Ohio* (1961).

1950 *United States v. Rabinowitz*, 339 U.S. 56. The Supreme Court upheld the constitutionality of a warrantless search that covers "all parts of the premises" and that results in the seizure of property.

Cassell v. Texas, 339 U.S. 282. The Supreme Court struck down a jury selection system that effectively excluded black jurors even though blacks appeared on lists of potential jurors.

American Communications Association v. Douds, 339 U.S. 382. Sustaining a provision of the Taft-Hartley Act, the Supreme Court held that the federal government could withhold National Labor Relations Board services from unions with Communist officers.

Sweatt v. Painter, 339 U.S. 629. The Supreme Court ordered the desegregation of the University of Texas School of Law, even though the state had recently established a segregated law school for blacks.

The Internal Security Act (McCarran Act), passed over President Harry Truman's veto, established a Subversive Activities Control Board and registration requirements for American Communists, and provided for the detention of Communists in the event of a national emergency.

1951   *Dennis v. United States*, 341 U.S. 494. With Justices Hugo Black and William O. Douglas dissenting, the Supreme Court upheld the Smith Act conviction of eleven Communist Party leaders. ACLU director Roger Baldwin called the decision "the worst single blow to civil liberties in all our history."

Ratification of the Twenty-Second Amendment, which limits American Presidents to two terms in office.

1952   *Adler v. Board of Education of City of New York*, 342 U.S. 485. The Supreme Court upheld a state law barring members of "subversive" organizations from public employment. The decision was later overruled in *Keyishian v. Board of Regents* (1967).

Carlson v. Landon, 342 U.S. 524. By a vote of 5–4, the Supreme Court upheld a lower court ruling that sanctioned the incarceration of (and denied bail to) five "Communist" aliens awaiting a deportation decision, even though none of the five had been charged with a crime.

Beauharnais v. Illinois, 343 U.S. 250. By a vote of 5–4, the Supreme Court upheld an Illinois group-libel law prohibiting publications that depict certain religious or racial groups as depraved or virtueless. The decision was effectively nullified by *New York Times v. Sullivan* (1964).

Zorach v. Clauson, 343 U.S. 306. The Supreme Court upheld the constitutionality of a New York City "released time" program which allowed public school students to attend religious courses funded by a religious body and held outside the public school building.

Burstyn v. Wilson, 343 U.S. 495. The Supreme Court ruled that a film cannot be censored because it is allegedly "sacrilegious." Overruling *Mutual Film Corp v. Industrial Commission* (1915), the Court held that motion pictures are "included within the free speech and free press guaranty of the First and Fourteenth Amendments."

The Immigration and Nationality Act (McCarran-Walter Act) reinstituted a strict quota system designed to control immigration levels.

1953   Earl Warren became Chief Justice of the U.S. Supreme Court.

1954   *Brown v. Board of Education of Topeka, Kansas,* I, 347 U.S. 483. Citing the equal protection clause of the Fourteenth Amendment, the Supreme Court unanimously overturned the "separate but equal" doctrine established in *Plessy v. Ferguson* (1896). The Court ruled that "separate educational facilities are inherently unequal."

The Communist Control Act relieved the Communist Party of the United States of its "privileges and immunities," placing it under the jurisdiction of the Internal Security Act. This all but outlawed membership in the party.

1955   *Brown v. Board of Education of Topeka, Kansas,* II, 349 U.S. 294. In the school desegregation implementation decision, the Supreme Court called for desegregation "with all deliberate speed."

1956   *Ullmann v. United States,* 350 U.S. 422. The Supreme Court ruled that the Fifth Amendment's protection against self-incrimination applies to the innocent as well as the guilty. However, the Court sustained the power of the Immunity Act of 1954 to compel testimony.

Pennsylvania v. Nelson, 350 U.S. 497. The Supreme Court invalidated all state sedition laws. According to the Court, only the federal government possessed the sovereignty necessary for constitutional prosecution of sedition.

1957   *Schware v. Board of Bar Examiners,* 353 U.S. 232. The Supreme Court held that an attorney could not be barred from practicing law because he or she had been a member of the Communist Party.

Jencks v. United States, 353 U.S. 667. In overturning the perjury conviction of labor leader Clinton E. Jencks, the Supreme Court insisted that FBI informant reports must be made available to defense counsels. Justice Thomas Clark's vigorous dissent led to the passage of the 1957 Jencks Act, which limited the defense's access to the pretrial testimony and files of government witnesses.

Watkins v. United States, 354 U.S. 178. The Supreme Court prohibited congressional investigative committees from requiring witnesses to answer questions that were not demonstrably relevant to pending or proposed legislation. Chief Justice Warren admonished the House Un-American Activities Committee for its record of using "congressional power to expose for the sake of exposure."

Sweezy v. New Hampshire, 354 U.S. 234. By a vote of 6–2, the Supreme Court ruled that a state legislative committee could not compel a university professor to answer questions about a lecture he had delivered at the University of New Hampshire. Justice Frankfurter offered a seminal discussion of academic freedom and constitutional law.

Yates v. United States, 354 U.S. 298. Amending the "clear and present danger" doctrine, the Supreme Court ruled that successful criminal prosecution for advocacy required proof that a specific future action was involved. A statement that future action is desirable is not sufficient to warrant prosecution and conviction.

Roth v. United States, 354 U.S. 476; *Alberts v. California*, 354 U.S. 476. In two companion cases, the Supreme Court ruled that obscenity is not constitutionally protected speech. Justices William O. Douglas and Hugo Black dissented in both cases.

The Civil Rights Act of 1957 created the Civil Rights Commission (limiting its powers to investigation and reportage) and the Civil Rights Division of the Department of Justice; it also made it unlawful to harass citizens exercising their voting rights in federal elections.

1958   *NAACP v. Alabama*, 357 U.S. 449. The Supreme Court ruled that the State of Alabama could not legally compel the NAACP to divulge the names of its members. The incorporation of the First Amendment through the due process clause of the Fourteenth Amendment guaranteed NAACP members freedom of association and expression.

1959   *Frank v. Maryland*, 359 U.S. 360. In a case involving residential inspections by the Baltimore City Health Department, the Supreme Court reiterated the importance of the Fourth Amendment's protection against unreasonable searches.

Uphaus v. Wyman, 360 U.S. 72. By a vote of 5–4, the Supreme Court upheld the right of a New Hampshire legislative committee to obtain the names of participants in a summer study camp sponsored by a left-wing organization called World Fellowship. A majority of the Court ruled that the government's interest in self-preservation overruled the participants' First Amendment rights.

Barenblatt v. United States, 360 U.S. 109. With Chief Justice Earl Warren and Justices Hugo Black and William O. Douglas dissenting, the Supreme Court upheld the contempt conviction of Vassar College instructor Lloyd Barenblatt, who had refused to answer HUAC's questions about the Communist Party.

1960   The Civil Rights Act of 1960 expanded the authority of federal officials to investigate voting rights violations, instituted criminal penalties for obstruction of court orders, and provided for the prosecution of individuals crossing state lines to avoid prosecution for committing acts of violence.

1961   *Communist Party v. Subversive Activities Control Board*, 367 U.S. 1. The Supreme Court rejected the Communist Party's complaint that the Party's required "registration" (which included the submission of a list of officers and members) with the SACB violated the First and Fifth Amendments.

Scales v. United States, 367 U.S. 203. The Supreme Court upheld the Smith Act conviction of Communist Party member Junius Scales. The only American ever to be imprisoned for mere membership in the Communist Party, Scales was pardoned in 1962 after serving fourteen months of a seven-year sentence.

Mapp v. Ohio, 367 U.S. 643. The Supreme Court ruled that the Fourth Amendment's protection against illegal search and seizure is extended to the states through the Fourteenth Amendment. The "exclusionary rule" applies to all court proceedings—federal, state, and local.

Hoyt v. Florida, 368 U.S. 57. The Supreme Court upheld the conviction of a Florida woman even though she was convicted in a county court system that effectively excluded women jurors.

Ratification of the Twenty-Third Amendment, which gives the District of Columbia representation in the Electoral College.

1962   *Baker v. Carr*, 369 U.S. 186. Invalidating Georgia's county-unit system, which discriminated against urban voters, the Supreme Court affirmed the "one man, one vote" principle.

Engel v. Vitale, 370 U.S. 421. The Supreme Court held that compulsory school prayer violated the First Amendment.

1963   *Bantam Books, Inc. v. Sullivan*, 372 U.S. 58. The Supreme Court voided a Rhode Island statute empowering a state commission to censor "objectionable" reading materials deemed unfit for young readers.

Gideon v. Wainright, 372 U.S. 335. The Supreme Court ruled unanimously that the equal protection clause of the Fourteenth Amendment requires state governments to provide legal counsel for indigent criminal defendants.

Douglas v. California, 372 U.S. 353. By a vote of 6–3, the Supreme Court required states to provide appellate counsel for convicted indigents.

Abington School District v. Schempp, 374 U.S. 203. The Supreme Court ruled that daily Bible reading in public schools violated the First Amendment's required separation of church and state.

Sherbert v. Verner, 374 U.S. 398. The Supreme Court ruled that a Seventh Day adventist who had refused to work on the sabbath was entitled to unemployment compensation.

1964   *New York Times v. Sullivan*, 376 U.S. 254. In a landmark decision that belatedly closed the book on the 1798 Sedition Act, the Supreme Court restricted the ability of public officials to sue members of the press for libel.

Malloy v. Hogan, 378 U.S. 1. Overturning *Twining v. New Jersey* (1908), the Supreme Court ruled that the Fifth Amendment protection against self-incrimination was an essential element of due process, and that it was incorporated into state law through the Fourteenth Amendment.

Escobedo v. Illinois, 378 U.S. 478. The Supreme Court disallowed confessions extracted from criminal defendants who have been denied prior access to legal counsel.

The Civil Rights Act of 1964 empowered the federal government to eliminate racial discrimination from American public life. The Act includes eleven Titles.

Ratification of the Twenty-Fourth Amendment, which abolished the poll tax in federal elections.

1965   *Pointer v. Texas*, 380 U.S. 400. Rejecting an alleged exception to the "hearsay rule," the Supreme Court ruled that the Sixth Amendment "right of an accused to confront the witnesses against him is a fundamental right" incorporated into state law through the Fourteenth Amendment.

        Griswold v. Connecticut, 381 U.S. 479. In striking down a state anti–birth control law, the Supreme Court declared that the "penumbras" of the Fourth, Fifth, Ninth, and Fourteenth Amendments established a constitutional right to privacy. Justice William O. Douglas wrote the Court's opinion.

        The Voting Rights Act of 1965 gave the federal government the authority to ensure the voting rights of minorities, especially in areas where racial discrimination had produced low voter turnout.

1966   *Miranda v. Arizona*, 384 U.S. 436. To ensure a criminal suspect's protection against self-incrimination, the Supreme Court ruled that the police must advise the suspect of his or her rights: the right to remain silent; the right to an attorney; etc. The "Miranda warning" subsequently became a requirement of American law enforcement.

1967   *Keyishian v. Board of Regents*, 385 U.S. 589. Rejecting the argument that access to public employment is a privilege, the Supreme Court overruled the 1952 *Adler* decision.

        In Re Gault, 387 U.S. 1. In a landmark decision involving a 15-year old "juvenile delinquent" committed to the Arizona Industrial School, the Supreme Court extended the due process requirements of the Bill of Rights to the juvenile court system.

        Katz v. United States, 389 U.S. 347. Overruling the 1928 *Olmstead* decision, the Supreme Court held that laws relating to electronic surveillance have to conform to the Fourth and Fifth Amendments' constitutional protections against unreasonable searches and self-incrimination.

        Ratification of the Twenty-Fifth Amendment, which altered the Presidential succession process by giving a President the power to nominate a Vice President whenever there is a vacancy in the office of Vice President.

1968   *Duncan v. Louisiana*, 391 U.S. 145. By a vote of 7–2, the Supreme Court held that the Sixth Amendment right to trial by jury was incorporated into state law through the Fourteenth Amendment.

United States v. O'Brien, 391 U.S. 367. By a vote of 8–1, the Supreme Court ruled that the burning of draft registration cards is not protected by the free speech clause of the First Amendment. The Court upheld a 1965 amendment to the Selective Service Act, which made it a crime to mutilate or destroy a draft card.

Board of Education v. Allen, 392 U.S. 236. The Supreme Court upheld the constitutionality of a New York program which loaned public school textbooks to parochial schools.

Jones v. Alfred H. Mayer Co., 392 U.S. 409. Citing the Thirteenth Amendment, the Supreme Court sustained the federal government's authority to prohibit private racial discrimination in housing.

Epperson v. Arkansas, 393 U.S. 97. The Supreme Court struck down a law prohibiting the teaching of evolution in the public schools of Arkansas.

Burton v. Sills, 28 ALR 3d 829. The New Jersey Supreme Court upheld the constitutionality of a 1966 state gun-control law.

Congress enacted the Omnibus Crime Control and Safe Streets Act.

The passage of the Civil Rights Act of 1968 provided new legal protections for nonviolent civil rights activists and Native Americans, harsh penalties for rioting protestors, and an open-housing law that prohibited racial discrimination in the sale, rental, financing, and advertising of real estate.

1969   *Tinker v. Des Moines Independent Community School District*, 393 U.S. 503. The Supreme Court upheld the First Amendment right of schoolchildren to wear black armbands in school as a protest against the Vietnam War.

Brandenburg v. Ohio, 395 U.S. 444. Reversing its 1927 Whitney decision, the Supreme Court held that radical political speech is protected by the First Amendment, even when that speech advocates violence. In effect, the Court accepted the "imminent harm" requirement first postulated by Justice Oliver Wendell Holmes, Jr., in his 1919 *Abrams* dissent.

Benton v. Maryland, 395 U.S. 784. Overruling the 1937 *Palko* decision, the Supreme Court extended the Fifth Amendment's protection against double jeopardy to defendants tried in state and local courts.

Albertson v. Holmes County Board of Education, 396 U.S. 19. In a belated but important footnote to the 1954 *Brown* decision, the Supreme Court held that all school boards must "terminate dual school systems at once." The era of "all deliberate speed" was over.

Warren E. Burger became Chief Justice of the U.S. Supreme Court.

1971   *Boddie v. Connecticut*, 401 U.S. 371. By a vote of 8–1, the Supreme Court held that an indigent unable to pay a $60 filing fee in a divorce case could not be denied access to a state court.

Swann v. Charlotte-Mecklenburg Board of Education, 402 U.S. 1. The Supreme Court sustained a district-wide school busing program in North Carolina.

Cohen v. California, 403 U.S. 15. The Supreme Court upheld the right of an anti-Vietnam War protester to wear a jacket sporting the slogan, "Fuck the Draft." Expressive conduct, however distasteful, was protected by the First Amendment.

Bivens v. Six Unknown Named Agents of the Federal Bureau of Narcotics, 403 U.S. 388. In a case involving an unconstitutional search, the Supreme Court sustained the doctrine of implied rights of action. Bivens could sue for damages even though no specific federal statute provided him with a cause of action.

Lemon v. Kurtzman, I, 403 U.S. 602; II, 411 U.S. 192 (1973). The Supreme Court established a three-pronged test for the resolution of established clause cases. A constitutional violation of the separation of church and state could be avoided if the action in question: (1) was non-coercive; (2) had a clear secular purpose; and (3) did not entangle church and state.

New York Times v. United States, 403 U.S. 713. Following the "no prior restraint" doctrine established in *Near v. Minnesota*, the Supreme Court, by a vote of 6–3, rejected the Nixon Administration's request for a court order banning the publication of the "Pentagon Papers."

Reed v. Reed, 404 U.S. 71. Citing the equal protection clause of the Fourteenth Amendment, the Supreme Court struck down an Idaho estate administrator statute that gave preference to men.

Ratification of the Twenty-Sixth Amendment, which lowered the voting age in federal and state elections to eighteen.

1972   *Eisenstadt v. Baird*, 405 U.S. 438. The Supreme Court struck down a Massachusetts law prohibiting the distribution of contraceptives to unmarried persons.

Argersinger v. Hamlin, 407 U.S. 25. The Supreme Court held that the constitutional right to counsel applies to all cases involving potential imprisonment.

Barker v. Wingo, 407 U.S. 514. The Supreme Court established a balancing test (involving four factors) to be used in determinations of whether or not a defendant has received a speedy trial.

Furman v. Georgia, 408 U.S. 238. The Supreme Court ruled that the administration of capital punishment was arbitrary and capricious, violating the Eighth Amendment's protection against cruel and unusual punishment. The *Furman* decision did not eliminate the death penalty, but it forced many states to redraft their death penalty statutes.

Branzburg v. Hayes, 408 U.S. 665. By a vote of 5–4, the Supreme Court rejected the claim that reporters have a First Amendment privilege not to testify before grand juries when the information sought can be obtained elsewhere or when the confidentiality of news sources is threatened.

The Equal Rights Amendment, outlawing discrimination on the basis of gender, was approved by Congress.

1973   *Roe v. Wade*, 410 U.S. 113. Citing the right to privacy established in *Griswold v. Connecticut* (1965), the Supreme Court affirmed a woman's right to terminate pregnancy during the first trimester. Speaking for the Court, Justice Harry Blackmun invalidated a Texas law banning abortions except when the mother's life is in danger.

San Antonio Independent School District v. Rodriguez, 411 U.S. 1. The Supreme Court upheld a Texas law that based public school financing on local property taxes and other local taxes. Rodriguez contended that the law discriminated against poorer districts, which often had a large proportion of minority students.

Frontiero v. Richardson, 411 U.S. 677. In sustaining a claim of sex discrimination, the Supreme Court cited the due process clause of the Fifth Amendment and ruled that gender is a suspect classification.

Miller v. California, 413 U.S. 15. The Supreme Court established "contemporary community standards" as the legal standard in obscenity cases.

Paris Adult Theatre I v. Slaton, 413 U.S. 49. In a companion case to *Miller v. California*, the Supreme Court upheld the restriction of public exhibitions of obscenity, if the standards in *Miller* were met.

1974   *DeFunis v. Odegaard*, 416 U.S. 312. In a case involving a challenge to the affirmative-action admissions program of the University of Washington Law School, the Supreme Court ruled that the case was moot due to DeFunis's impending graduation from the school.

Kahn V. Shevan, 416 U.S. 351. The Supreme Court upheld a Florida statute granting widows, but not widowers, a $500 annual property tax exemption.

Geduldig v. Aiello, 417 U.S. 484. The Supreme Court upheld a state disability income protection program that excluded pregnancy benefits. Despite the equal protection clause of the Fourteenth Amendment, the Court rejected the claim that women have the right to collect disability pay for work absences caused by pregnancy.

1975   Congress passed the Age Discrimination Act (Title III of the Older Americans Amendments), and the Developmentally Disabled and Bill of Rights Act.

1976   *Buckley v. Valeo*, 424 U.S. 1. The Supreme Court struck down all limits on campaign expenditures of political candidates.

Massachusetts Board of Retirement v. Murgia, 427 U.S. 307. The Supreme Court upheld a Massachusetts law requiring uniformed state police officers to retire at the age of fifty. Despite the equal protection clause of the Fourteenth Amendment, the Court ruled that not all forms of age classification are ''suspect.''

Nebraska Press Association v. Stuart, 427 U.S. 539. The Supreme Court upheld a court order barring news reporters from a Nebraska courtroom, but made it clear that in future cases specific threats to a fair trial would have to be present before reporters could be legally barred.

Planned Parenthood of Central Missouri v. Danforth, 428 U.S. 52. In a series of split votes, the Supreme Court clarified its position on state laws regulating abortion. By a vote of 6–3, the Court disallowed a requirement that a woman's husband must give his consent before she can receive a legal abortion. By a vote of 5–4, the Court invalidated a parental-consent requirement for unmarried women under the age of eighteen.

Gregg v. Georgia, 428 U.S. 153. In *Gregg* and five companion cases, the Supreme Court upheld some state death penalty statutes and struck down others. But, in its most important judgment, the Court ruled that the death penalty *per se* is not cruel and unusual punishment. Justices William Brennan and Thurgood Marshall dissented.

Craig v. Boren, 429 U.S. 190. The Supreme Court struck down an Oklahoma law that allowed women to buy beer at the age of eighteen but did not give the same privilege to men, who had to be twenty-one. This case set the standard of review for sex discrimination cases.

1977   *Arlington Heights v. Metropolitan Housing Development Corporation*, 429 U.S. 252. The Supreme Court upheld the right of community zoning to limit multiple-family dwellings, even when such zoning results in racial discrimination.

Bounds v. Smith, 430 U.S. 817. Citing the Fourteenth Amendment, the Supreme Court ruled that prison inmates have a constitutional right to enjoy access to legal research facilities. In this case, the Court asserted a ''fundamental constitutional right of access to the courts.''

Carey v. Population Services International, 431 U.S. 678. By a vote of 7–2, the Supreme Court struck down three New York statutes that restricted the sale and advertisement of contraceptives.

1978   *First National Bank of Boston v. Bellotti*, 435 U.S. 765. The Supreme Court held that a corporation's right to influence elections by making campaign contributions cannot be restricted by state statutes.

Regents of the University of California v. Bakke, 438 U.S. 265. Citing the equal protection clause of the Fourteenth Amendment, the Supreme Court struck down an affirmative action/racial quota admissions program at the medical school of the University of California at Davis.

1979   *Personnel Administrator of Massachusetts v. Feeney*, 442 U.S. 256. The Supreme Court sustained a state civil service employment law that gave absolute preference to military veterans, even though the Court acknowledged that the law inadvertently discriminated against women.

Gannett Co., Inc. v. DePasquale, 443 U.S. 368. By a vote of 5–4, the Supreme Court upheld a court order closing a courtroom to the press and public during a pretrial hearing. A majority of the Court rejected the argument that the Sixth Amendment gives the public a guaranteed constitutional right to attend criminal trials.

1980   *Harris v. McRae*, 448 U.S. 297. By a vote of 5–4, the Supreme Court upheld the constitutionality of the Hyde Amendment, which prohibited federally funded abortions.

Fullilove v. Klutznick, 448 U.S. 448. By a vote of 6–3, the Supreme Court upheld the constitutionality of a federal public works statute requiring a 10 percent "set aside" for "minority business enterprises." In certain circumstances, the Court ruled, the federal government can impose racial quotas to ameliorate past discrimination.

Richmond Newspapers, Inc. v. Virginia, 448 U.S. 555. Clarifying and revising the constitutional questions raised in the 1979 *Gannett* case, the Supreme Court, by a vote of 7–1, acknowledged a limited constitutional right of public and press access to criminal trials.

1982   *Quilici v. Morton Grove*, 695 Federal Reports 2d 261. The Seventh Circuit Court of Appeals rejected the argument that the

Second Amendment applies to state governments, reaffirming *Presser v. Illinois* (1886).

Plyer v. Doe, 457 U.S. 202. Citing the equal protection clause of the Fourteenth Amendment, the Supreme Court ruled that illegal or undocumented aliens could not be excluded from the public schools of Texas.

The period (extended) for ratification of the Equal Rights Amendment expired.

Congress approved the renewal of the 1965 Voting Rights Act. The Act was renewed previously in 1970 and 1975.

1983   *Bob Jones University v. United States*, 461 U.S. 574. By a vote of 8–1, the Supreme Court sustained the right of the Internal Revenue Service to deny a federal tax exemption to a racially discriminatory private educational institution.

Marsh v. Chambers, 463 U.S. 783. The Supreme Court upheld the practice of initiating legislative sessions with a chaplain's prayer.

Lynch v. Donnelly, 465 U.S. 668. By a vote of 5–4, the Supreme Court ruled that the placement of a crèche in a public park does not violate the establishment clause of the First Amendment.

1984   *New York v. Quarles*, 467 U.S. 649. The Supreme Court approved a "public safety" exception to the Miranda warning requirement. Police officers have the right to ask questions about the location of a weapon before they inform the suspect about the right to remain silent.

United States v. Leon, 104 S. Ct. 3405. The Supreme Court established the "good faith exception" to the exclusionary rule. Evidence obtained in a reasonable search conducted in "good faith" was ruled admissible, even if the probable cause basis of the search warrant proved to be unfounded.

American Booksellers Association v. Hudnut, 598 F. Supp. 1316. U.S. District Judge Sarah Barker struck down an Indianapolis anti-pornography ordinance as an unconstitutional infringement of the First Amendment.

1985   *Tennessee v. Garner*, 471 U.S. 1. Citing the Fourth Amendment's protection against unreasonable search and seizure, the

Supreme Court invalidated a Tennessee law that sanctioned the use of deadly force against unarmed "fleeing felons."

Wallace v. Jaffree, 472 U.S. 38. The Supreme Court refused to allow the practice of requiring a voluntary moment of silent prayer in public schools.

Aguilar v. Felton, 105 S. Ct. 3232 and *Grand Rapids School District v. Ball*, 102 S. Ct. 3216. By a vote of 5–4, the Supreme Court disallowed the use of public school teachers in parochial schools. In these companion cases, the Court found "excessive entanglement of church and state."

1986   *Meritor Savings Bank v. Vinson*, 477 U.S. 57. The Supreme Court ruled that Title VII of the 1964 Civil Rights Act provides constitutional protection against sexual harassment in the workplace.

Ansonia Board of Education v. Philbrook, 479 U.S. 60. The Supreme Court ruled that public school systems do not have to provide employees with a paid leave when the employees observe religious holidays.

Colorado v. Connelly, 479 U.S. 157. Weakening the requirements of the *Miranda* rule, the Supreme Court held that confessions prompted by nonviolent subterfuge could be classified as "voluntary" (and thus admissible) confessions.

William H. Rehnquist became Chief Justice of the U.S. Supreme Court.

1987   *Hobbie v. Unemployment Appeals Commission of Florida*, 480 U.S. 136. Reaffirming its earlier ruling in the 1963 *Sherbert* case, the Supreme Court held that employees who refuse to work on the sabbath cannot be denied unemployment compensation.

Tison v. Arizona, 481 U.S. 137. The Supreme Court upheld the constitutionality of state statutes that imposed the death penalty on felons who were only indirectly involved in a capital crime. Accessories to murder could be put to death, even if they had no direct participation in the murder.

McCleskey v. Kemp, 481 U.S. 279. The Supreme Court ruled that a death row inmate attempting to set aside a death sentence could not base his appeal on an aggregate, overall pattern of racial bias. Instead, each defendant would be required to prove that racial bias had influenced his particular case.

Edwards v. Aguillard, 482 U.S. 578. The Supreme Court invalidated a state law requiring the teaching of "creation science" in public schools. The Court held that the law violated the establishment clause of the First Amendment.

1988   *Hazelwood School District v. Kuhlmeir*, 483 U.S. 299. The Supreme Court ruled that a high school principal had the right to remove "objectionable" stories from a school-sponsored student newspaper.

1989   *Texas v. Johnson*, 109 S. Ct. 2533. By a vote of 5–4, the Supreme Court struck down a state law prohibiting the burning of the American flag.

National Treasury Employees Union v. Von Raab, 109 S. Ct. 1384. The Supreme Court ruled that a drug-testing program for customs workers must satisfy the reasonableness requirement of the Fourth Amendment.

Skinner v. Railway Labor Executives Association, 109 S. Ct. 1402. Citing the government's interest in ensuring the safety of travelers, the Supreme Court upheld a Federal Railroad Administration drug-testing program.

Price Waterhouse v. Hopkins, 490 U.S. 228. The Supreme Court held that an employment decision based in part on racial or sexual prejudice does not violate Title VII of the 1964 Civil Rights Act if the employer can prove that the same decision could be justified on nondiscriminatory grounds.

Lorance v. AT&T Technologies, 490 U.S. 900. By a vote of 5–3, the Supreme Court altered the burden-of-proof formula in some discrimination cases, making it more difficult for plaintiffs to prove that employee seniority systems promote racial or sexual discrimination.

Patterson v. McLean Credit Union, 491 U.S. 164. By a vote of 5–4, the Supreme Court denied relief to a black woman who was refused promotion after being subjected to racial harassment. To gain promotion she was required to prove that she was better qualified than her competitors.

Webster v. Reproductive Health Services, 109 S. Ct. 3040. The Supreme Court upheld the constitutionality of a Missouri statute that prohibited the use of public funds and public facilities for abortions.

Court of Allegheny v. ACLU of Greater Pittsburgh Chapter, 109 S. Ct. 3086. Sustaining its decision in *Lynch v. Donnelly* (1983), the Supreme Court upheld the constitutionality of Christian nativity scenes in public parks.

Martin v. Wilks, 110 S. Ct. 11. In a case pitting black firefighters against the city government of Birmingham, Alabama, the Supreme Court declared that individual plaintiffs and third-party unions can challenge the advisability of an affirmative action consent decree, a decision that drew criticism from several national civil rights organizations.

Wards Cove Packing Company, Inc. v. Atonio, 110 S. Ct. 38. The Supreme Court rejected the claims of nonwhite salmon processing workers that the perpetuation of a racially stratified workforce violated Title VII of the 1964 Civil Rights Act.

1990   *University of Pennsylvania v. Equal Employment Opportunity Commission*, 110 S. Ct. 577. The Supreme Court ruled that universities possess no special privilege against disclosure of faculty peer review materials to a public agency investigating a tenure decision. The lawyers for the University of Pennsylvania argued unsuccessfully that this privilege is grounded in common law and the tradition of academic freedom.

James v. Illinois, 110 S. Ct. 648. Clarifying the exclusionary rule, the Supreme Court disallowed the use of evidence obtained in violation of the Fourth Amendment when that evidence is used to discredit the testimony of defense witnesses other than the defendant.

Blystone v. Pennsylvania, 110 S. Ct. 1078. The Supreme Court sustained a state death-penalty statute that requires juries to impose the death sentence if the jury unanimously concludes that the capital crime under review involved at least one aggravating circumstance and no mitigating circumstances.

Butterworth v. Smith, 110 S. Ct. 1376. Citing the First Amendment, the Supreme Court invalidated a Florida law that prohibited grand jury witnesses from making their testimony public after the grand jury's dissolution.

Austin v. Michigan Chamber of Commerce, 110 S. Ct. 1391. The Supreme Court upheld the constitutionality of a state law prohibiting corporations, including non-profit corporations, from using general corporate treasury funds for political campaign contributions.

Osborne v. Ohio, 110 S. Ct. 1691. The Supreme Court upheld the constitutionality of a state statute that makes it a criminal offense to possess or view child pornography in one's home.

Horton v. California, 110 S. Ct. 2301. The Supreme Court ruled that the "plain view" exception to the warrant requirement of the Fourth Amendment can be applied even when the discovery of evidence or contraband is not inadvertent.

Board of Education of Westside Community Schools v. Mergens, 110 S. Ct. 2356. Clarifying the restriction imposed by the Equal Access Act, the Supreme Court ruled that allowing Bible study groups to hold meetings in federally assisted public schools does not violate the establishment clause of the First Amendment.

United States v. Eichman, 110 S. Ct. 2404. By a vote of 5–4, the Supreme Court reaffirmed its decision in *Texas v. Johnson*, i.e., flag burning is constitutionally protected expression.

Employment Division, Department of Human Resources of Oregon v. Smith, 110 S. Ct. 2605. In a case involving the free exercise clause of the First Amendment, the Supreme Court upheld the constitutionality of an Oregon law prohibiting the use of peyote, even when the usage is religiously motivated.

Milkovich v. Lorain Journal, 110 S. Ct. 2695. The Supreme Court ruled that columnists can be held accountable for libelous opinions if the column in question involves "implied" factual situations.

Cruzan v. Director, Missouri Department of Health, 110 S. Ct. 2841. In an important "right to die" case, the Supreme Court affirmed a patient's right to refuse life-sustaining medical treatment. But the Court also held that a state may insist that the patient's wishes be confirmed by "clear and convincing" evidence: in the absence of such evidence, the Court ruled, the state can prevent a family from acting on the patient's behalf.

Hodgson v. Minnesota, 110 S. Ct. 2926. The Supreme Court upheld the overall constitutionality of a Minnesota abortion law, but struck down a provision requiring notification of both parents when a minor is involved.

Ohio v. Akron Center for Reproductive Health, 110 S. Ct. 2972. The Supreme Court upheld an Ohio abortion law that places parental notice and other restrictions on unmarried women under the age of eighteen seeking abortions.

Maryland v. Craig, 110 S. Ct. 3157. The Supreme Court ruled that in cases involving child abuse the Sixth Amendment's requirement of a face-to-face confrontation between witness and defendant can be waived, but only after it is established that such a confrontation would inflict substantial emotional trauma on a child witness.

Metro Broadcasting, Inc., v. Federal Communications Commission, 111 S. Ct. 15. The Supreme Court upheld the constitutionality of the FCC's practice of giving special consideration to minorities when awarding new broadcast licenses.

Minnick v. Mississippi, 111 S. Ct. 486. The Supreme Court held that after a criminal suspect in custody invokes his Fifth Amendment right to counsel, authorities cannot legally reinitiate questioning in the absence of counsel.

President George Bush vetoed the 1990 Civil Rights Act.

1991 *Board of Education of Oklahoma City Public Schools v. Dowell*, 111 S. Ct. 630. The Supreme Court ruled that a school desegregation order can be terminated if school district officials have made a sustained "good faith" effort to eliminate the effects of de jure segregation.

International Union, United Automobile, Aerospace and Agricultural Implement Workers of America, United Auto Workers v. Johnson Controls Inc., 111 S. Ct. 1196. The Supreme Court invalidated an employer's fetal protection plan that barred fertile female employees from jobs involving exposure to lead. The Court held that the plan discriminated against women on the basis of gender.

Arizona v. Fulminante, 111 S. Ct. 1246. The Supreme Court ruled that under certain circumstances police-coerced confessions may be considered "harmless error" and thus admissible as evidence.

McCleskey v. Zant, 111 S. Ct. 1454. The Supreme Court ruled that the government can place certain limitations on the filing of habeas corpus petitions by state prisoners.

Rust v. Sullivan, 111 S. Ct. 1759. By a vote of 5–4, the Supreme Court upheld a federal regulation prohibiting employees of federally-funded family-planning clinics from providing patients with abortion counseling.

Barnes v. Glen Theatre, Inc., 59 U.S.L.W. 4745. Upholding a South Bend, Indiana, indecent exposure ordinance, the Supreme Court, by a vote of 5–4, rejected the argument that nude dancing in bars is protected by the First Amendment.

Payne v. Tennessee, 59 U.S.L.W. 4814. By a vote of 6–3, the Supreme Court ruled that at sentencing hearings in capital cases prosecutors have the right to introduce testimony on the victim's character and on the effect of the crime on surviving family members and friends.

About the Editor
and Contributors

Raymond Arsenault is Professor of History at the University of South Florida, St. Petersburg. He is the author of *The Wild Ass of the Ozarks: Jeff Davis and the Social Bases of Southern Politics* (1984); *St. Petersburg and the Florida Dream, 1888–1950* (1988); and "The End of the Long Hot Summer: The Air Conditioner and Southern Culture," in Raymond A. Mohl, ed., *Searching for the Sunbelt: Historical Perspectives on a Region* (1990).

David J. Bodenhamer is Professor of History and Director of POLIS at Indiana University at Indianapolis. He is the author of *The Pursuit of Justice: Crime and Law in Antebellum Indiana* (1986); *Fair Trial: Rights of the Accused in American History* (1991); and "Trial Rights of the Accused," in Kermit L. Hall, ed., *By and For the People: Constitutional Rights in American History* (1991).

James W. Carey is Dean of the College of Communications at the University of Illinois, Urbana-Champaign. He is the editor of *Media, Myth and Narratives: Television and the Press* (1988); and the author of *Communication as Culture: Essays on Media and Society* (1989).

John Hope Franklin is James B. Duke Professor Emeritus of History and Law at Duke University. His publications include *The Militant South, 1800–1861* (1956); *From Slavery to Freedom* (sixth edition, co-authored by Alfred A. Moss, 1988); and *Race and History* (1990).

Kermit L. Hall is Professor of History and Law at the University of Florida. He is the author of *The Magic Mirror: Law in American History*

(1989); the editor of *By and For the People: Constitutional Rights in American History* (1991); and the co-editor, with William Wiecek, of *A History of American Legal Culture* (1991).

Paul L. Murphy is Regents Professor of History at the University of Minnesota. He is the author of *The Constitution in Crisis Times, 1918– 1969* (1972); *The Meaning of Free Speech: First Amendment Freedoms from Wilson to Roosevelt* (1972); and *The Shaping of the First Amendment* (1991).

Samuel Walker is Professor of Criminal Justice at the University of Nebraska, Omaha. He is the author of *A Critical History of Police Reform* (1977); *Popular Justice: A History of American Criminal Justice* (1980); and *In Defense of American Liberties: A History of the ACLU* (1990).

Stephen J. Whitfield is Max Richter Professor of American Civilization at Brandeis University. He is the author of *Into the Dark: Hannah Arendt and Totalitarianism* (1980); *A Death in the Delta: The Story of Emmett Till* (1988); and *The Culture of the Cold War* (1990).

Selected Bibliography and Suggested Reading

1: The Crucible of Liberty

Alderman, Ellen, and Caroline Kennedy. *In Our Interest: The Bill of Rights in Action.* New York: William Morrow, 1991.

Barnette, Randy, ed. *The Rights Retained by the People: The History and Meaning of the Ninth Amendment.* Lanham, Md.: University Press of America, 1989.

Calvert, Robert E., ed. *"The Constitution of the People": Reflections on Citizens and Civil Society.* Lawrence: University of Kansas Press, 1991.

Cox, Archibald. *The Court and the Constitution.* Boston: Houghton Mifflin, 1987.

Currie, David P. *The Constitution in the Supreme Court: The Second Century, 1888–1986.* Chicago: University of Chicago Press, 1991.

Cushman, Robert E. *Civil Liberties in the United States.* Ithaca: Cornell University Press, 1956.

Douglas, William O. *A Living Bill of Rights.* New York: Doubleday, 1961.

Dumbauld, Edward. *The Bill of Rights and What It Means Today.* Norman: University of Oklahoma Press, 1957.

Glendon, Mary Ann. *Rights Talk: The Impoverishment of Political Disclosure.* New York: Free Press, 1991.

Grossman, Joel B. "Teaching Civil Liberties in the Bicentennial Year." *Focus on Law Studies* (American Bar Association) VI (Spring 1991): 1, 9.

Hall, Kermit L., ed. *By and For the People: Constitutional Rights in American History.* Arlington Heights, Ill.: Harlan Davidson, 1991.

Hand, Learned. *The Bill of Rights.* Cambridge: Harvard University Press, 1958.

Hickock, Eugene W., Jr. *The Bill of Rights: Original Meaning and Current Understanding.* Charlottesville: University of Virginia Press, 1991.

Hoffer, Peter Charles. *The Law's Conscience: Equitable Constitutionalism in America*. Chapel Hill: University of North Carolina Press, 1990.

Hutson, James H. "A Nauseous Project." *Wilson Quarterly* XV (Winter 1991): 57–70.

Kammen, Michael. *A Machine That Would Go of Itself: The Constitution in American Culture*. New York: Knopf, 1986.

———. *Sovereignty and Liberty: Constitutional Discourses in American Culture*. Madison: University of Wisconsin Press, 1988.

Kelly, Alfred H., Winfred A. Harbison, and Herman Belz. *The American Constitution: Its Origins and Development*. Seventh Edition. New York: W. W. Norton, 1991.

Levy, Leonard. *Constitutional Opinions: Aspects of the Bill of Rights*. New York: Oxford University Press, 1986.

Levy, Leonard, et al., eds. *Encyclopedia of the American Constitution*. New York: Macmillan, 1986.

McDowell, Gary L. "Rights Without Roots." *Wilson Quarterly* XV (Winter 1991): 71–79.

Melusky, Joseph A. *The Constitution: Our Written Legacy*. Melbourne, Fla.: Krieger, 1991.

Neely, Mark E., Jr. *The Fate of Liberty: Abraham Lincoln and Civil Liberties*. New York: Oxford University Press, 1991.

Ollmann, Bertell, and Jonathan Birnbaum, eds. *The U.S. Constitution: Two Hundred Years of Anti-Federalist, Abolitionist, Feminist, Muckraking, Progressive, and Especially Socialist Criticism*. New York: New York University Press, 1990.

Peters, William. *A More Perfect Union*. New York: Crown Publishers, 1987.

The Public Interest 86 (Winter 1987). A Special Issue. "The Constitutional Order 1787–1987."

Sarat, Austin, and Thomas R. Kearns, eds. *The Fate of Law*. Vol. 1 of The Amherst Series in Law, Jurisprudence, and Social Thought. Ann Arbor: University of Michigan Press, 1991.

Siegel, Fred. "Nothing in Moderation." *Atlantic Monthly* (May 1990): 108–110.

Snowiss, Sylvia. *Judicial Review and the Law of the Constitution*. New Haven: Yale University Press, 1990.

Sunstein, Cass R. *After the Rights Revolution: Reconceiving the Regulatory State*. Cambridge: Harvard University Press, 1990.

Tribe, Lawrence H. *God Save This Honorable Court: How the Choice of Supreme Court Justices Shapes Our History*. New York: Random House, 1985.

Tribe, Lawrence H., and Michael C. Dorf. *On Reading the Constitution*. Cambridge: Harvard University Press, 1991.

Urofsky, Melvyn I. *A March of Liberty: A Constitutional History of the United States.* New York: Knopf, 1988.

Veit, Helen E., Kenneth R. Bowling, and Charlene Bangs Bickford, eds. *Creating the Bill of Rights: The Documentary Record from the First Federal Congress.* Baltimore: Johns Hopkins University Press, 1991.

"We the People." *Time* (Special Edition) 130, No. 1 (July 6, 1987).

Weinberger, Andrew D. *Freedom and Protection: The Bill of Rights.* San Francisco: Chandler, 1962.

Wellington, Harry H. *Interpreting the Constitution: The Supreme Court and the Process of Adjudication.* New Haven: Yale University Press, 1991.

2: The Bill of Rights, Liberty, and Original Intent

Adams, Willi Paul. *The First American Constitutions: Republican Ideology and the Making of the State Constitutions in the Revolutionary Era.* Chapel Hill: University of North Carolina Press, 1980.

Bloom, Allan, ed. *Confronting the Constitution: The Challenge to Locke, Montesquieu, and the Federalists from Utilitarianism, Historicism, Marxism, Freudianism, Pragmatism, Existentialism . . .* Washington, D.C.: American Enterprise Institute Press, 1990.

Brant, Irving. *The Bill of Rights: Its Origin and Meanings.* Indianapolis: Bobbs-Merrill, 1965.

———. *James Madison.* 6 Vols. Indianapolis: Bobbs-Merrill, 1941–1961.

Buel, Richard, Jr. *Securing the Revolution: Ideology and American Politics, 1789–1815.* Ithaca: Cornell University Press, 1972.

Curry, Thomas J. *The First Freedoms: Church and State in America to the Passage of the First Amendment.* New York: Oxford University Press, 1986.

Hall, Kermit L. *The Magic Mirror: Law in American History.* New York: Oxford University Press, 1989.

Levy, Leonard. *Emergence of a Free Press.* New York: Oxford University Press, 1985.

———. *The Establishment Clause: Religion and the First Amendment.* New York: Macmillan, 1986.

———. *Original Intent and the Framers' Constitution.* New York: Macmillan, 1988.

Lutz, Donald S. *The Origins of American Constitutionalism.* Baton Rouge: Louisiana State University Press, 1988.

McClosky, Herbert, and Alida Brill. *Dimensions of Tolerance: What Americans Believe About Civil Liberties.* New York: Russell Sage Foundation, 1983.

McCoy, Drew R. *The Elusive Republic: Political Economy in Jeffersonian America.* Chapel Hill: University of North Carolina Press, 1980.

Mee, Charles L., Jr. *The Genius of the People*. New York: Harper and Row, 1987.

Miller, William Lee. *The First Liberty: Religion and the American Republic*. New York: Knopf, 1986.

Pfeffer, Leo. *Church, State, and Freedom*. Boston: Beacon Press, 1953.

Rakove, Jack N., ed. *Interpreting the Constitution: The Debate Over Original Intent*. Boston: Northeastern University Press, 1990.

Reid, John Phillip. *The Concept of Liberty in the Age of the American Revolution*. Chicago: University of Chicago Press, 1988.

———. *Constitutional History of the American Revolution: The Authority of Rights*. Madison: University of Wisconsin Press, 1986.

Rutland, Robert A. *The Birth of the Bill of Rights, 1776–1791*. Chapel Hill: University of North Carolina Press, 1955.

Schwartz, Bernard. *The Great Rights of Mankind: A History of the American Bill of Rights*. New York: Oxford University Press, 1977.

Schwartz, Bernard, ed. *Roots of the Bill of Rights*. 5 vols. New York: Chelsea House, 1980.

Smith, James Morton. *Freedom's Fetters: The Alien and Sedition Laws and American Civil Liberties*. Ithaca: Cornell University Press, 1956.

Wood, Gordon S. *The Creation of the American Republic, 1776–1789*. Chapel Hill: University of North Carolina Press, 1969.

3: African-Americans and the Bill of Rights

Berlin, Ira. *Slaves Without Masters: The Free Negro in the Antebellum South*. New York: Pantheon, 1974.

Berwanger, Eugene H. *The Frontier Against Slavery: Western Anti-Negro Prejudice and the Slavery Extension Controversy*. Urbana: University of Illinois Press, 1967.

Bodenhamer, David J., and James W. Ely, Jr., eds. *Ambivalent Legacy: A Legal History of the South*. Jackson: University Press of Mississippi, 1984.

Campbell, Stanley W. *The Slave Catchers: Enforcement of the Fugitive Slave Law, 1850–1860*. Chapel Hill: University of North Carolina Press, 1968.

Davis, David Brion. *The Problem of Slavery in the Age of Revolution, 1770–1823*. Ithaca: Cornell University Press, 1975.

Fehrenbacher, Don E. *The Dred Scott Case: Its Significance in American Law and Politics*. New York: Oxford University Press, 1978.

Finkelman, Paul. *An Imperfect Union: Slavery, Federalism, and Comity*. Chapel Hill: University of North Carolina Press, 1981.

———. "Slavery and the Constitutional Convention: Making a Covenant with Death." In *Beyond Confederation*, ed. Richard Beeman, 188–225. Chapel Hill: University of North Carolina Press, 1987.

Franklin, John Hope. "Slavery and the Constitution." In *Encyclopedia of the American Constitution,* ed. by Leonard Levy et al., Vol. I, 1688–1695. New York: Macmillan, 1986.

Franklin, John Hope, and Alfred A. Moss. *From Slavery to Freedom.* Sixth Edition. New York: Knopf, 1988.

Fredrickson, George M. *The Black Image in the White Mind: The Debate on Afro-American Character and Destiny, 1817–1914.* New York: Harper and Row, 1971.

Genovese, Eugene D. *Roll, Jordan, Roll: The World the Slaves Made.* New York: Pantheon, 1974.

Greenberg, Jack. *Race Relations and American Law.* New York: Columbia University Press, 1959.

Hall, Kermit L., and James W. Ely, Jr., eds. *An Uncertain Tradition: Constitutionalism and the History of the South.* Athens, Ga.: University of Georgia Press, 1989.

Harding, Vincent. *There Is a River: The Black Struggle for Freedom in America.* New York: Harcourt Brace Jovanovich, 1981.

Higginbotham, A. Leon, Jr. *In the Matter of Color: Race and the American Legal Process: The Colonial Period.* New York: Oxford University Press, 1978.

Hopkins, Vincent C. *Dred Scott's Case.* New York: Fordham University Press, 1951.

Huggins, Nathan Irvin. *Black Odyssey: The Afro-American Ordeal in Slavery.* New York: Pantheon, 1977.

Jordan, Winthrop D. *White Over Black: American Attitudes Toward the Negro, 1550–1812.* Chapel Hill: University of North Carolina Press, 1968.

Kalven, Harry, Jr. *The Negro and the First Amendment.* Columbus: Ohio State University Press, 1965.

Kluger, Richard. *Simple Justice: The History of Brown v. Board of Education and Black America's Struggle for Equality.* New York: Knopf, 1976.

Kutler, Stanley I. *The Dred Scott Decision: Law or Politics?* Boston: Houghton Mifflin, 1967.

Levy, Leonard. "Sims' Case: The Fugitive Slave Law in Boston in 1851." *Journal of Negro History* 35 (1950): 39–74.

Levy, Leonard, and Douglas L. Jones, eds. *Jim Crow in Boston: The Origin of the Separate But Equal Doctrine.* New York: Da Capo Press, 1974.

Litwack, Leon F. *North of Slavery: The Negro in the Free States, 1790–1860.* Chicago: University of Chicago Press, 1961.

Maltz, Earl M. *Civil Rights, the Constitution, and Congress, 1863–1869.* Lawrence: University of Kansas Press, 1991.

Miller, John Chester. *The Wolf by the Ears: Thomas Jefferson and Slavery*. New York: Free Press, 1977.

Nash, Gary B., and Jean R. Soderlund. *Freedom by Degrees: Emancipation and Its Aftermath in Pennsylvania*. New York: Oxford University Press, 1990.

Nieman, Donald G. *Promises to Keep: African Americans and the Constitutional Order, 1776 to the Present*. New York: Oxford University Press, 1991.

———. *To Set the Law in Motion: The Freedmen's Bureau and the Legal Rights of Blacks, 1865–1868*. Millwood, N.Y.: KTO Press, 1979.

Oakes, James. *Slavery and Freedom: An Interpretation of the Old South*. New York: Knopf, 1990.

Patterson, Orlando. *Slavery and Social Death: A Comparative Study*. Cambridge: Harvard University Press, 1982.

Pease, Jane H., and William H. *They Who Would Be Free: Blacks' Search for Freedom, 1830–1861*. Urbana: University of Illinois Press, 1974.

Robinson, Donald. *Slavery in the Structure of American Politics, 1765–1820*. New York: W. W. Norton, 1979.

Stampp, Kenneth M. *The Peculiar Institution: Slavery in the Ante-Bellum South*. New York: Random House, 1956.

Stewart, James Brewer. *Holy Warriors: The Abolitionists and American Slavery*. New York: Hill and Wang, 1976.

Takaki, Ronald. *Iron Cages: Race and Culture in 19th-Century America*. New York: Oxford University Press, 1982.

Tannenbaum, Frank. *Slave and Citizen: The Negro in the Americas*. New York: Knopf, 1946.

Voegeli, V. Jacque. *Free But Not Equal: The Midwest and the Negro During the Civil War*. Chicago: University of Chicago Press, 1967.

Watson, Alan. *Slave Law in the Americas*. Athens, Ga.: University of Georgia Press, 1989.

Wyatt-Brown, Bertram. *Southern Honor: Ethics and Behavior in the Old South*. New York: Oxford University Press, 1982.

Zilversmit, Arthur. *The First Emancipation: The Abolition of Slavery in the North*. Chicago: University of Chicago Press, 1967.

4: The Growth of Civil Liberties, 1900–1945

Chafee, Zechariah, Jr. *Free Speech in the United States*. Cambridge: Harvard University Press, 1941.

Cohen, Jeremy. *Congress Shall Make No Law: Oliver Wendell Holmes, the First Amendment, and Judicial Decision Making*. Ames: Iowa State University Press, 1989.

Daniels, Roger. *Concentration Camps USA: Japanese Americans and World War II*. New York: Holt, Rinehart and Winston, 1971.

Daniels, Roger, Sandra C. Taylor, and Harry H. L. Kitano, eds. *Japanese Americans, From Relocation to Redress.* Salt Lake City: University of Utah Press, 1986.

Friendly, Fred. *Minnesota Rag.* New York: Random House, 1981.

Ginger, Ray. *Six Days or Forever? Tennessee v. John Thomas Scopes.* Boston: Beacon Press, 1958.

Grodzins, Morton. *Americans Betrayed.* Chicago: University of Chicago Press, 1949.

Hall, Kermit L. *The Magic Mirror: Law in American History.* New York: Oxford University Press, 1989.

Hays, Arthur Garfield. *Let Freedom Ring.* Revised Edition. New York: Liveright, 1937.

Irons, Peter H. *Justice at War.* New York: Oxford University Press, 1983.

Irons, Peter H., ed. *Justice Delayed: The Record of the Japanese Internment Cases.* Middletown, Conn.: Wesleyan University Press, 1989.

Jensen, Joan M. *The Price of Vigilance.* Chicago: Rand McNally, 1968.

Johnson, Donald. *The Challenge to American Freedoms: World War I and the Rise of the American Civil Liberties Union.* Lexington: University of Kentucky Press, 1963.

Lamson, Peggy. *Roger Baldwin: Founder of the American Civil Liberties Union.* Boston: Houghton Mifflin, 1976.

Manwaring, David. *Render Unto Caesar: The Flag Salute Controversy.* Chicago: University of Chicago Press, 1962.

Marchand, Roland. *The American Peace Movement and Social Reform, 1898–1918.* Princeton: Princeton University Press, 1972.

Murphy, Paul L. *The Constitution in Crisis Times, 1918–1969.* New York: Harper and Row, 1972.

―――. *The Meaning of Freedom of Speech: First Amendment Freedoms from Wilson to Roosevelt.* Westport, Conn.: Greenwood Press, 1972.

―――. *World War I and the Origin of Civil Liberties in the United States.* New York: W. W. Norton, 1979.

Murray, Robert K. *Red Scare: A Study in National Hysteria, 1919–1920.* New York: McGraw-Hill, 1964.

Novick, Sheldon M. *Honorable Justice: The Life of Oliver Wendell Holmes.* Boston: Little, Brown and Company, 1989.

Polenberg, Richard. *Fighting Faiths: The Abrams Case, The Supreme Court, and Free Speech.* New York: Viking, 1987.

Preston, William. *Aliens and Dissenters: Federal Suppression of Radicals, 1903–1933.* New York: Harper and Row, 1966.

Pritchett, C. Herman. *The Roosevelt Court: A Study of Judicial Politics and Values, 1937–1947.* Chicago: Quadrangle Books, 1969.

Reitman, Alan, ed. *The Pulse of Freedom: American Liberties, 1920–1970s.* New York: W. W. Norton, 1975.

Smith, Donald L. *Zechariah Chafee, Jr.: Defender of Liberty and Law.* Cambridge: Harvard University Press, 1986.

ten Broek, Jacobus, et al. *Prejudice, War, and the Constitution.* Berkeley: University of California Press, 1970.

Walker, Samuel. *In Defense of American Liberties: A History of the ACLU.* New York: Oxford University Press, 1990.

5: Civil Liberties and the Culture of the Cold War

Aronson, James. *The Press and the Cold War.* Indianapolis: Bobbs-Merrill, 1970.

Bayley, Edwin R. *Joe McCarthy and the Press.* New York: Pantheon, 1982.

Belknap, Michael R. *Cold War Political Justice: The Smith Act, the Communist Party, and American Civil Liberties.* Westport, Conn.: Greenwood Press, 1977.

Bentley, Eric, ed. *Thirty Years of Treason: Excerpts from Hearings before the House Committee on Un-American Activities, 1938–1968.* New York: Viking, 1971.

Buckley, William F., Jr., and L. Brent Bozell. *McCarthy and His Enemies: The Record and Its Meaning.* New Rochelle, N.Y.: Arlington House, 1954.

Caute, David. *The Great Fear: The Anti-Communist Purge under Truman and Eisenhower.* New York: Simon & Schuster, 1978.

Ceplair, Larry, and Steven Englund. *The Inquisition in Hollywood: Politics in the Film Community, 1930–1960.* Garden City, N.Y.: Doubleday, 1980.

Fried, Richard. *Nightmare in Red: The McCarthy Era in Perspective.* New York: Oxford University Press, 1990.

Goodman, Walter. *The Committee: The Extraordinary Career of the House Committee on Un-American Activities.* New York: Farrar, Straus & Giroux, 1968.

Griffith, Robert, and Athan Theoharis, eds. *The Specter: Original Essays on the Cold War and the Origins of McCarthyism.* New York: Franklin Watts, 1974.

Griswold, Erwin. *The Fifth Amendment Today.* Cambridge: Harvard University Press, 1955.

Hook, Sidney. *Political Power and Personal Freedom: Critical Studies in Democracy, Communism, and Civil Rights.* New York: Criterion, 1959.

Kanfer, Stefan. *A Journal of the Plague Years.* New York: Atheneum, 1973.

Kempton, Murray. *America Comes of Middle Age: Columns, 1950–1962.* Boston: Little, Brown, and Company, 1963.

Konvitz, Milton R. *Expanding Liberties: The Emergence of New Civil Liberties and Civil Rights in Postwar America.* New York: Viking, 1967.

Kutler, Stanley I. *The American Inquisition: Justice and Injustice in the Cold War.* New York: Hill & Wang, 1982.

Latham, Earl. *The Communist Controversy in Washington: From the New Deal to McCarthy.* Cambridge: Harvard University Press, 1966.

Mitgang, Herbert. *Dangerous Dossiers.* New York: Donald I. Fine, 1988.

Murphy, Paul L. *The Constitution in Crisis Times, 1918–1969.* New York: Harper & Row, 1972.

Navasky, Victor S. *Naming Names.* New York: Viking, 1980.

Oshinsky, David M. *A Conspiracy So Immense: The World of Joe McCarthy.* New York: Free Press, 1983.

Powers, Richard Gid. *G-Men: Hoover's FBI in American Popular Culture.* Carbondale, Ill.: Southern Illinois University Press, 1983.

———. *Secrecy and Power: The Life of J. Edgar Hoover.* New York: Free Press, 1987.

Pritchett, C. Herman. *Civil Liberties and the Vinson Court.* Chicago: University of Chicago Press, 1954.

Radosh, Ronald, and Joyce Milton. *The Rosenberg File: A Search for the Truth.* New York: Vintage Books, 1984.

Roche, John P. *The Quest for the Dream: The Development of Civil Rights and Human Relations in Modern America.* New York: Macmillan, 1963.

Schrecker, Ellen W. *No Ivory Tower: McCarthyism and the Universities.* New York: Oxford University Press, 1966.

Shils, Edward A. *The Torment of Secrecy: The Background and Consequences of American Security Policies.* New York: Free Press, 1966.

Steinberg, Peter L. *The Great "Red" Menace: United States Prosecution of American Communists, 1947–1952.* Westport, Conn.: Greenwood Press, 1984.

Stone, I. F. *The Haunted Fifties.* New York: Vintage Books, 1969.

———. *The Truman Era.* New York: Monthly Review Press, 1953.

Theoharis, Athan, and John Stuart Cox. *The Boss: J. Edgar Hoover and the Great American Inquisition.* Philadelphia: Temple University Press, 1988.

Wechsler, James A. *The Age of Suspicion.* New York: Random House, 1953.

Weinstein, Allen. *Perjury: The Hiss-Chambers Case.* New York: Knopf, 1978.

White, G. Edward. *Earl Warren: A Public Life.* New York: Oxford University Press, 1983.

Whitfield, Stephen. *The Culture of the Cold War.* Baltimore: Johns Hopkins University Press, 1990.

Ziegler, Benjamin Munn, ed. *Communism, the Courts, and the Constitution.* Lexington, Mass.: D. C. Heath, 1964.

6: Equal Justice Under Law, 1932–1991

Allen, Frances L. *The Borderland of Criminal Justice.* Chicago: University of Chicago Press, 1964.

Baker, Liva. *Miranda: Crime, Law, and Politics.* New York: Atheneum, 1983.

Bayley, David, and Harold Mendelsohn. *Minorities and the Police.* New York: Free Press, 1969.

Bedau, Hugo. *The Courts, the Constitution, and Capital Punishment.* Lexington, Mass.: Lexington Books, 1977.

Berger, Mark. *Taking the Fifth: The Supreme Court and the Privilege against Self-Incrimination.* Lexington, Mass.: Lexington Books, 1980.

Berns, Walter. *For Capital Punishment: Crime and the Morality of the Death Penalty.* New York: Basic Books, 1979.

Black, Charles L., Jr. *Capital Punishment: The Inevitability of Caprice and Mistake.* New York: W. W. Norton, 1974.

Blasi, Vincent, ed. *The Burger Court: The Counter-Revolution That Wasn't.* New Haven: Yale University Press, 1983.

Bodenhamer, David J. *Fair Trial: Rights of the Accused in American History.* New York: Oxford University Press, 1991.

Brennan, William J., Jr. *Constitutional Adjudication and the Death Penalty: A View from the Court.* Cambridge: Harvard University Press, 1986.

Carr, James G. *The Law of Electronic Surveillance.* Revised Edition. New York: Clark Boardman, 1983.

Carter, Dan T. *Scottsboro: A Tragedy of the American South.* Baton Rouge: Louisiana State University Press, 1979.

Clark, Ramsey. *Crime in America: Observations on Its Nature, Causes, Prevention, and Control.* New York: Simon & Schuster, 1970.

Cortner, Richard C. *The Supreme Court and the Second Bill of Rights: The Fourteenth Amendment and the Nationalization of Civil Liberties.* Madison, University of Wisconsin Press, 1981.

Cox, Archibald. *The Warren Court.* Cambridge: Harvard University Press, 1968.

Davis, Sue. *Justice Rehnquist and the Constitution.* Princeton: Princeton University Press, 1989.

Fellman, David. *The Defendant: Rights Today.* Second Edition. Madison, University of Wisconsin Press, 1975.

Flaherty, David H. *Protecting Privacy in Surveillance Societies: The Federal Republic of Germany, Sweden, France, Canada, and the United States.* Chapel Hill : University of North Carolina Press, 1989.

Frankel, Marvin. *Criminal Sentences: Law Without Order.* New York: Hill and Wang, 1973.

Graham, Fred. *The Due Process Revolution: The Warren Court's Impact on Criminal Law.* New York: Hayden, 1970.

Griswold, Erwin N. *The Fifth Amendment Today.* Cambridge: Harvard University Press, 1955.

Harris, Richard. *The Fear of Crime.* New York: Praeger, 1969.

Heller, Francis Howard. *The Sixth Amendment to the Constitution of the United States: A Study in Constitutional Development.* Lawrence: University of Kansas Press, 1969.

Hook, Sidney. *Common Sense and the Fifth Amendment.* Criterion, 1957.

Kamisar, Yale. *Police Interrogations and Confessions: Essays in Law and Policy.* Ann Arbor: University of Michigan Press, 1980.

LaFave, Wayne R. *Search and Seizure: A Treatise on the Fourth Amendment.* 3 Vols. St. Paul, Minn.: West Publishing Co., 1978.

Levy, Leonard. *Against the Law: The Nixon Court and Criminal Justice.* New York: Harper & Row, 1974.

————. *Origins of the Fifth Amendment: The Right Against Self-Incrimination.* New York: Oxford University Press, 1968.

Lewis, Anthony. *Gideon's Trumpet.* New York: Random House, 1964.

Marx, Gary T. *Undercover Police Surveillance in America.* Berkeley: University of California Press, 1988.

Meltsner, Michael. *Cruel and Unusual: The Supreme Court and Capital Punishment.* New York: Random House, 1973.

Meltzer, Milton. *The Right to Remain Silent.* New York: Harcourt Brace Jovanovich, 1972.

Morgan, Richard E., and Christian P. Potholm, eds. *Focus on Police: Police in American Society.* Cambridge: Schenkman, 1976.

Oaks, Dallin H. "Studying the Exclusionary Rule." *University of Chicago Law Review* 37 (1970): 665–757.

President's Commission on Law Enforcement and Administration of Justice. *The Challenge of Crime in a Free Society.* New York: Avon, 1968.

Prettyman, Barret. *Death and the Supreme Court.* New York: Harcourt, Brace, and World, 1961.

Reiss, Albert. *The Police and the Public.* New Haven: Yale University Press, 1971.

Schwartz, Herman, ed. *The Burger Years: Rights and Wrongs in the Supreme Court, 1969–1986.* New York: Viking, 1987.

————. *Taps, Bugs, and Fooling the People.* New York: Field Foundation, 1977.

Sellin, Thorstein. *The Penalty of Death.* Beverley Hills, Cal.: Sage Publications, 1980.

Skolnick, Jerome. *Justice Without Trial.* New York: John Wiley, 1967.

Sommer, Robert. *The End of Imprisonment.* New York: Oxford University Press, 1976.

Stephens, Otis. *The Supreme Court and Confessions of Guilt.* Knoxville: University of Tennessee Press, 1973.

Stewart, Potter. "The Road to *Mapp v. Ohio* and Beyond: The Origins, Development, and Future of the Exclusionary Rule in Search-and-Seizure Cases." *Columbia Law Review* 83 (1983): 1365–1404.

Urofsky, Melvyn I. *The Continuity of Change: The Supreme Court and Individual Liberties, 1953–1986.* Belmont, Cal.: Wadsworth, 1991.

Walker, Samuel. *A Critical History of Police Reform: The Emergence of Professionalism.* Lexington, Mass.: Lexington Books, 1977.

————. *Popular Justice: A History of American Criminal Justice.* New York: Oxford University Press, 1980.

Westley, William A. *Violence and the Police: A Sociological Study of Law, Custom, and Morality.* Cambridge: MIT Press, 1970.

White, Welsh S. *The Death Penalty in the Nineties: An Examination of the Modern System of Capital Punishment.* Ann Arbor: University of Michigan Press, 1991.

7: Balancing Acts, 1965–1991

Bell, Derrick A. *And We Are Not Saved: The Elusive Quest for Racial Justice.* New York: Basic Books, 1987.

————. *Race, Racism, and American Law.* Boston: Little, Brown and Company, 1973.

Berry, Mary F. *Why the ERA Failed: Politics, Women's Rights, and the Amending Powers of the Constitution.* Bloomington: Indiana University Press, 1986.

Block, W. E., and M. A. Walker, eds. *Discrimination, Affirmative Action, and Equal Opportunity: An Economic and Social Perspective.* Vancouver, B.C.: Fraser Institute, 1982.

Bork, Robert H. *The Tempting of America: The Political Seduction of the Law.* New York: Free Press, 1990.

Bronner, Ethan. *Battle for Justice: How the Bork Nomination Shook America.* New York: W. W. Norton, 1989.

"The Civil Rights Act of 1990." *Congressional Digest* 69 (August–September 1990): 196–224.

Dorsen, Norman. *The Evolving Constitution.* Middletown, Conn.: Wesleyan University Press, 1987.

Dworkin, Ronald. *Taking Rights Seriously*. Cambridge: Harvard University Press, 1977.

Eisenstein, Zillah R. *The Female Body and the Law*. Berkeley: University of California Press, 1988.

Fox-Genovese, Elizabeth. *Feminism Without Illusions: A Critique of Individualism*. Chapel Hill: University of North Carolina Press, 1990.

Freyer, Tony. *Justice Hugo Black and Modern America*. Tuscaloosa: University of Alabama Press, 1989.

Fried, Charles. *Order and Law: Arguing the Reagan Revolution—A Firsthand Account*. New York: Simon & Schuster, 1991.

Ginsburg, Ruth Bader. "The Burger Court's Grapplings with Sex Discrimination." In *The Burger Court: The Counter-Revolution That Wasn't*. ed. V. Blasi, 132–156. New Haven: Yale University Press, 1983.

Glazer, Nathan. *Affirmative Discrimination*. New York: Basic Books, 1976.

Gordon, Linda. *Woman's Body, Woman's Right: Birth Control in America*. New York: Penguin Books, 1976.

Graber, Mark A. *Transforming Free Speech: The Ambiguous Legacy of Civil Libertarianism*. Berkeley: University of California Press, 1991.

Gubar, Susan, and Joan Hoff, eds. *For Adult Users Only: The Dilemma of Violent Pornography*. Bloomington: Indiana University Press, 1989.

Haiman, Franklyn S. *Speech and Law in a Free Society*. Chicago: University of Chicago Press, 1981.

Hirsch, Marianne, and Evelyn Fox Keller, eds. *Conflicts in Feminism*. New York: Routledge, 1991.

Hoff, Joan. *Unequal Before the Law: A Legal History of U.S. Women*. New York: New York University Press, 1989.

Hopkins, W. Wat. *Actual Malice: Twenty-Five Years After Times v. Sullivan*. New York: Praeger, 1989.

Irons, Peter. *The Courage of Their Convictions: Sixteen Americans Who Fought Their Way to the Supreme Court*. New York: Free Press, 1988.

Kalven, Harry, Jr. *A Worthy Tradition: Freedom of Speech in America*. New York: Harper & Row, 1988.

Kanowitz, Leo. *Equal Rights: The Male Stake*. Albuquerque: University of New Mexico Press, 1981.

———. *Women and the Law*. Albuquerque: University of New Mexico Press, 1969.

Karst, Kenneth L. *Belonging to America: Equal Citizenship and the Constitution*. New Haven: Yale University Press, 1989.

Karst, Kenneth L., and Harold W. Horowitz. "Affirmative Action and Equal Protection." *Virginia Law Review* 60 (1974): 955–974.

Labunski, Richard. *Libel and the First Amendment: Legal History and Practice in Print and Broadcasting.* New Brunswick: Transaction Books, 1987.

Law, Sylvia. "Rethinking Sex and the Constitution." *University of Pennsylvania Law Review* 132 (1984): 955–1040.

Maveety, Nancy. *Representation Rights and the Burger Years.* Ann Arbor: University of Michigan Press, 1991.

McKinnon, Catherine A. *Feminism Unmodified: Discourses on Life and Law.* Cambridge: Harvard University Press, 1988.

Mohr, James C. *Abortion in America: The Origins and Evolution of National Policy, 1800–1900.* New York: Oxford University Press, 1978.

Morgan, Richard E. *Disabling America: The "Rights Industry" in Our Time.* New York: Basic Books, 1984.

Murphy, Paul L. *The Shaping of the First Amendment.* New York: Oxford University Press, 1991.

Neier, Aryeh. *Defending My Enemy: American Nazis, The Skokie Case, and the Risks of Freedom.* New York: Dutton, 1979.

O'Neill, Robert M. *Discriminating Against Discrimination.* Bloomington: Indiana University Press, 1975.

Powe, Lucas A., Jr. *American Broadcasting and the First Amendment.* Berkeley: University of California Press, 1987.

Rae, Douglas. *Equalities.* Cambridge: Harvard University Press, 1981.

Rhode, Deborah L. *Justice and Gender: Sex Discrimination and the Law.* Cambridge: Harvard University Press, 1989.

Rosenberg, Norman L. *Protecting the Best Men: An Interpretive History of the Law of Libel.* Chapel Hill: University of North Carolina Press, 1986.

Rossum, Ralph A. *Reverse Discrimination: The Constitutional Debate.* New York: Marcel Dekker, 1980.

Schauer, Frederick F. *Free Speech: A Philosophical Enquiry.* New York: Cambridge University Press, 1982.

Schwartz, Bernard. *Behind Bakke: Affirmative Action and the Supreme Court.* New York: New York University Press, 1988.

———. *The New Right and the Constitution: Turning Back the Legal Clock.* Boston: Northeastern University Press, 1990.

Smith, Rodney K. *Public Prayer and the Constitution: A Case Study in Constitutional Interpretation.* Wilmington, Del.: Scholarly Resources, 1987.

Sowell, Thomas. *Affirmative Action Reconsidered: Was It Necessary in Academia?* Washington, D.C.: American Enterprise Institute, 1975.

Steiner, Gilbert Y. *Constitutional Inequality: The Political Fortunes of the ERA.* Washington, D.C.: Brookings Institution, 1985.

Swanson, Wayne R. *The Christ Child Goes to Court.* Philadelphia: Temple University Press, 1989.

Tedford, Thomas L. *Freedom of Speech in the United States.* Carbondale: Southern Illinois University Press, 1985.

Tribe, Lawrence H. *Abortion: The Clash of Absolutes.* New York: W. W. Norton, 1990.

————. *American Constitutional Law.* Second Edition. Mineola, N.Y.: Foundation Press, 1988.

Urofsky, Melvyn I. *A Conflict of Rights: The Supreme Court and Affirmative Action.* New York: Charles Scribner's Sons, 1991.

————. *The Continuity of Change: The Supreme Court and Individual Liberties, 1953–1986.* Belmont, Cal.: Wadsworth, 1991.

Van Alstyne, William W. "Rites of Passage: Race, the Supreme Court, and the Constitution." *University of Chicago Law Review* 46 (1979): 775–810.

Walton, Hanes, Jr. *When the Marching Stopped: The Politics of Civil Rights Regulatory Agencies.* Albany: State University of New York Press, 1988.

Weber, Paul J., ed. *Equal Separation: Understanding the Religious Clauses of the First Amendment.* Westport, Conn.: Greenwood Press, 1990.

Williams, Patricia J. *The Alchemy of Race and Rights.* Cambridge: Harvard University Press, 1991.

Wills, Garry. *Under God: Religion and American Politics.* New York: Simon & Schuster, 1990.

Woodward, Bob, and Scott Armstrong. *The Brethren: Inside the Supreme Court.* New York: Simon & Schuster, 1979.

8: "A Republic, If You Can Keep It"

Adler, Mortimer J. *Haves Without Have-Nots: Essays for the 21st Century on Democracy and Socialism.* New York: Macmillan, 1991.

Anderson, Walter Truett. *Reality Isn't What It Used To Be: Theatrical Politics, Ready-to-Wear Religion, Global Myths, Primitive Chic, and Other Wonders of the Postmodern World.* San Francisco: Harper and Row, 1990.

Baranczak, Stanislaw. *Breathing Under Water and Other East European Essays.* Cambridge: Harvard University Press, 1990.

Billias, George Athan, ed. *American Constitutionalism Abroad: Selected Essays in Comparative Constitutional History.* Westport, Conn.: Greenwood Press, 1990.

Blumenthal, Sidney. *Pledging Allegiance: The Last Campaign of the Cold War.* New York: HarperCollins, 1990.

Bollinger, Lee C. *The Tolerant Society: Freedom of Speech and Extremist Speech in America.* New York: Oxford University Press, 1986.

Brandys, Kazimierz. *Warsaw Diary.* Translated from the Polish by Richard Lourie, New York: Random House, 1983.

Carey, James W. *Communication as Culture: Essays on Media and Society.* Boston: Unwin Hyman, 1988.

Carey, James W., ed. *Media, Myths and Narrative: Television and the Press.* Beverly Hills: Sage, 1987.

Chomsky, Noam, and Edward S. Herman. *Manufacturing Consent: The Political Economy of the Mass Media.* New York: Pantheon, 1988.

Clurman, Richard M. *Beyond Malice: The Media's Years of Reckoning.* Revised and Updated Edition. New York: New American Library, 1990.

Davis, David Brion. *Revolutions: Reflections on American Equality and Foreign Liberations.* Cambridge: Harvard University Press, 1990.

Demac, Donna A. *Liberty Denied: The Current Rise of Censorship in America.* Revised Edition. New Brunswick: Rutgers University Press, 1991.

Ehrenreich, Barbara. *The Worst Years of Our Lives: Irreverent Notes from a Decade of Greed.* New York: Pantheon, 1990.

Emerson, Thomas I. *The System of Freedom of Expression.* New York: Random House, 1970.

———. *Toward a General Theory of the First Amendment.* New York: Random House, 1966.

Feldman, Daniel L. *The Logic of American Government: Applying the Constitution to the Contemporary World.* New York: William Morrow, 1990.

Garton Ash, Timothy. *The Magic Lantern: The Revolution of '89 in Warsaw, Budapest, Berlin, and Prague.* New York: Random House, 1990.

———. *The Uses of Adversity: Essays on the Fate of Central Europe.* New York: Random House, 1989.

Gastil, Raymond D. "What Kind of Democracy?" *Atlantic Monthly* (June 1990): 92–96.

Halberstam, David. *The Next Century.* New York: William Morrow, 1991.

Hartz, Louis, *The Liberal Tradition in America.* New York: Harcourt, Brace and Company, 1955.

Havel, Vaclav. *Disturbing the Peace: A Conversation with Karel Hvizdala.* Translated from the Czech with an introduction by Paul Wilson. New York: Knopf, 1990.

———. *Letters to Olga.* New York: Henry Holt, 1989.

Heller, Agnes, and Ferenc Feher. *From Yalta to Glasnost: Dismantling of Stalin's Empire.* Cambridge: Blackwell, 1991.

Hentoff, Nat. *The First Freedom: The Tumultuous History of Free Speech in America.* New York: Delacorte, 1980.

Kundera, Milan. *The Book of Laughter and Forgetting.* Translated from the Czech by Michael Henry Heim. New York: Knopf, 1980.

Lasch, Christopher. *The True and Only Heaven: Progress and Its Critics.* New York: W. W. Norton, 1991.

Lee, Martin A., and Norman Solomon. *Unreliable Sources: A Guide to Detecting Bias in News Media.* New York: Lyle Stuart, 1990.

Lichtenberg, Judith K., ed. *Democracy and the Mass Media.* Cambridge, U.K.: Cambridge University Press, 1990.

Lichter, S. Robert, Stanley Rothman, and Linda S. Lichter. *The Media Elite: America's New Powerbrokers.* New York: Hastings House, 1986.

Lippmann, Walter. *Public Opinion.* New York: Harcourt, Brace and Company, 1922.

Lukacs, John. *Outgrowing Democracy: A History of the United States in the Twentieth Century.* Garden City, N.Y.: Doubleday, 1984.

Michnik, Adam. *Letters from Prison and Other Essays.* Translated by Maya Latynski. Foreword by Czeslaw Milosz. Introduction by Jonathan Schell. Berkeley: University of California Press, 1985.

Oakeshott, Michael Joseph. *Rationalism in Politics: And Other Essays.* London: Rowan and Littlefield, 1977.

Orwell, George. *1984.* New York: Harcourt, Brace Jovanovich, 1949.

Pfaff, William. "Redefining World Power." *Foreign Affairs* 70, No. 1 (1991): 34–48.

Postman, Neil. *Amusing Ourselves to Death: Public Discourse in the Age of Show Business.* New York: Viking Penguin, 1985.

Powe, Lucas A., Jr. *The Fourth Estate and the Constitution: Freedom of the Press in America.* Berkeley: University of California Press, 1991.

Rosen, Jay. "Making Journalism More Public." *Communication* 12, No. 4 (1990): 1–18.

Sakharov, Andrei. *Memoirs.* Translated from the Russian by Richard Lourie. New York: Knopf, 1990.

———. *Moscow and Beyond, 1986 to 1989.* New York: Knopf, 1991.

Scheer, Robert. *Thinking Tuna Fish, Talking Death: Essays on the Pornography of Power.* New York: Hill and Wang, 1988.

Schultz, Bud, and Ruth Schultz. *It Did Happen Here: Recollections of Political Repression in America.* Berkeley: University of California Press, 1989.

Shiffrin, Steven H. *The First Amendment, Democracy, and Romance.* Cambridge: Harvard University Press, 1990.

Slater, Philip E. *A Dream Deferred: America's Discontent and the Search for a New Democratic Ideal.* Boston: Beacon Press, 1991.

Smith, Bruce James. *Politics and Remembrance: Republican Themes in Machiavelli, Burke, and Tocqueville.* Princeton: Princeton University Press, 1985.

Smith, Hedrick. *The New Russians.* New York: Random House, 1990.

Smolla, Rodney A. *Suing the Press: Libel, the Media and Power.* New York: Oxford University Press, 1986.

Solzhenitsyn, Aleksandr. *The Oak and the Calf: Sketches of Literary Life in the Soviet Union*. Translated from the Russian by Harry Willetts. New York: Harper and Row, 1980.

————. *Prussian Nights: A Poem*. Translated by Robert Conquest. New York: Farrar, Straus and Giroux, 1977.

Theiner, George. *They Shoot Writers, Don't They?* London: Faber and Faber, 1984.

Westin, Alan F. *Privacy and Freedom*. New York: Atheneum Press, 1967.

Will, George. *Suddenly: The American Idea Abroad and At Home, 1986–1990*. New York: Free Press, 1990.

Zinn, Howard. *Declarations of Independence: Cross-Examining American Ideology*. New York: HarperCollins, 1990.

Index